TRADE UNIONS AND THE BRITISH ELECTORATE

For Susan

Trade Unions and the British Electorate

PAUL WEBB

Dartmouth
Aldershot · Brookfield USA · Hong Kong · Singapore · Sydney

Published by
Dartmouth Publishing Company Limited
Gower House
Croft Road
Aldershot
Hants GU11 3HR
England

Dartmouth Publishing Company Limited
Distributed in the United States by Ashgate Publishing Company
Old Post Road
Brookfield
Vermont 05036
USA

A CIP catalogue record for this book is available from the British Library and the US Library of Congress

ISBN 1 85521 217 X

Printed in Great Britain by
Billing & Sons Ltd, Worcester

Contents

Acknowledgements

While any responsibility for what follows rests solely with myself, I must acknowledge the helpful advice and comments that I have received from a number of academic sources at various stages of this book's preparation. I am particularly indebted to Ian Budge, Peter Mair, Gosta Esping-Andersen, Bo Sarlvik and Duncan Gallie for their constructive observations on earlier drafts. Neither should I overlook the constant support that I have always been able to count on receiving from my wife, Susan, and my parents. For what it is worth, this is for you.

PDW,
London,
November 1991.

List of Tables and Figures

Glossary of Acronyms

ACTAT	Association of Cinematograph, Television and Allied Technicians
APEX	Association of Professional, Executive, Clerical and Computer Staff
ASLEF	Associated Society of Locomotive Engineers and Firemen
ASTMS	Association of Scientific, Technical and Managerial Staffs
AUEW	Amalgamated Union of Engineering Workers
CAC	Conference Arrangements Committee (Labour Party)
CATU	Ceramic and Allied Trade Union
CIR	Commission on Industrial Relations
CLPD	Campaign for Labour Party Democracy
COHSE	Confederation of Health Service Employees
DEA	Department of Economic Affairs
EETPU	Electrical, Electronic, Telecommunication and Plumbing Union
FBU	Fire Brigades Union
FTAT	Furniture, Timber and Allied Trades Union
GMBATU	General, Municipal, Boilermakers' and Allied Trades Union
GALO	General Association of Loom Overlookers
IMF	International Monetary Fund
ISTC	Iron and Steel Trades Confederation
MSC	Manpower Services Commission
MU	Musicians Union
NACODS	National Association of Colliery Overmen, Deputies and Shotfirers
NBPI	National Board of Prices and Incomes
NCCL	National Council for Civil Liberties
NCU	National Communications Union
NEA	National Economic Assessment
NEDC	National Economic Development Council ('Neddy')
NIRC	National Industrial Relations Court
NGA	National Graphical Union
NLB	National League of the Blind and Disabled
NUDAGO	National Union of Domestic Appliances and General Operatives
NUFLAT	National Union of Footwear, Leather and Allied Trades Union
NUM	National Union of Mineworkers
NUPE	National Union of Public Employees
NUR	National Union of Railwaymen
NUS	National Union of Seamen
NUTGWU	National Union of Tailors and Garment Workers
OPEC	Organisation of Petroleum Exporting Countries

PLCTWU	Power Loom Carpet Weavers' and Textile Workers' Union
RUBSSO	Rossendale Union of Boot, Shoe and Slipper Operatives
SOGAT'82	Society of Graphical and Allied Trades 1982
TASS	Technical, Salaried and Supervisory Staff (AUEW affiliate)
TGWU	Transport and General Workers' Union
TSSA	Transport Salaried Staffs Association
TWU	Tobacco Workers' Union
TULO	Trade Union Liaison Officer
UCATT	Union of Construction, Allied Trades and Technicians
UCW	Union of Communications Workers
USDAW	Union of Shop, Distributive and Allied Workers

1 Trade Unions and Electoral Mobilisation

Despite the abundance of literature and comment upon the political significance of trade unions in Britain, surprisingly little detailed attention has been paid to their impact on the national electorate (though for a little known exception see Freyman, 1980). Yet given that the burgeoning field of voting studies has for some time clearly indicated the widespread state of flux in which the British electorate finds itself, it is not unreasonable to assume that unions could comprise one element in this pattern of electoral change. Like churches in other European societies, trade unions in Britain are *non-electoral* organisations which nevertheless play an important role in mobilising political consciousness and action. Indeed, trade unions have been crucial to the development of politics in modern British industrial society. In founding and sustaining the Labour party they have played a seminal role in the crystallisation and institutionalisation of the class politics which has so manifestly characterised British political culture since before the Great War. Moreover, and notwithstanding some speculation to the contrary, there is reputable and cogent research to remind us that Peter Pulzer's well known dictum that 'class is the basis of British politics - all else is embellishment and detail', remains appropriate (Pulzer 1967: 98; Marshall, Newby, Rose and Vogler 1988).

One could imagine a variety of ways in which unions might affect electoral outcomes. For a start, it is conceivable that they could have an impact on the way that voters *assess salient public issues* at election time; or again, they might plausibly be regarded as a potential source of influence on the *ideological profile* of parties and electors. Of course, they have long since been presumed to play some part in mobilising class linked attitudes and identities which might sustain support for the Party. Clearly, also, British unions maintain a capacity for providing *organisational input* into Labour's election campaign efforts. In all these contexts they should be regarded as institutions which share a mobilisational capacity and role with political parties. Indeed, it has been pointed out that, for a number of European states, '...union membership is at least as important, if not more important, than occupational class in predicting socialist versus non-socialist support' (Mair 1983: 423)[1]. In this book, we shall be endeavouring to see how far it is possible to unravel the effect that British trade unions have had in this continuing political process of electoral mobilisation, in particular since the 1960s.

Despite - or maybe because of - the growing number of trade unionists in Britain over the past twenty five years, a decreasing proportion of them have been willing to maintain their traditional allegiance towards the Labour Party at election time. Thus, in the general election of 1964 fully three-fifths of all trade union members voted for Labour, yet less than two decades later the corresponding proportion was down to barely one-third (see table 5.1, below). This fact has been observed and commented upon not infrequently by politicians, commercial pollsters, journalists and academics alike. Yet, to reiterate, detailed analysis of this phenomenon has been virtually non-existent. This leaves a gap which it is the central objective of this book to fill. Precisely how and why have trade union members turned away from the Labour Party since its triumphant return to power in 1964 after 'thirteen wasted years' in the wilderness of frustrating political opposition? In 1964 the millions of ordinary trade unionists were a vital part of the constituency that swept Labour back into national governmental office. In the 1990s, Labour again anticipates just such a return to power, and is fully aware that a successful appeal to the union constituency may be important if that dream is to come true.

Despite the lack of detailed treatment, many studies have touched upon the electoral consequences of trade unionism in Britain. These frequently confine themselves to the observation that the union electorate is subject to the effects of social change. Colin Crouch, for instance, informs us that:

> The proportion of union members who automatically support the Labour Party is declining...(this) follows the changing social composition of union membership - a factor which also explains the declining proportion of members in unions affiliated to the party. The great increase in unionisation of the past decade has occurred primarily in white collar and professional unions, most of which are not affiliated, while

> unions in decline as a result of a shrinkage in their occupational base have been Labour strongholds (Crouch 1982: 171).

Crouch makes an important point, yet to concentrate purely upon factors related to the social context is not really enough, as we shall see. A further example of academic interest in the question of why Labour has lost the political support of trade unionists has been provided by the work of Andrew J. Taylor (Taylor 1987a: 242-252). Taylor provides a rather different focus to Crouch, but one which is equally problematic from the perspective of electoral analysis. Perhaps this is because his approach is limited to a brief review of research which is potentially relevant to the specific question of the voting behaviour of unionists. Consequently, Taylor grasps at various factors which may have possible explanatory value, but he fails to evaluate their importance with any precision. We are not provided with a parsimonious and coherent interpretation, for there is simply too much in there. In short, in explanatory terms he seems to say everything and yet he says nothing. Thus, the list of possible factors that he adduces might explain Labour's loss of support among union members includes:

i. Weakening affective loyalty for the party.
ii. Increasingly negative instrumental assessments of the party's performance in government and opposition.
iii. Various aspects of social change, such as the growing relevance of sectoral cleavages, the growing number of white collar, women and unskilled manual union members, and the disruption of communal solidarity that accompanies the divorce of residential from working locations.
iv. Labour's loss of credibility as an alternative governing team.
v. Labour's unpopular policies.

These factors are not necessarily uninformative in themselves - indeed, I shall be drawing upon several of them myself, in one way or another - though they are not very helpful as presented by Taylor, in my view. The reasons for this vary. In the first place, some of the factors he mentions help us understand the *general* electoral decline of the Labour Party rather than its *particular* decline within the union constituency. This is true of the points concerning Labour's policies and its widely perceived 'credibility gap' for large sections of the electorate during the 1980s. Moreover, some electoral analysts have effectively questioned just how important direct assessment of policy alternatives by voters really is, which further undermines the plausibility of the policy voting explanation (see, for example, Heath, Jowell and Curtice 1985: chapter 7). Then again, whilst social change certainly provides an important contextual setting against which to consider the weakening of Labour's support among trade unionists, it supplies few directly helpful explanations. Take the question of the impact of the private/public sector cleavage, for example. Though an interesting line of enquiry that developed in British psephology during the 1980s, we shall see that the question of whether one is an employee in the public sector or the private sector has little direct explanatory relevance for voting behaviour (see chapter 6, below). Similarly, the presence of greater numbers of female and unskilled employees within the ranks of union memberships proves to be something of a red herring (chapter 5). And so it is with regards to the growth of white collar unionism, for it is my contention that the most notable phenomenon requiring explanation is the heavy swing against Labour among *blue collar* union members (chapter 5). (Not that the growth of white collar membership is entirely irrelevant to the problem of political mobilisation faced by Labour, however, as we shall be seeing in chapter 2).

None of this is said to denigrate the valuable contributions made by writers like Crouch or Taylor; on the contrary, it is merely to suggest that this book aims to build upon the work of research such as theirs, which has hitherto concentrated largely upon other aspects of the party-union relationship in Britain. Consideration of the union electorate is usually tangential to the main thrust of these efforts.[2] The work of Crouch and Taylor simply serves as a preliminary illustration of the gaps in the existing literature. Clearly, from the point of view of electoral studies, there is a need to sharpen the analysis and specify explanations.

Trade unions and the sources of electoral mobilisation

The mobilisational role played by trade unions entails practical collaboration of some kind with political parties, and this may be so regardless of whether we are talking about class-left, christian democratic or right wing parties (all of which have links with unions in various European countries). Such ties as exist between parties and unions may be relatively loosely drawn, however, reflecting the desire of union bodies to maintain a certain distance. Many unions are wary of casting all their eggs into one party political basket; such a strategy would run the risk of attracting hostility from governments of contrary political hue, and can draw unions into the morass of internal party politics. On the other hand, unions with a clear ideological or social group identity may willingly become immersed in a close 'organic' relationship with a party.

Historically, the union movement in Britain has experienced both types of relationship, though throughout the twentieth century this experience has far more closely approximated the latter, 'organic' alternative. From 1900 until well into the post World War Two era the Labour Party and many of the unions affiliated to the TUC unquestionably stood together as the institutional expression of the working class community's political consciousness.

Broadly speaking, there would seem to be three major potential sources of change in the voting behaviour of union members - *social, political and organisational*. In general terms social change, political change and organisational change can all play their distinct, though often inter-related, parts in producing electoral change. Consequently, in the course of this book various possible explanations of electoral change that fall into these broad categories are considered. To take *social* factors, for instance, the question of the changing social profile of the trade unions must be broached; for example, does the growth of white collar unionism explain Labour's losses among members? This is an issue we shall be addressing during the course of the book. It is, moreover, a question the mention of which offers an early opportunity of issuing a brief caveat regarding the phenomenon of *class dealignment* in British electoral behaviour. Stated simply, class dealignment refers to the apparent decline in the proportion of electors willing to vote according to the social class to which they belong, and this is a phenomenon which is by no means exclusive to trade unionists. But, given that British trade unionism has historically been associated with class mobilisation we would expect change in unionist voting behaviour to reflect, perhaps to a large extent, processes of class dealignment. This illustrates the point that we clearly cannot attribute all unionist electoral change to causes *specifically* connected with trade unions. To some extent, more general electoral change explains the behaviour of the particular constituency in which we are interested. It has to be made clear then, that to some extent, the behaviour we shall focus upon is simply an adjunct of broader phenomena of change which have often been examined in great detail elsewhere. However, one of the things which can be demonstrated is that there is far more to change in union members' voting behaviour than this. Methodologically, it is not difficult to control for the effect of (changing) social background influences, and this consequently allows us to suggest *union-specific* explanations. In this regard, the major theme to be developed in the course of the book is that union-specific factors interact with the processes of social change that underlie class dealignment to offer an explanation of the changing voting patterns of trade unionists. Thus, while accepting that the changing nature of class identities and values affects the working class community as a whole, its real significance for us lies in setting the context within which union members react to the political activity of their leaderships. This latter phenomenon constitutes a union-specific effect, of course.

There is, of course, no simple one to one relationship between social change and electoral change. Other factors intervene to mediate the effect of the former upon the latter, factors which may be more purely 'political' or 'organisational' in nature. It is the purpose of this book to examine how far the political and organisational activity of trade unions might be important in this respect. To consider the *organisational* factor, for instance, it would seem appropriate to pose the question of whether a weakening of the organisational linkage between the party and the unions might have undermined the capacity of the movement to mobilise trade unionist support for Labour. This will be considered in the next chapter; as will be seen, there is little or no convincing evidence to suggest that this is in fact the case. Consequenctly, we are left with the possibility that *political* factors best account for the behaviour of union members at the polls. In particular, I shall argue that political conflict between party and union elites since the 1960s offers a convincing explanation for the exceptional electoral swing against Labour shown by manual union members over the period. This is not to say that social change has no part to play in our explanation; on the contrary, social changes already evident by the middle of the 1960s were important in undermining deep-seated affective loyalty previously felt for the Labour Party by many working class people in Britain. It is only in the context of these relatively weak psychological bonds that more purely instrumental evaluations of political factors like party-union relations gain in significance for the voting decision. And it was in the 1960s, of course, that union and industrial affairs were thrust to a position near the top of the political agenda; in brief, these became salient issues, and from time to time have again been since, especially for trade unionists. This argument, along with supporting evidence, will be revealed in detail as the book unfolds. The essential message is that social and political factors *interact* in structuring electoral choices, and it is our purpose to demonstrate just how this has been so in the context of the trade union movement.

Conclusion

To recap briefly, then; it has been established, firstly, that the electoral impact of trade unions is a subject worthy of attention given the important mobilisational role that they have assumed in many nations - especially Britain. This impact, it has been suggested, is likely to flow from the ways in which unions affect factors such as issue assessments, social identities, ideological profiles and flows of organisational resources. The central object of this study is to explain the shift away from the Labour Party of a large part of the British trade union constituency since the 1960s, and we shall focus upon the possible impact of social, political and organisational factors. In the course of our study it will become clear that strictly organisational explanations are unconvincing; rather, it is the interaction of social change and political factors such as the state of party-union relations which best accounts for the changing partisan preferences of trade unionists.

It is time to begin putting the flesh onto the bare bones of the interpretation that has been sketched. Over the course of the next two chapters the organisational, political and social contexts of the relationship between the party and the unions are considered in detail, since these are assumed to be the major potential sources of electoral change among union members. In chapter 4 we review the work that has been conducted on British electoral change; this provides both a context and a practical theoretical basis upon which to proceed with the actual data analysis of unionists' electoral behaviour which ensues in chapters 5 and 6.

Notes

1. A basic illustration of the relative significance of the trade union variable in structuring voting behaviour during the post-war era is provided by Table 1.1n. This table has been constructed using information first gathered by Richard Rose in the mid-1970s (Rose 1974), and provides an indication of the situation in various European countries during the early part of the period covered by our own study of the British case. The table reveals that in no case did trade union membership account for more than one-third of the total variance explained by selected social background variables. However, it can be seen that in half of the eight relevant cases drawn from Rose's book (including Sweden), union membership accounted for a higher degree of the variance than occupational class. An examination of a more recently gathered source of data, the *Eurobarometer* survey of European Community electorates undertaken in the late 1980s, reveals that the relationship between vote and unionisation was statistically significant at the 1% level in each of the 'big four' European democracies - Britain, (West) Germany, France and Italy. The percentage of union members who reported voting for the left in each of these countries was as follows:

Britain -	41.2% (Labour)
France -	73.7% (Socialists, Communists, Unified Socialists)
W. Germany -	52.1% (Social Democrats)
Italy -	58.7% (Communists, Socialists, Proletarian Democracy)

In short, it would seem that the capacity of union membership to structure electoral alignment is often significant in western democracies.

Moreover, a brief glance at Table 1.2n, which draws largely on a study of working class mobilisation by Walter Korpi, indicates broad prima facie support for the idea that trade union strength and working class politics go together. It is notable that the level of unionisation and the strength of electoral

Table 1.1n

The percentage of variance in voting behaviour explained by trade union membership: selected post-war examples

	Total variance explained (TV)	Variance explained by union membership (UV)	UV/TV	Variance explained by class (CV)	CV/TV
Belgium 1972	34.5	1.6	4.6	4.2	12.1
W.Germany 1967	19.7	5.6	28.4	2.1	10.6
Italy 1968	28.3	4.9	17.3	0.3	1.1
Finland 1966	33.2	0.3	0.9	31.8	95.7
Australia 1967	14.6	1.8	12.3	8.9	60.1
Britain 1970	12.0	3.3	27.5	N.A	N.A
Ireland 1969	3.1	0.9	29.0	N.A	N.A

Note: All figures are percentages. Percentage of variance explained by union membership is not reported in the case study on Swedish voting behaviour in Rose's book. However, it is possible to ascertain the order of explanatory importance of the different independent variables for the country, and this reveals that union membership had less impact on vote than occupational class. For an account of the *Automatic Interaction Detector (AID)* technique employed in these studies see Sonquist and Morgan, 1964.

Source: AID analyses published in Rose 1974, passim.

support for class-left parties appear to be associated in western Europe. (The cause of the relative weakness of the Labour Party in the Republic of Ireland reflects, to a significant extent, the fact that the struggle for national independence coincided with a period critical to the potential mobilisation of the working class there. As a result, union members tended to develop strong loyalties for Fianna Fail, the decisive party of Republicanism.)

Table 1.2n
Unionisation and left wing voting in European democracies, 1946-1976

Country	National rate of unionisation	Percentage of votes cast for left
Austria	55	45
Sweden	71	43
Norway	46	41
Denmark	49	39
Finland*	39	37
United Kingdom	44	35
Italy	23	34
Belgium	47	32
France	24	32
West Germany	35	31
Netherlands	32	31
Switzerland	24	18
Ireland	37	9

Sources: Korpi 1981: 308; Lane & Ersson 1991: 95

2. Other examples of books on the Labour Party and the unions which largely bypass the question of the electoral significance of the relationship between the two include the following: Harrison 1960, Richter 1973, Simpson 1973, May 1975, Panitch 1976, Taylor 1978, Dorfman 1979, Coates and Topham 1985, Fatchett 1987.

2 Party-union Linkages Since 1964: The Organisational Dimension

> No idea has ever made much headway without an organisation behind it...wherever ideologies seem to be important in politics they have a firm organisational basis (Barnes 1966: 522).

Organisation is a sine qua non of political mobilisation. Scholars have deployed this intuitively plausible generalisation in a variety of ways in the attempt to gauge more precisely the political impact that organisational resources can have - through, for instance, estimating the effect of electoral campaigns on voting behaviour (Weir 1985) or considering the electoral consequences of local constituency input (Bochel and Denver 1971). By and large these studies have confirmed the general message that organisation matters. The British Labour Party has historically depended greatly upon the unions for organisational resources, and this provokes the question of whether Labour's electoral decline among trade unionists is to some extent a reflection of weaker organisational links between the party and the unions.

The landmark study on this subject remains that of Martin Harrison, although it is more than thirty years old now (Harrison 1960). This is not to say that the topic has been ignored since the time Harrison wrote, but rather that nobody has dealt with it so comprehensively or impressively in the succeeding period. Authors such as May did, however, go some way towards updating Harrison's work in the 1970s (May 1978). May, essentially, adopted the skeleton of Harrison's original framework as a baseline for his own, less substantial, study. Where Harrison provided a book length treatment of the subject, May concentrated his efforts into a chapter of a book with a wider substantive scope. Such is, clearly, also the situation with this book. Whilst it is not my intention to follow precisely the format offered by either Harrison or May, the area covered in this chapter is in many ways similar to that which their work encompasses. Important material relating to the organisational relationship between the Labour Party and the trade unions requires updating; in certain respects - for instance, with regard to TULV or TUFL - this book necessarily breaks newer ground.

There are at least seven distinct aspects of the organisational linkage between the party and the unions which merit attention - party membership, finance, the party's annual conference and the National Executive Committee, the sponsorship of MPs, TULV, and TUFL's role in electoral organisation and political education. We shall consider these in turn. But by way of introduction, it is useful to make some introductory observations concerning the general historical importance of the unions for the Labour Party organisation.

The historical basis of the party-union link in Britain

It is of fundamental significance that the British Labour Party has never really developed into a genuine mass membership party in the way that some of its continental European counterparts have. For classic observers of European political parties like Maurice Duverger and Otto Kirchheimer, a mass membership organisation (or as Kirchheimer put it, a party of mass integration) was one whose most important resource was its individual membership. It was therefore vital that this membership be as large as possible, and that it was isolated from alternative ideological influences. The classic party of mass integration attempted to deploy all the organisational resources at its disposal in order to 'encapsulate' a target community within an extensive network of interlinking social, economic and political organisations; this strategy of 'organising and incorporating within the political party as many of the every day activities of the membership as possible' (Wellhofer 1979: 171) was adopted in Italy, for instance, with the object of isolating the nascent industrial working classes from the influence of the dominant culture which was catholic and socially conservative (Barnes 1974). In Giovanni Sartori's terms, the goal of the class-left mass membership party was to 'pass from class conditions to class consciousness and action' by encapsulating and mobilising a community of 'class devotees who actually live a class ideology'.

In this sense the party or union playing on the class appeal was an instrument of 'class persuasion' that concentrated on radicalising the underlying values of a social group (Sartori 1968: 12-16).

In Britain, however, Labour did not attempt to encapsulate the working class community through the development of its own widespread and thoroughgoing organisational presence. Though it has been a source of regret for some on the left, the party has never been ambitious enough to attempt the ideological isolation of the working class. Instead, it has been more inclined to accept the organisational and ideological domination of its own structures by the trade unions. Its organisational strength lay with the unions, who really mobilised the working class in Britain - at first industrially and later politically. The British Labour Party has had the rare distinction among European class-left parties of having grown out of 'the bowels of the trade union movement', to employ the famous and somewhat graphic phrase coined by Ernest Bevin. In fact, as Colin Crouch has said, the Labour Party has traditionally 'solved' the problem of its weak organisational condition by 'extreme dependence upon the unions' (Crouch 1982: 175). Consequently, for example, it is almost commonplace to observe that the party has consistently had the lowest ratio of members to voters of any of the major European social democratic parties - even before the party reformed the practices which produced habitual official overestimation of the true individual membership position (Hodgson 1981: 56). At its inception the Labour Representation Committee (as the party was known in its pre-1906 incarnation) accepted recommendations that no uniform system of constituency organisation be instituted, in favour of a strategy of simply leaving the task to affiliating bodies in the locality. In the earliest days of the new party the role of the Independent Labour Party (like the unions, an important corporate affiliate of Labour's federal structure) was particularly important in this regard:

> The ILP provided most of the speakers in the country, it did most of the campaigning and practically all the propaganda (Williams 1950: 203).

Indeed, by 1918 there were 672 ILP branches spread around the country compared to just 158 local LRCs. However, most of these cells were tiny, and McKibbin has argued that after 1910, in particular, it was the unions who were really responsible for the Labour Party's growth. The ILP could not hope to match the contribution and input of the unions, especially in the financial sphere (McKibbin 1975). Thus Sidney Webb reported Ramsay-MacDonald as having said that, 'only by them (the unions) could the party have got mass support and money' - whilst, incidentally, lamenting the 'terrible incubus' this represented for Labour (Forester 1975: 96). Compare also Arthur Henderson's comment to the editor of the *Manchester Guardian* in December 1918 on the party's new-found potential to run 500 candidates at the impending general election:

> They (the party activists) were better equipped for this than either of the two great parties because they had an existing trades union organisation in every town (Wrigley 1982: 86).

It seems clear enough, then, that the trade unions have made a very significant impact on Labour's organisational structure since early days. But the consequences of this organisational influence have been apparent at the ideological level too. Historically, the union-party nexus was born only after socialist attempts to mobilise the working class had proved disappointing. Tom Nairn has written of the attitude of the leaders of the ILP, which was clearly the foremost socialist body of the turn of the century:

> They speedily realised that...they must either induce the trade unions to throw in their lot with them or be content to build up very slowly a party based on individual membership on the continental socialist model...most of them preferred the shorter cut of a Labour party based on trade union affiliations, even though they realised that they could get such a party only by considerable dilution of their socialist objectives (Nairn 1965: 169).

This view is to some extent confirmed by contemporary observers such as Wertheimer, whose own roots lay in the experience of the continental European mass membership social democratic party (Wertheimer 1929). As Tom Forester has much more recently commented, the Labour Party's aim was never to create a 'clean break with the British political culture' (Forester 1976: 38). From its inception the party had a more limited and explicitly electoralist remit. Thus the founding conference of the LRC in 1900 declared among its aims the 'securing of better representation of labour in the House of Commons (and) promoting legislation in the direct interest of labour.' Beyond this, there was little or no explicit articulation of ideological, cultural or normative purpose. The consequences of this have been felt even after the party did adopt a formal commitment to socialism in 1918. Commenting on political activity within a core section of Labour's constituency during this period, a Durham mining village, RS Moore concluded that the party's approach was essentially 'opportunist': 'Labour in fact compromised with existing social outlooks in order to win votes' (Moore 1975: 50). As a result of this strategy, Forester argues that Labour has exerted little 'social control' over the working class 'beyond habitual electoral allegiance' (Forester 1976: 94). As we shall see in chapter 5, it is doubtful whether the party can honestly be said to manage even this any more.

HM Drucker has pointed out that there is another level on which the unions have also influenced the Labour Party's organisation and values. Though less immediately tangible it is none the less significant for that. It is the level of *ethos*, which is to be distinguished from the purely *doctrinal*, but which contributes equally to the overall ideology of the party. An ethos incorporates a set of values arising out of the 'experience of the people whom it characterises', and it affects personal and political relationships. This highly implicit spirit of a party, its 'traditions and habits, its feel' reflects the experience of the dominant group within it - in this case, the British industrial working class. Whereas doctrine characterises the way that intellectuals think, ethos exemplifies the 'less demanding, less articulate level' at which the workers typically operate in a political context. Consequently,

> The centre of gravity in the Labour Party is located in working class institutions - overwhelmingly in the trade unions (Drucker 1979: 11).

As a result, many of the organisational principles adopted in the earliest days of party development were taken 'unreflectively from the characteristic practices of the unions'. For example, Drucker is inclined to the view that certain typical party expressions of internal democracy, solidarity and loyalty are derived from the unions. Similarly, notions such as responsibility to the party conference, delegated representation and the need for loyalty to the elected party leader owe much to the ethos of the unions themselves. More especially, the belief that an organisation requires a declared principle to guide it - such as Clause 4 of the party constitution - has been bequeathed by the unions. Drucker summarises what lies at the heart of union - and therefore party - ethos in the following way. He is worth quoting at some length:

> Notoriously, the rules and practices of unions vary...But..they all exemplify a form of democracy. The unions, especially the older unions, were formed by people who had slowly built them in a hostile world. Thus the unions tend to be slow moving, defensive organisations. Their rules are remarkably elaborate and self-contained. They leave little to the initiative of the unions' own leaders and

> less to the public law. They often incorporate generous universalistic aspirations and narrow formalistic procedures (Drucker 1982: 261).

So the unions have dominated the organisation of the Labour Party virtually from the time of its inception, and consequently have been in a position to influence its strategy, doctrine and ethos. This has necessarily had an important effect upon the political and ideological mobilisation of the British working class. What of the details of the unions' input into the organisation of the Labour Party since the early 1960s. Has the party-union organisational link been eroded in any significant way?

1. Party membership

It is almost a cliché of British politics that Labour's mass membership base is a 'myth'. This assertion rests on the distinction between individual and affiliated membership of the party. To be an individual member, it is necessary, firstly, to be a member of an affiliated organisation for which one is eligible (a union or socialist society), and secondly, to actually obtain direct membership of a Constituency Labour Party (CLP). On the other hand, organisations affiliated to the Labour Party are also entitled to take a political levy off those of their members who are happy to pay it. This money can be passed on to the Labour Party in affiliation fees, and the levy payers designated the 'affiliated membership'. Whilst trade unions are not obliged to affiliate for all who pay the levy it is nonetheless clear that the bulk of Labour's claimed national membership over the years has comprised this affiliated element rather than the individual element. It is, furthermore, almost certain that many who pay the political levy do so out of apathy rather than out of conviction; that is, they pay the levy automatically unless they can be bothered to specifically 'contract out'. (When it was necessary to specifically 'contract in' in order to pay this levy between 1927 and 1945, affiliated membership income declined significantly, as table 2.1 demonstrates.) Thus the true indicator of committed membership must be taken to be the individual membership, not the affiliated membership.

To understand just how significant affiliated membership is, it is enough simply to cast a cursory glance over the figures presented in table 2.2. It is immediately obvious that by far and away the greatest component of total party membership is that comprising trade union affiliated membership. More to the point, it is equally evident that there has been little or no change over the years; the unions' affiliated members have generally accounted for around 90%

Table 2.1
Affiliated membership income for the Labour Party, selected years

Year	Total union affiliation fees
1918	20,000
1926	56,000
1927	43,000
1928	33,000
1939	44,000
1946	51,000
1947	81,000
1948	130,000

Source: Pinto-Duschinsky 1980: 76

of total party membership since the foundation of the Labour Representation Committee. It is clear that the Labour Party remains as dependent on the unions for its nominal membership as ever it did, and by implication for its financing too, as we shall see. Moreover, this dependence is largely focused on a few major trade unions. 'The dominance of a few is not a recent phenomenon', as Upham and Wilson have pointed out, but it has probably become more exaggerated. In the mid-1950s, the top six affiliates accounted for two-thirds of the total membership of the party, whereas thirty years later the top four amounted to 60% of the total (Upham and Wilson 1989: 14).

Interestingly, although it may be the case that the membership links between the Labour Party and its affiliated unions are as close as ever, it does not necessarily follow that those between the party and the TUC as a whole are. Somewhat curiously, if typically, whilst the TUC as a body founded the Labour Representation Committee at the turn of the century, it is not the case that all its member unions are individually affiliated to the party, nor that the TUC as a body is. The TUC has always resisted any pressure for the fragmentation of the union movement along ideological lines; it has never lost sight of its primary goal of presenting a comprehensive and relatively united national federation of labour in the industrial arena. Consequently, Britain is not characterised by the model often found in continental Europe of rival union federations that are divided by ideological and political identity. Thus the TUC can reasonably claim all-inclusiveness but not political coherence.[1] The inevitable corollary of the scope of its membership is a certain amount of internal political tension that the TUC has to live with. There are those who are happy to affiliate to the TUC in order to be a part of its combined

Table 2.2
Labour party membership, selected years

Year	Individual membership	Affiliated union membership	Affiliated socialist societies' membership	Total membership	Union membership as a % of total membership
1900	NA	353,070	22,861	375,931	93.9
1945	487,04	2,510,369	41,281	3,038,697	82.6
1964	830,116	5,502,001	21,146	6,439,893	85.4
1966	775,693	5,538,744	21,285	6,086,625	90.1
1970	690,191	5,518,520	23,869	6,222,580	88.7
1974	691,889	5,787,467	39,101	6,518,451	88.8
1979	666,091	6,511,179	58,328	7,235,598	90.0
1983	295,344	6,101,438	58,955	6,455,737	94.5
1987	288,829	5,564,477	54,843	5,908,149	94.2

Note: Estimates of individual membership levels have fallen in the 1980s since CLPs are no longer required to affiliate for a minimum number of 1000 members.

Source: Report of the Annual Conference of the Labour Party, 1987.

industrial muscle, while resisting the further step of explicitly identifying the Labour Party as their political flagship. Taylor has claimed that the influence of these types of union may be increasing within the TUC given the growth of white collar unionism: 'As so few white collar unions are affiliated to both the TUC and the Labour Party this hints at a growing separation between the two...' (Taylor 1987a: 170) This is especially pertinent in the case of private sector white collar union members who might be inclined to regard politics as a thing divorced from purely industrial concerns. There are certainly many examples of the officials of white collar unions, mindful of their own memberships, nervously reminding delegates at annual congress that the TUC must always retain a separate identity from the party which it founded.[2] However, we must take care not to exaggerate the size of the potential wedge that some perceive being driven between the TUC and the party. Significantly, table 2.3 indicates that these 'non-partisan' - though not necessarily non-political - unions are by no means necessarily a growing component of the TUC. Unions affiliated to the Labour Party today account for around three-fifths of TUC membership, just as they did twenty years ago.

Table 2.3
TUC membership and affiliation to the Labour Party, selected years

Year	Unions in TUC	Total TUC memb'ship	Unions affiliated to the Labour Party	Total Labour affiliated union memb'ship	Number of Labour affiliates as a % of TUC total	Labour's affiliated memb'ship as a % of TUC total
1900	184	1,250,000	41	353,070	22.3	28.2
1945	191	6,575,654	69	2,510,369	36.1	38.2
1964	175	8,325,790	81	5,502,001	46.3	66.1
1966	170	8,867,522	79	5,538,744	46.5	62.5
1970	150	9,402,170	67	5,518,520	44.7	58.7
1974	109	10,002,224	63	5,787,467	57.8	57.9
1979	112	12,128,078	59	6,511,179	52.7	53.7
1983	102	10,510,157	47	6,101,438	46.1	58.1
1987	87	9,243,297	40	5,564,477	46.0	60.2

Sources: TUC Annual Reports; Reports of the Annual Conference and the NEC of the Labour Party.

This brief analysis seems to suggest that the link between the Labour Party and the unions remains as important as ever in so far as party membership is concerned. Labour's affiliated membership is proportionately as significant as ever it was, the proportion of the TUC affiliating to the party has not weakened notably and the TUC still encompasses the vast bulk of union membership in Britain. Nonetheless, it is interesting to note that the party may well consider that this is no longer good enough. As a corollary of the party's much-vaunted policy review it has been suggested that the traditional myth of a mass membership (while in reality power lies with a relatively small number of constituency activists and union barons who dominate the annual conference) needs to be seen for what it is. The only way to curb the influence of radical activists may be to generate an authentic mass membership of a million or more individuals who are socially and attitudinally representative of the wider electorate. To be effective, it follows that it it is also necessary to diminish the power of the unions at conference; what is the attraction of joining a party as an enthusiastic individual member if real influence continues to lie with a few union leaders? Similar logic has been used to explain the political inactivity of trade union members themselves:

> The very existence of the block vote seemed to hinder the development of a politically active trade union membership. The party's own internal surveys showed that very few active trade unionists devoted much time to the Party. Out of 6 million union members and 10,000 union branches affiliated to the party, possibly no more than 4,000 trade union activists were similarly active in the Party. The trade unions with the busiest Labour Party members were white collar professional unions which were not affiliated...The manual unions, the life-blood of the party, had relatively few members in the party (Hughes and Wintour 1990: 190).

Hence, we may expect to see the national drive for individual party members accompanied by the modification of the union block vote at party conference in the future. The 1988 conference empowered the party's NEC to look into the reform of the block vote, and the 1990 conference agreed to the principle of diminishing its overall weight. Whether the goal of an active mass membership is a realistic target or simply an anchronistic illusion is another matter, of course. However, none of this necessarily implies that the unions will no longer have a place in the business of building party membership in the future. Indeed, if the projected recruiting drive is to become manifest, the opposite is quite likely given the growing feeling within the movement that unions' own memberships are an untapped mine of potential recruits to the party. The process of joining the Party has been simplified and trade unionists are now entitled to a temporary discount on subscription rates. But we should not be deceived into imagining that this holds out the real prospect of the unions losing their traditional significance as the party's pay masters.

2. Financial links between the party and the unions

The aspect of organisational interlinkage which has always attracted most attention in the case of the Labour Party and the unions is, of course, that of finance. It has often been controversial at the level of partisan rhetoric; occasionally, it has been thrust onto the centre of the agenda of national politics, notably in the middle of the 1980s. But is the financial dependence of the party upon the unions as strong as ever? This is the essential question that we shall try to answer in this section. It is naturally crucial to the broader question of the continuing organisational input of the unions.

In the main, I intend to concentrate upon the financial connection between the party and the unions at the national level. It is, perhaps, simplest and most appropriate to split the discussion between the party's *General Fund*, its *General Election Fund* and various other miscellaneous spending projects. How far do the unions contribute to these different funds?

Table 2.4
Trade union affiliation fee contributions to the Labour Party's General Fund, 1964-1987 (£)

Year	Total income	Total affiliation fee income	Trade union affiliation fees	Union % of affiliation fee income	Union fees as a % of total income
1964	385,576	315,539	276,237	87.5	71.6
1966	386,945	313,976	273,716	87.2	70.7
1970	516,110	443,625	401,792	90.6	77.9
1974	869,027	743,208	670,488	90.2	77.2
1979	2,151,238	2,112,830	1,842,383	87.2	85.6
1983	3,776,000	3,568,000	2,969,000	83.2	78.6
1987	5,873,000	5,328,000	4,180,000	78.5	71.2

Source: Annual Reports of the National Executive Committee of the Labour Party.

Table 2.4 shows at a glance just how important the unions remain to the Labour Party's general finances. Unsurprisingly, given the foregoing discussion of membership, it can be seen that the vast bulk of all affiliation fee income that the party earns comes from the trade unions; comparatively little is contributed by the party's other affiliated organisations, the cooperative and socialist societies, although it has to be said that these bodies do contribute a slightly greater proportion of all affiliation fees than formerly. Nonetheless, the proportion of the total General Fund represented by union affiliation fees has remained fairly steady since the early 1960s. That it has not actually increased - as it threatened to do in the 1970s - is only due to the substantial real increase in individual membership fees that was imposed in the 1980s. The annual party membership fee was 30 pence per member in 1964, rising to 60 pence in 1966, and £1.20 in 1974. But as recorded individual membership plummetted in the 1980s, the party forced up the subscription rate to £6 in 1983 and £10 in 1987. The only other possible source of General Fund revenue is that derived from returns on investment. In 1960 Martin Harrison complained that the Labour Party was relatively unadventurous in this respect ('The insignificance of investment income is remarkable' Harrison 1960: 61), and in all honesty it appears that little has changed in this respect. Thus, for example, in 1983 the entire contribution to the party's general revenue of £3,776,000 made by investment income amounted to just £7,000. (The situation vis a vis the General Election Fund was little different, investment returns totalling £23,000 out of £2,590,000.) To reiterate then, the unions surely remain as important to the Labour Party's general financing as ever they did.

The second major national party fund is the General Election Fund. The Labour Party appears to be a little less forthcoming in reporting details of the sources of this fund. Table 2.5 simply informs of the total donations to the fund in general election years.

Table 2.5
Total donations to General Election Funds, 1964-1987 (£)

Year	Total donations
1964	611,464
1966	357,085
1970	513,035
1974	914,998
1979	857,592
1983	2,183,000
1987	3,760,000

Source: Annual Reports of the National Executive Committee of the Labour Party.

For most of these years, the party's annual report tends to satisfy itself - if not the inquisitive reader - with somewhat vague comments to the effect that these donations were made 'principally by trade unions' (1964) or derived 'mainly from the unions' (1966). Such comments are not completely uninformative, but they lack precision, of course. However, we are able to be a great deal more exact about the situation since 1979. Table 2.6 indicates that the unions have been no less responsible for funding Labour's election campaigning than for its general operations. As Pinto-Duschinsky says:

> Despite the use of direct mail fund-raising, the party still relied overwhelmingly on trade union contributions. The main story of Labour Party fund-raising during 1983-7 and in the 1987 campaign was the success in attracting money from the unions. This was achieved despite the sharply falling membership of trade unions...(Pinto-Duschinsky 1989: 17).

Table 2.6
Sources of Labour's General Election Fund, 1979-1987

	Trade unions	Other	Total	Union % of total
1979	834,870	102,722 *	937,592	89.0
1983	2,147,000	36,000	2,183,000	98.4
1987	3,775,228	300,000	4,075,228	92.6

* This figure includes a grant to the election fund from the General Fund, which itself is heavily dependent upon union sources, of course. Consequently, the percentage figure in the final column of the 1979 entry is something of an underestimate of the true degree of union input.

Source: Annual Reports of the National Executive Committee, Pinto-Duschinsky 1989: 18.

Table 2.7 breaks down the overall figure for union donations by major individual contributions for 1983 and 1987. From this it becomes clear that seven trade unions alone (plus the TULV in 1983), accounted for over 70% of the total union input for each of these elections. (Moreover, this ignores far from insubstantial efforts made by unions like COHSE, the NUR and ASTMS.) Clearly, some major unions are still quite prepared to regard the connection with Labour as something serious enough to pay big money for.

Quite apart from the financing of Labour's General and General Election Funds, the unions have also shown themselves willing to foot bills which benefit the party in various other, not insignificant, ways. The most notable such example in recent years probably concerns the provision of a party headquarters. For many years lodgings were provided at Transport House in Smith Square, Westminster, the national headquarters of the Transport and General Workers' Union. Towards the end of the 1970s, however, it was decided that the party should be re-housed in new premisses of its own. A site

Table 2.7
Major individual contributions to Labour's General Election Fund, 1983 and 1987

1983		1987	
1. TGWU	508,252	1. TGWU	1,279,000
2. GMBATU	306,805	2. GMBATU	630,750
3. NUM	234,150	3. NUPE	260,000
4. NUPE	220,048	4. AUEW	250,000
5. AUEW	217,500	5. NUM	207,000
6. TULV Levy Fund	100,000	6. NUR	161,000
7. UCW	87,163	7. UCW	158,000
8. USDAW	80,000	8. USDAW	62,150

Sources: Annual Report of the National Executive Committee; Pinto-Duschinsky 1989: 23.

was secured south of the Thames at Walworth Road, and a comfortable new building erected. The precise cost of the exercise has never been published but, needless to say, the price of development in London has never been cheap; the project was financed by a consortium of major trade unions which now holds a 999 year lease on the property. Other examples of union spending which benefit the party are provided by the specific issue campaigns that certain unions run from time to time. Most notable in this respect are the anti-privatisation and anti-spending cuts campaigns which have been run since 1979 by some of the public sector unions. Obviously in the unions' own interest, these campaigns nonetheless undeniably dovetail with Labour's philosophy and political rhetoric. Such would be true of, for instance, NALGO's *Stop The Cuts* campaign of 1983.

Martin Harrison posed the question in 1960 of whether the unions really 'pulled their weight' in funding the Labour Party as a political organisation. He concluded that, broadly speaking, they probably did not ('..the unions have been enjoying the benefits of political action on the cheap' [Harrison 1960: 100-102]), but one might contend that the material we have considered so far all tends to suggest the unions have paid a substantial price for their political link with Labour. At the very least, it is worth noting that their financial input has been maintained in real terms in spite of the frequent tensions in the relationship that they have enjoyed with the party over the past thirty years. In the first three decades after the war the unions benefited from the steady growth of trade union membership in Britain, which permitted them to increase the contributions they made to the party without actually pushing up the contribution per member in line with inflation (Fatchett 1987: 48). However, they have been obliged to demonstrate the real extent of their commitment to Labour in hard financial terms over the course of the most recent decade. This has been accomplished mainly through boosting affiliation levels to the party. In 1979 the amount of money paid to the party by the unions amounted to 84% of all income that they were actually able to generate through the political levy. Nine years later the unions were affiliating for 105% of the numbers paying the levy. Thus, although the number of levy paying union members declined by 29% during the period, actual affiliation levels dropped by just 11%. Moreover, affiliation fees increased by more than 80% in real terms between the elections of 1979 and 1987, and the levy increased as a proportion of total union subscriptions. Overall, union contributions increased by more than 50% in real terms, even though they lost a quarter of their levy-paying members in this time (Upham and Wilson 1989: 7). One final piece of evidence which underlines the sense of commitment that many unions manifestly demonstrate about the organic link with Labour cannot be ignored. This is provided by the fight to save their political funds during the mid-1980s.

The story of the battle over trade union political funds is one that has received much coverage in the media as well as in academic circles (Coates and Topham 1986, Fatchett 1987, Grant 1987). In the early 1900s the unions financed the Labour Representation Committee out of their general funds or, occasionally, out of special parliamentary funds. The former required no special balloting of members in order that it be established, though the latter did. During these years the battle lines were drawn up over various issues involving the legal rights and liabilities of unions; the notorious 'Osborne Judgement' of 1909 was one such instance which focused on the rights of unions to continue financing the Labour Party. A lay official of the Amalgamated Society of Railway Servants sought to legally restrain his union's right to levy and distribute money for political ends, and the House of Lords acceded to his demand.

A rash of similar injunctions was subsequently and quickly imposed on other unions seeking to support the Labour Party, but the Liberal government returned to office in 1910 required Labour's parliamentary support; as a quid pro quo it introduced the Trade Union Act of 1913 which largely continued to define the legal parameters of union activity until the 1980s, (this despite the fact that, according to Coates and Topham, it was '..regarded by the whole movement at the time of its passage as an unfair and discriminatory piece of law', [Coates and Topham 1986: 118]). The new law permitted the establishment of special political funds which could be used by unions for, amongst other objects, the purpose of making contributions to the Labour Party.[3] However, these funds had first to be approved by union memberships in secret ballots. This was to be a once and for all time consultation procedure, though dissenting union members were subsequently to have the right to contract out of participating in the political fund.

With the notable exception of the hiatus created by the Trade Disputes and Trade Unions Act of 1927 (which replaced the 'contracting-out' proviso with a 'contracting-in' one, until its repeal in 1946) little changed, legally speaking, until the 1980s. In January 1983, however, the Employment Secretary Norman Tebbit introduced the Green Paper *Democracy In Trade Unions* (Cmnd 8778: 1983). This criticised the traditional arrangements and argued that there should be a regular re-balloting of members on the question of the maintenance of political funds, that the present definition of 'political' was no longer adequate and that contracting-in should be re-established since there were too many practical hindrances to the act of contracting out. Subsequent to the election that summer, legislation was introduced which was broadly based on the rhetoric and recommendations of the Green Paper, although contracting-in was not proposed. The TUC managed to avoid this after consulations with Tebbit and his successor, Tom King; as a result of these negotiations, the TUC produced a new 'code of practice' which promised to make the contracting-out procedure fairer and easier for union members who wished to follow this course of action. Nevertheless, the Trade Union Act of 1984 appeared to do the unions and the Labour Party very few favours. Amongst other things, this new piece of legislation introduced a new provision requiring unions to reballot their members every decade on the question of political funds, whilst also redefining the meaning of the term 'political' within the context of the law. This latter point promised to be crucial since it threatened to prevent individual unions running specific issue campaigns which might in some way conceivably benefit the public standing of a party - unless that campaign was also financed out of the political fund (Taylor 1987a: 214-215). In retrospect, it is possible to argue that this provided many unions with a vital key to the strategy they were to adopt in going to their memberships on the matter of the retention of the political funds. Unions such as NALGO, for instance, were able to claim that under the provisions of the new Act, efforts like their *Stop The Cuts* campaign of 1983 would have been outlawed unless the political fund was retained - even though it did not specifically involve contributions to, or polemic on behalf of, the Labour Party. Opinion polls commissioned at the time all tended to reveal how unpopular the link with Labour was amongst ordinary union members, and yet a closer reading of some of them indicated that clear majorities were in favour of union involvement in certain political issues, especially those which 'directly' affected members' interests. Table 2.8 provides an illustration of how union members felt about the different forms of political activity that unions engage in.

Table 2.8
Affiliated union memberships' level of approval of various forms of trade union political action, 1982-1984

	Approve	Disapprove
Of political activities on behalf of members	44%	45%
Of affiliation and donation of money to the Labour Party	38%	52%
Of using up to 5p. of a member's weekly contribution for political activities	42%	47%
Of supporting MPs in the interest of the union's members	63%	27%
Of campaigns which directly affect members' pay and jobs	60%	32%
Of campaigns which indirectly affect members' pay and jobs	26%	61%
Of industrial action against government economic policies	37%	53%
Of full participation in key decisions affecting economy	57%	34%

Sources: MORI 1982; Taylor 1987a: 210

Writing in *The Guardian* in 1984, the journalist John Torode succinctly summarised the position emerging from data of this nature:

> ..what MORI suggests is that most trade union members want their unions to be able to indulge in political campaigning. They also want to be able to fund MPs of their choice. What most trade unionists object to is specifically the direct and exclusive constitutional link with the Labour Party (Torode 1984: 21).

Following the passage of the new legislation the unions started mobilising amongst their members for the campaigns on the retention of political funds. The *Trade Union Coordinating Committee* (TUCC) was established as an umbrella organisation of the 37 unions required to ballot their memberships. Although this might have seemed a duplication of the functions of the TULV (see below), it was felt that a new single-purpose body was needed since the NUM and AUEW had both quit TULV through concern over the political direction it was taking. TULV therefore took the step of establishing a TUCC which incorporated both these unions, and donated an initial grant of £50,000 towards it costs. It was chaired by the former general secretary of SOGAT'82, Bill Keys, and he was assisted by two full time officers who were seconded from individual unions (Graham Allen and Sheila Field). The TUCC had a General Management Committee and an Executive Committee (representing just the major unions) at national level, and a regional structure. In total it spent around £200,000 which made it a comparatively inexpensive national campaign vehicle; this largely reflected the fact that it relied far more on the existing structures of the union movement in order to communicate with the rank and file, than it did on high profile media advertising. The workplace branch was the crucial focus of the campaign, in which five major lines of argument were stressed to members:

i. The government's legislation was unfair and undemocratic.
ii. The political background influenced most of the issues affecting ordinary working people.
iii. Important gains were made on behalf of members through the political action that unions were involved in.
iv. The central issue was not how the political fund was spent, but its very existence.
v. Even those not paying the levy should vote for the funds in order that others had the freedom to choose whether or not to pay (Fisher 1988: 69-70).

The TUCC preferred not to hold all individual union ballots simultaneously, partly for fear that it would provide the opportunity for a hostile media campaign to focus on 'national polling day', and partly because, by commencing with the unions most likely to retain the funds, a bandwagon effect might be created. Campaign literature was produced by the TUCC and the individual unions, videos released and meetings held. The Labour Party itself played a fairly low-key role in the campaign, unsurprisingly given the nature of a strategy which made relatively little play of the party link. This held at local level as well as nationally, as Fatchett has taken pains to illustrate (see table 2.9).

Table 2.9
Constituency Labour involvement in political fund ballot campaigns, 1984-1985

No involvement	44.6%
Internal CLP discussion, but no external activity	31.2%
Offered assistance, but not taken up	6.9%
Assistance with facilities	6.9%
Involved in actual union campaign work	8.4%
No response	2.0%

Source: Fatchett 1987: 78.

As the first ballot results became known - all affirming the intention of maintaining political funds - some Conservatives complained that the campaigns were misleading, and had sought to to divert members' attention from the underlying nature of the link with Labour (Fatchett 1987: 79). However, criticism was somewhat restrained, possibly out of a desire to avoid drawing heavy counterfire over the sources of Conservative Party funding. Voting took place either in the workplace or through postal balloting, turnout generally being higher in the former case. In no case did a union reject the idea of continuing an established fund, as table 2.10 illustrates; indeed, in fully eighteen subsequent cases unions which had not previously had any political fund decided to hold ballots on the matter and voted to establish new funds (Upham and Wilson 1989: 9). Interestingly, however, many of these unions with new political funds chose not to affiliate to the Labour Party, which perhaps indicates a growing partisan independence of unions generally, though not a weakening commitment to Labour among its own affiliates (Fisher 1991).

The lowest 'yes' vote in a political fund ballot was 59% by the ACTT, and regional variations were not great, although the south of England was slightly less positive in support for the funds (Fisher 1988: 85-93). Moreover, the whole process of mobilising support for the retention of the funds has demonstrated a point which may have long term ramifications for Labour's electoral strategy in the future. The unions were forced to go to their grass roots memberships and justify their political activities and, to a degree, their link with the Labour Party (Leopold 1986). This inspired the sort of political

Table 2.10
Political fund ballot results, 1985-1986

Union	In Favour	Against	Turnout
SOGAT'82	78.0%	22.0%	56.0%
ISTC	87.0%	13.0%	67.0%
FTAT	72.0%	28.0%	30.0%
UCW	75.5%	24.5%	69.0%
NCU (Engineers)	81.0%	19.0%	79.0%
GMBATU	89.0%	11.0%	61.0%
APEX	73.0%	27.0%	60.0%
EETPU	84.0%	16.0%	45.0%
AUEW	84.0%	16.0%	37.0%
NUR	87.0%	13.0%	61.0%
NUS	86.5%	13.5%	34.0%
PLCTWU	75.0%	25.0%	98.0%
ASLEF	93.0%	7.0%	85.0%
TSSA	69.0%	31.0%	67.0%
CATU	77.0%	23.0%	73.0%
National Union of Scalemakers	77.0%	23.0%	54.0%
TGWU	81.0%	19.0%	49.5%
COHSE	91.0%	9.0%	40.0%
NUDAGO	84.5%	15.5%	68.0%
NUTGWU	91.0%	9.0%	87.0%
NLB	90.0%	10.0%	83.0%
NUFLAT	78.0%	22.0%	84.0%
USDAW	88.0%	12.0%	39.5%
ACTT	59.0%	41.0%	49.0%
NGA	78.0%	22.0%	73.0%
TWU	90.0%	10.0%	76.0%
NACODS	87.0%	13.0%	76.0%
TASS	76.0%	24.0%	55.0%
NUPE	84.5%	15.5%	9.0%
RUBSSO	78.0%	22.0%	40.0%
GALO	84.0%	16.0%	92.0%
MU	76.0%	24.0%	36.5%
NUM	91.0%	9.0%	76.0%
FBU	80.0%	20.0%	87.0%
ASTMS	81.0%	19.0%	32.0%
UCATT	91.5%	8.5%	25.0%

awareness campaign among ordinary union members that had never taken place before. The lessons of this were by no means lost on Party and union activists; in the wake of the political fund campaigns the Trades Union For Labour organisation (TUFL) was established, a body whose work we shall be considering in greater detail subsequently. Its basic goal, however, was to build upon the momentum generated by TUCC's work in order to develop a consistent political education effort amongst union members. Although there are those who are disappointed that this work has not really gone far enough, it may yet prove a significant departure in Labour's electoral strategy. It has already been claimed that TUFL helped win the party new electoral support in 1987 (see below).

There is little or nothing in this review of financial links that suggests a weakened organisational connection between the party and the unions. In real terms the unions seem to pour as much money into the party as ever they did; the campaigns over political funds clearly demonstrates how important the financial link continues to be to them. Moreover,it has arguably had the spin-off effect of generating an extra strand to the organisational nexus between the party and the unions via TUFL. There remains, perhaps, the question of union views on the matter of state aid to political parties. A groundswell of opinion within the union movement in favour of state financial aid might be taken as evidence of a shift towards a weaker link. For sure, a Labour Party that could rely upon the state to pay a major proportion of its bills would not be so beholden to the unions politically, and there are many who would regard such a development as beneficial to both sets of actors in the relationship. The journalist John Lloyd provides an example that encapsulates this position. Lloyd has argued quite plausibly that the unions' memberships have been changing, and this has forced them to become more flexible and competitive in seeking members from new industrial and occupational sectors in a context of high unemployment, low inflation and hostile governmental and employer relationships. Allied with a process of longer term social change this has produced union memberships which are 'more diverse and individualised', and an inevitable consequence of this has been the declining demand on the part of those memberships for '..the unions to provide a political service of which the majority do not approve and which, even if they did, they would normally wish to do for themselves.' It is hard to break the party-union relationship for it is founded on solid foundations of 'money, power and a certain corruption', but on the whole it would be better for both if this relationship was now sundered. The unions dominate the party's policy making process through the conference block vote, and this inevitably kills the incentive of all but the extreme few to join and be active in the constituencies. Lloyd concludes that there is a need for the union role and input to be greatly downgraded so that the membership would have a real task to undertake in raising funds and running the party. To make their targets realistic, their work would have to be underpinned by the substantial state funding of party expenses. All this could have the effect of stimulating a new membership drive and rendering the party and the unions 'at least semi-detached', and so freer to act. The party would not be seen to be the puppet of the unions, and would not thereby suffer from the virtually permanent unpopularity of the latter, though nothing would actually prevent the unions from making contributions to the party or engaging in a constructive and friendly relationship with it. The point is simply that the organic link between the two would be weakened, but this would have the paradoxical effect of revitalising the party (Lloyd 1988: 34-39). An essentially similar argument has been proposed by Eric Hammond, General Secretary of EETPU, who has complained about the way that certain public sector unions have used their political influence 'unreasonably' within the party. He too hopes that 'Britain will soon follow the rest of Europe towards a level of state aid for political parties', yet it is interesting to note the limits he imposes on his case. Controversial and right wing he may have been regarded as by many within the labour movement, and yet he is happy to state emphatically enough that, during the course of the political fund campaigns:

> Not only did we argue that our union needed a political voice but, in particular, both ourselves and the AEU argued that that voice needed to find expression through the Labour Party (Hammond 1988: 25-27).

Maybe this is an example of the 'sentimentality' that Lloyd regards as continuing to bind the party and the unions to one another; others like Geoffrey Goodman prefer to speak of the shared 'ethos' they manifest (Goodman 1988: 28-29). Either way, they both make an important point. The sheer cultural legacy of the shared history the party and the unions enjoy makes it highly unlikely that the two will undergo some process of organisational divorce in the forseeable future, no matter how politically estranged they appear to be from time to time. None of this is meant to imply that the party and the unions have set themselves irreversibly against all possibility of an increase in the level of state aid beyond the contribution to parliamentary parties that is presently maintained. Indeed, it has been noted that, during the consultations preceding the publication of the Houghton Report on political finance in 1976, affiliated unions 'strongly supported' state aid, 'fully conscious that this would reduce the party's dependence on them' (Crouch 1982: 178). Moreover, the party has recently affirmed that it is 'committed to a major extension of state aid to benefit the activities of political parties' (Labour Party 1988: 5). The point is, however, that state aid is regarded by neither the party nor the unions as a potential replacement for union contributions. It is merely a possible complement to the unions' input. Whatever, it has to be said that there is little immediate prospect of the extension of state financial aid to political parties in Britain. Even if the notion of a 'semi-detached' relationship sustained by state aid becomes a logically compelling scenario in the long term, its arrival is far from imminent; in the meantime it is hard to argue that the unions are gradually withdrawing meaningful financial backing from the Labour Party. The political funds question more than exemplifies this point.

Broadly then, the unions put as much into the party financially, at national level, as they ever did. What of the local linkage? In this respect, the published sources provide somewhat sketchy information. Labour's annual reports tend to gloss over connections with unions in the regions and constituencies in rather broad terms; few statistics are provided. To take one of the election years of interest to us, for example, in 1979 three out of the eleven regional organisations of the party actually made no reference whatsoever to the unions in their contributions to the NEC Annual Report (1979: 33-38). Of the remainder, most were satisfied with brief and on the whole rather uninformative comments; for instance, we learn simply that the Labour Party in the South West conducted 'regular consultations with trade union officers', or that 'excellent efforts by our trade union colleagues could not stem the tide' against the party in the Southern region during the general election. Only the North West, North East and Greater London Labour Parties actually report how many union members were affiliated to the regions (1,150,000, 645,430 and 729,963 respectively). None say anything about the financial implications of sub-national relationships. Such lack of emphasis may either reflect the fact that connections with the unions in the regions are so obvious a political fact of life as to be taken largely for granted in such official accounts, or alternatively they may indicate the paucity of union input on this level. Certainly, we have no basis for analysing the financial commitments of local and regional union organisations if we rely solely upon party publications.

Fortunately, some helpful academic research on this theme has been conducted. For instance, Martin Harrison felt able to conclude in 1960 that around two-thirds to three-quarters of the Labour Party's regional funds originated with the trade unions (Harrison 1960: 76). More recently, Derek Fatchett has generated a rare data set on the direct contributions that unions make towards the funding of local CLPs. As a general rule local parties do not generate more than a few thousand pounds a year in income, and of this only a certain amount comes directly from unions. Pinto-Duschinsky has explained that this follows from the traditional demand from the NEC for union money to be directed towards the centre, rather than risk 'frittering it away on various local Labour causes' (Pinto-Duschinsky 1980: 175). Therefore, presuming that this demand is generally adhered to, it would be surprising if Pinto-Duschinsky's claim that 'every level of the Labour Party organisation (is) heavily dependent on the unions' actually holds true. Thus, Fatchett found that less than 2% of CLPs relied on union contributions for more than half of their income; nearly 90% of parties obtained less than a quarter of their income from this source. On the basis of this information he went on to conclude that 'it can be tentatively estimated that some 60% of the Labour Party's total income at all levels comes from the trade unions' (Fatchett 1987: 50-51). Interestingly, he claims that the pattern of greater union input at the central level rather than the local level tends to be repeated in the sphere of party policy making. Thus, it was rare in his experience for union branch delegations to constitute a majority of either constituency General Management Committees or Executive Committees. Indeed, in as many as 36% of cases, affiliated unions could not even find enough delegates to fill all the places to which they were entitled on these bodies. Nonetheless, nearly a third of constituency party chairmen, and a quarter of party secretaries came from the unions (Ibid: 54-55). Clearly, the party-union organisational relationship has traditionally been, and continues to be, concentrated at the centre rather than in the locality. Unions are as happy as ever to finance the party nationally, but do not regard the local and regional organisations as important enough to invest heavily in - and they probably never have done. At once this explains the weakness of Labour's local organisation in general and illustrates the extent of the party's reliance on the unions for organisational development. It is worth observing, however, that it is one of the objectives of TUFL, a relatively new forum of party-union linkage, to try and strengthen the local connection. We shall return to this later.

3. Labour's annual conference

Table 2.2, by showing how more than 90% of Labour's membership is still affiliated union membership, reminds us of the capacity of the unions to influence the party's annual conference through the block vote. This system affords the unions voting power at conference in direct proportion to the weight of their membership; obviously, as a combined group this confers upon them an overwhelming numerical advantage vis a vis the delegates from the constituency parties. The major unions, in particular, have tremendous potential leverage through this voting power. The TGWU alone is able to account for around one fifth of the conference's total voting strength. For many years the party leadership was able to stave off the advance of radicals in the constituency parties by drawing on the support of major union leaders at conference. None of these leaders had to worry about their union's delegation splitting its vote; all members of a delegation were obliged to vote the same way. It was simply a matter of successfully influencing the decision about how the delegation was to vote. A combination of the block vote and the influence of the unions on the Conference Arrangements Committee (on which they are in a majority) habitually ensured that 'much of what emerged as the decisions of the conference' bore marks of the interaction between party and union elites (Minkin 1980: 317).

Over the past twenty years, however, the major unions have not always made such reliable allies for the party leadership. As we shall see in the next chapter, the leadership has often come under severe pressure over questions of incomes policy and industrial relations legislation. Moreover, during the 1970s and early 1980s the left wing Campaign For Labour Party Democracy (CLPD) began to make notable inroads into the ranks of union activists and officials over questions of Labour Party constitutional reform (Kogan and Kogan 1982). This too produced occasional differences at conference between the party leadership and some of the major unions. Indeed, even at the best of times, as far as the party-union elite relationship is concerned, Lewis Minkin - the author of the definitive work to date on the party conference - has taken pains to stress that 'it was difficult for the party leadership to make positive commitments which ran counter to the policy boundaries set by the unions' (Minkin 1980: 317). He has spoken of the 'delicate interaction with the unions' which which has produced a characteristic 'pattern of collective restraint' in the party power structure; this obliges the party leadership - particularly when in opposition - to make major accommodations over a range of policy issues extending well beyond the narrower industrial matters of direct interest to the unions. Thus, the apparent 'passivity' of the major union leaderships in the 1950s and most of the 1960s was 'always a contingent and not an endemic feature' of the power structure. In fact, Minkin insists, each separate issue produces a different relationship and balance of power between the party leadership, the unions and the constituencies.

Since its inception the block vote has come in for criticism, often from radical constituency activists. Yet it is only recently that the prospect of its reform has actually become tangible. The reason for this change of heart within the labour movement's elite has much to do with the wide ranging policy review that the party embarked upon following its third consecutive general election defeat in 1987. The general thrust of the review, stated crudely, has been to produce policies that will be more likely to attract the support of the ordinary and, it is assumed largely moderate, voters rather than the political enthusiasts who run Labour's constituency parties. As part of the strategy developed to make this new policy package workable, and in order to dilute the influence of the activists, the leadership has decided that certain constitutional changes are required of the party. Most notable is the proposal to reform the block vote (refer again to pages 18-19, or Lloyd's views outlined on page 30 above). This is ironic in some senses, since the block vote has been important to the passage of the policy review, and yet many regard the proposal to reform it as unavoidable if a new mass membership is to be developed. Curiously, such a strategic shift might seem a virtual anachronism, since Kirchheimer warned of the demise of the mass membership model of a social democratic party over twenty years ago (Kirchheimer 1969). Nonetheless, the Labour leadership in Britain has decided that individual members are to have greater power within the movement, above all at the heart of the party's democratic policy making process - its annual conference - in order that more are inspired to join and participate. Consequently, the relative importance of the unions in such a policy process must be down-graded. The 1990 conference finally chose to endorse the retention of the union block vote in principle, whilst reducing its overall weight to 70% of the total conference electorate. The precise details of how this is to be done will only emerge after the next general election, but it is obvious that they may have implications for the structure of power and organisation within the Labour Party. However, we need not speculate further on this. Our purpose is limited to explaining the changing electoral behaviour of union members between 1964 and 1987; obviously, the imminent reform of the unions' role at party conference can in no way account for this. In these terms, then, we can really only say that there is no evidence of diminished trade union input into Labour's annual conference over the course of the period which interests us. Organisationally, the party-union linkage has been maintained in this respect, and it can therefore hardly help explain the apparent political divorce between Labour and the trade union constituency. Indeed, the impression of a union role of continuing significance at party conference is reinforced when we consider the available data on agenda-setting and debates. Minkin argues strongly that the Conference Arrangements Committee, the organisational nucleus of the agenda-setting process at conference, is not only genuinely independent of the PLP leadership, but is moreover 'the preserve of the largest unions' (Minkin 1980: 321). Though always certain to 'sound out' the party leadership in the months preceding conference, the Arrangements Committee has consistently been prepared to place potentially contentious issues - such as incomes policy - on the agenda.

Conference is, formally speaking, the summit of party policy formulation. It is central, but not the only arena of policy making, of course. In particular, the various committees of the party - and above all the NEC - are crucially important to the policy process. What role have the unions played here?

4. The National Executive Committee

Table 2.11 makes it readily apparent that the unions are as well represented on Labour's NEC as ever; indeed, their formal representation has increased slightly from around 32% to 37.5% of the total committee membership. When allowance is made for the fact that some of those sitting on the NEC in *non*-union representational capacity often have union backgrounds also, it becomes obvious that the unions are quite able to articulate their views at this level of the party structure. For instance, in 1987 two out of the five NEC members who sat as women's representatives were also trade union officials.

Table 2.11
Union representation on Labour's NEC, 1964-1987

Year	Unions	Socialist and cooperative societies	CLPs	Women	LPYS	% union representation on NEC *
1964	9	1	7	5	0	32.1
1966	11	1	7	4	0	37.9
1970	12	1	7	5	0	38.7
1974	12	1	7	5	0	38.7
1979	12	1	7	5	1	37.5
1983	12	1	7	5	1	37.5
1987	12	1	7	5	1	37.5

* In addition to the members included here, NEC membership is always supplemented by the Chair and Vice-chair of the party, the Leader and Deputy Leader, plus the General Secretary and the Treasurer. These have been taken into account in calculating the union proportion of NEC membership.

Source: NEC Annual Reports

Moreover, the NEC has a number of permanent sub-committees upon which the unions are represented. Five of these have existed throughout the period under investigation (some under a variety of titles), while the once important TUC-PLP Liaison Committee has been around since the early 1970s. The number and proportion of places on these committees taken up by union officials are reported in table 2.12. Once again, it is clear that there is no obvious pattern of declining involvement on the part of the unions. Indeed, with the exception of the Liaison Committee, the rate of participation by union

Table 2.12
Union representation on NEC sub-committees, 1964-1987

Year	Finance	Home	Organisation	International	Campaign	Liaison
1964	7/16	5/19	4/18	5/25	4/14	-
	(43.8%)	(26.3%)	(22.2%)	(20.0%)	(28.6%)	-
1966	8/16	7/18	5/18	7/21	3/14	-
	(50.0%)	(38.9%)	(27.8%)	(33.3%)	(21.4%)	-
1970	5/16	6/19	6/19	5/18	2/16	-
	(31.3%)	(31.6%)	(31.6%)	(27.8%)	(12.5%)	-
1974	6/15	4/23	7/18	6/21	3/15	8/22
	(40.0%)	(17.4%)	(38.9%)	(28.6%)	(20.0%)	(36.4%)
1979	5/11	2/16	4/16	7/16	3/11	N.A
	(45.5%)	(12.5%)	(25.0%)	(43.8%)	(27.3%)	N.A
1983	6/10	8/18	8/18	8/14	6/15	5/9
	(60.0%)	(44.4%)	(44.4%)	(57.1%)	(40.0%)	(55.6%)
1987	12/22	12/26	7/18	12/20	6/17	3/10
	(54.5%)	(46.2%)	(38.9%)	(60.0%)	(35.3%)	(30.0%)

Note: Finance - Finance and General Purposes; Home - Home policy; International - Overseas/International; Campaign - Press and Publicity/Campaign and Communications; Liaison - TUC-PLP Liaison.

These calculations are based upon a system of counting only those who are known trade union officials during the year under consideration; thus, ex-union officials who later become MPs, for example, are *not* considered union representatives. This gives a fairly conservative estimate of actual 'union representation'.

Source: NEC Annual Reports

officials has actually increased in all cases. The lowest recorded level of union representation on any of these committees is 12.5%, and the highest 60%. The average rates of union involvement for the various committees over the years are as follows:

Finance and General Purpose Committee	46.4%
Home Policy Committee	31.0%
Organisation Committee	32.7%
Overseas/International Committees	38.6%
Press & Publicity/Campaign & Communications Committees	26.4%
TUC-PLP Liaison Committee	40.7%

In addition, it should be said that each of these permanent committees sustains a structure of further sub-committees, all of which manifest similar levels of union representation. In short, there is no evidence that the unions have shown any inclination to withdraw from this level of party policy making.

Before concluding our brief discussion of the union presence in Labour's committee structure it is worth devoting a few comments to the TUC-PLP Liaison Committee, since this appeared for a while during the 1970s to be the crux of party-union organisational and political linkage. At the end of 1970, the committee was formed - largely at the instigation of Jack Jones of the TGWU - as a forum in which representatives of the NEC, the TUC and the Parliamentary Labour Party (PLP) could meet. Its initial brief was to consider the movement's response to the industrial relations legislation of the Heath government (see chapter 3). The scope of its work quickly expanded, however, and it was influential in the development of the policies proposed in the TUC's own *Economic Review* and *Labour's Programme For Britain* which emerged in the early 1970s. Indeed, these were succeeded by a series of documents which served as the basis of what was to develop into the Social Contract after 1974. For an experienced commentator such as Lewis Minkin, the Liaison Committee '..had good claim to be the most important committee in the party during this period' (Minkin 1980: 337). In a similar vein it has been emphasised that '..the main thrust of union activity in Labour policy making after 1970 took place in the Liaison Committee and not in the customary machinery of the party executive sub-committees' (Stallard 1987: 47). As a consequence, some tension was to develop between the NEC and the Liaison Committee; in some quarters the latter was, inevitably, regarded as a devious piece of chicanery through which Harold Wilson was able to bypass the NEC, on which he could not be assured of majority support. Nonetheless, Stallard has pointed out that there were few substantive policy differences between the two bodies at this stage. Once in government the Liaison Committee continued to serve as a forum of regular contact between union and governmental elites over matters of direct concern to the former; this institutional linkage alone was not enough to guarantee political convergence, however. It has been suggested that the TUC became increasingly uncertain of its institutional presence within the Labour Party hierarchy, and preferred to revert to the formal apparatus of the National Economic Development Council (Minkin 1980: 352), and this is perhaps hardly surprising, given that the TUC as a body has no formal affiliation to the party. Moreover, political divergence between the TUC and the government during the period made the committee less attractive to the unions; they were almost bound to re-emphasise their independence from the party as they came under pressure from their own rank and file memberships. The Liaison Committee never had a clear formal status within the party, and consequently its political star waxed and waned according to the prevalent political exigences of the day. There was nothing created to bind the body formally and conclusively into the institutional fabric of the Labour Party. Consequently, it was of little significance to the development of election manifestos in 1979 or after. It continues to exist as a forum for regular contact and consultation, but since the 1970s it has not challenged the formal policy formulating preeminence of the NEC and its sub-committees. This does not necessarily imply the weakening presence of the unions in the councils of the party, however.

5. The Trade Union Group in parliament

Writing in the 1970s, RW Johnson and John Ellis reported the rueful responses of union-sponsored MPs to the question of how they felt they were regarded by TUC leaders.

> They're amiable tyrants. They used us when they felt they needed us. In general they're suspicious of political action.
>
> As a bloody nuisance to them, to be used only when it suits their individual purposes...unions only have sponsored MPs for reasons of prestige (Johnson and Ellis 1974: 19).

The financial sponsoring and maintaining of MPs by trade unions is the oldest form of collaboration between unions and political parties in Britain. Initially, this did not involve the Labour Party, of course, but the Liberals. It was only in 1900 that the Labour Representation Committee was formed by the unions as a way of sending working men to parliament; even this did not automatically bring to an end the parliamentary links that were forged with the Liberals, especially in the case of the Miners (Pelling 1971: 126-128). Eventually, however, TUC affiliates interested in parliamentary links concentrated their efforts upon the new Labour Party. It is, of course, not the case that all members of the PLP are directly sponsored by unions, but a significant proportion continue to be. Why should this be so, given the jaundiced views of sponsored MPs like those referred to above?

The group of MPs who are sponsored by unions is not especially cohesive, though it does meet formally from time to time and elect officers. It rarely takes a united view of an issue, but is far more likely to be guided by the individual interests of its constituent sponsors. Johnson and Ellis pointed out that, although the sponsoring unions generally maintained fairly regular contact with their MPs, they were frequently loath to encourage energetic advocacy on their behalf in parliament. Since 1945 union leaders have been increasingly able to bypass the parliamentary channel and to concentrate on the corporate channel in their efforts to influence public policy. In George Woodcock's resonant phrase, the unions were hoping to move 'into Whitehall', and to elicit greater benefit from direct contact with ministers and civil servants. Given that this access has been considerably restricted since the return of Conservative government in 1979, one might expect the use of sponsored MPs has taken on renewed significance for unions; however, against such a resolutely hostile government the unions hardly need to single out the sponsored members for their defence. Almost any member of the PLP could be relied upon to reject Conservative employment amd industrial relations proposals during the 1980s. But unions have never shown any inclination to withdraw their commitment to sponsorships. In part this can be attributed to sheer habit and, as the anonymous MP quoted above suggested, prestige, but there are other, more tangible factors which come into play.

For a start, there is the claim that 'without the sponsorship system the actual representation of the working class would be virtually nil', as Johnson puts it (Johnson and Ellis 1974: 15). Presumably, some of the older industrial unions would wish to avoid such a development. Interestingly, more recent research into the social profile of the trade union group in fact shows two factors of note in this regard. Firstly, in terms of occupational class and educational experience the sponsored MPs are indeed more typically working class than the rest of the PLP (table 2.13); nonetheless, it also seems clear that the union group has moved somewhat away from its traditional working class profile over the years (table 2.14). One wonders, therefore, how much longer the traditional rationale for sponsorship that consisted of ensuring the place in parliament of men with a substantially similar background to ordinary union members can continue to be justified. The temptation to speculate along these

Table 2.13
Comparison of union-sponsored and other Labour MPs, 1983

	Union Group	Other MPs
MPs with higher education	34.7%	68.0%
MPs from professional occupations	24.8%	62.9%
MPs from working class occupations	37.6%	22.7%

Source: Park, Lewis and Lewis 1986: 311

lines is reinforced by the further information provided by Park and his colleagues that the proportion of union group members having no recorded experience of prior trade union work leapt from 12.3% in 1951 to 49% in 1983; furthermore, those who had actually been full time union officials before becoming sponsored MPs dropped from over one third to little more than one tenth in the same period (Park et al 1986: 310). This fact is particularly

Table 2.14
Social class characteristics of sponsored Labour MPs, 1951 and 1983

Characteristic	1951	1983
Experience of higher education	5.7%	34.7%
Professional, executive or managerial occupation	9.6%	43.6%
Supervisors and other non-manual grades	45.2%	34.7%
Manual workers	45.2%	21.8%

Source: Derived from Park, Lewis and Lewis 1986: 309.

interesting since it stands out as one of the few pieces of evidence we have so far uncovered which actually suggests a significant weakening of the *organisational* linkage between Labour and the unions. However, interesting as it is, it hardly constitutes a persuasive case in its own right, given that the sponsoring of MPs has long since been relatively unimportant to the party-union political relationship.

The most tangible reason of all for maintaining the sponsorship of Labour MPs is that it can directly benefit union interests. Despite the clear preference for negotiation with ministers and state bureaucrats, there are still likely to be occasions when the trade union group can be of service in this way. Johnson and Ellis cited a couple of examples from the 1960s which both illustrated how sponsored backbench MPs could be used to exert effective pressure on a Labour government; TGWU MPs were quietly influential in producing amendments to the Merchant Shipping Bill which followed the Seamen's strike of 1966, and the union group as a whole played a crucial role in the *In Place Of Strife* episode of 1969 (see chapter 3). In this latter instance the group acted with rare cohesion even though relatively little pressure was brought to bear upon it by the sponsoring unions (Johnson and Ellis 1974: 16-23). But this was a particular and unusual instance; May has pointed out that during the 1960s the sponsored MPs were twice as likely to respond to the call of the party whips as they were to the protests of their unions over the question of

Table 2.15
Parliamentary candidates and members sponsored by trade unions, 1964-1987

Year	Total number of candidates sponsored by unions	Total number of members sponsored by unions	Trade Union Group as a % of PLP
1964	138	120	37.9
1966	138	132	36.4
1970	137	114	39.6
1974 (February)	155	127	42.2
1974 (October)	141	127	39.8
1979	165	133	49.4
1983	153	114	54.5
1987	145	130	56.8

Source: NEC Annual Reports.

incomes policy (May 1978: 33). The final way in which the sponsored MPs can be of direct service to trade unions is through casework they conduct on behalf of individual union members. Nonetheless, in terms of general policy influence most union leaders seem to feel that there are better ways of approaching governments; given that, additionally, the background experience

Table 2.16
Major sponsoring unions, 1964-1987

1964	Candidates	MPs	1966	Candidates	MPs	1970	Candidates	MPs
1. NUM	29	28	1. NUM	28	27	1. TGWU	23	19
2. TGWU	23	21	2. TGWU	27	27	2. NUM	21	20
3. AEU	19	17	3. AEU	17	17	3. AUEW	21	16
4. USDAW	10	10	4. GMWU	10	10	4. GMWU	12	12
5. GMWU	7	7	5. USDAW	8	8	5. USDAW	7	7
6. TSSA	7	7	6. NUR	8	7	6. NUR	6	6
7. NUR	7	6				7. NUPE	6	6

Feb. 1974	Candidates	MPs	Oct. 1974	Candidates	MPs	1979	Candidates	MPs
1. AUEW	26	22	1. TGWU	23	22	1. TGWU	29	20
2. TGWU	23	22	2. NUM	18	18	2. NUM	18	16
3. NUM	21	18	3. AUEW	18	16	3. AUEW	18	16
4. ASTMS	14	9	4. GMWU	13	13	4. GMWU	14	14
5. GMWU	13	13	5. ASTMS	13	10	5. NUR	13	12
6. NUR	7	7	6. NUPE	7	6	6. ASTMS	12	8
7. NUPE	7	7	7. NUR	6	6			
			7. APEX	6	6			

1983	Candidates	MPs	1987	Candidates	MPs
1. TGWU	29	24	1. TGWU	34	31
2. AUEW	27	17	2. GMB	13	13
3. NUM	14	14	3. NUM	13	13
4. GMB	14	11	4. AEU	13	12
5. NUR	12	10	5. NUPE	12	9
6. ASTMS	11	10	6. USDAW	9	8

Source: NEC Annual Reports

of sponsored MPs is increasingly likely to distance them from their unions, one is bound to wonder if it has not occurred to union leaders and officials that sponsorship is an anachronism of, at best, marginal relevance. Is there any evidence that the unions are withdrawing from the sponsorship role? Table 2.15 reveals the broad picture since 1964; it is obvious that there are just as many sponsored candidates and members as ever. Moreover, the trade union group constitutes a greater proportion of the PLP than at the beginning of the period (partly a consequence of its reduction in size, no doubt). In this sense, the organisational link between Labour and the unions has in no way been diminished. In table 2.16 we are able to trace the half dozen major sponsoring unions at each of the general elections covered; the most notable features are the decline of the NUM, the growing importance of NUPE and ASTMS, and the steady commitment of the major general unions TGWU and GMBATU as sponsors. Though always important, the AEU has had a somewhat fluctuating record of sponsorship, whereas the NUR has maintained a constant commitment despite its declining membership.

Finally, it should be said that after the 1987 general election Labour elected a shadow front bench team more than three-quarters of which was sponsored by the trade unions.[4] This tends to reinforce the view that, if there has been any weakening of the organisational connection between the party and the unions, it certainly has not happened in the context of parliamentary sponsorship. Most of the present shadow cabinet are union members and union sponsored, and so is a good portion of the PLP.

6. Trade Unions For Labour Victory (TULV)

Since 1964 the relationship between the Labour Party and the trade unions has found expression in new institutional linkages beyond the traditional arenas of conference, executive and parliament. We have already mentioned the Liaison Committee, of course, which was a formal extension of the inevitable process of elite level accommodation within the labour movement. More interesting, in some ways, has been the development over the past decade of links which focus directly on the role that unions can play in renewing the party organisation and aiding electoral mobilisation. In the strictest sense this is literally an organisational role rather than a political one, and there are signs that the labour movement may even regard this as a more appropriate role for the unions in the future. While it would be unrealistic to expect the unions to withdraw from their positions on the NEC they do seem prepared to renounce the block vote in its present form, and the Liaison Committee clearly no longer threatens the supremacy of the NEC in the party's committee system; this raises the prospect that direct union involvement in party policy making may be replaced by a new emphasis on an organisational role to be played within the party. The chief institutional devices so far developed to facilitate such a role have been *Trade Unions For Labour Victory (TULV)* and *Trade Unions For Labour (TUFL)*.

TULV was largely the inspiration of the former leader of the General and Municipal Workers, the late David Basnett. It was initially launched in August 1978 (in mistaken anticipation of an autumn election) largely as a way of coordinating the unions' financial investment in, firstly, the new party headquarters at Walworth Road, and secondly, the forthcoming election effort. Previously, senior party officers had been obliged to contact individual unions and request donations. This was followed by a certain amount of informal union contact aimed at establishing the 'going rate' for contributions according to union size. The establishment of the TULV provided a more efficient apparatus through which this process could be coordinated. It was not long before the new body began to spread its wings, however, becoming more intimately bound up with the business of campaigning in particular. When it was formally constituted on a permanent basis in 1981 it announced its objectives in these terms:

> To establish a means by which trade unions can discuss matters of common interest in relation to the Labour Party and make recommendations on matters of finance, organisation and membership with the objective of ensuring the return of a Labour government (NEC Annual Report 1983: 22).

Clearly, the emphasis was placed upon the organisational and mobilisational tasks that the unions could undertake, rather than the policy making ones. Accordingly, in the 1979 general election the TULV concentrated largely upon coordinating the provision of full time union officials who could do campaign work for Labour in marginal seats; the TGWU and the GMWU proved particularly supportive in this respect. In addition, the TULV made some sort of an attempt to communicate in a more directly political way with the trade union rank and file than had hitherto been normal. This was illustrated by some of the publications that it issued for the campaign, which had titles like *Why Trade Unionists Must Vote Labour* and *The Tory Attack On The Unions*. As a result of this activity the TULV felt able to claim credit for having had some impact on the outcome of the election; for instance, it was stated that the seats where TULV had been involved suffered less from the anti-Labour swing in 1979 than did either surrounding seats or other marginals where TULV had no presence. Subsequently, the TULV set about developing its role and established the following goals:

i. The raising of political fund levels within unions.
ii. The improvement of Labour's financial management.
iii. The improvement of union membership and affiliation levels.
iv. The covering of key seats in all future elections.
v. The improvement of party organisation, structure and efficiency.

Before long, moreover, the TULV actively encouraged greater union-party rapport at regional level, for example through the generation of joint rallies, the birth of regional versions of the Liaison Committee and joint regional executive meetings. Indeed, by 1982 a regional TULV committee existed everywhere save Scotland. The recommendations of a party enquiry on finance and organisation presented to the 1980 conference clearly reflected the TULV's preoccupation with developing party-union links at grass roots level, moreover. These recommendations included a demand for an end to the practice of under-affiliation by some unions, an exhortation to publish greater political content in union journals, and a demand for more profound party-union communication in the constituencies and regions. As a result, TULV claimed that almost every major union, and most smaller unions, altered the basis of their political fund levies between 1979 and 1983. This did much to boost Labour's income, and helped to eradicate the net loss the party had become accustomed to incurring on its General Fund each year. The following figures tell briefly the story of Labour's net balance on its General Fund during the period.

1978	-£140,000	1979	-£153,000	1980	-£165,000
1981	-£320,000	1982	-£141,000	1983	+£132,000

TULV negotiated a substantial increase in affiliation fees paid to the party by unions; as a result, these fees rose by nearly 90% between 1980 and 1983, which clearly benefited the party enormously - though it did nothing to reduce general dependence on the unions, of course. Furthermore, the TULV was instrumental in the restructuring and computerisation of the party's Finance Department during this period. An attempt was also made about this time to recruit more individual members to the party from within the unions' own rank and file, although it was admitted that this was less successful an initiative than anticipated. Finally, TULV granted a request worth more than £30,000 per year in research assistance for the party's front bench spokesmen in parliament after the 1983 general election. In short, TULV had rapidly become very active in pursuit of its objective of rendering the party every possible assistance in its bid to augment its organisational and campaigning profile.[5]

In addition, the TULV became involved in the internal factional conflict of the Labour Party during the early 1980s, acting as a sort of 'party political ACAS', in the words of Andrew Taylor (Taylor 1987a: 145). In particular it took steps to encourage the resolution of such conflict by organising major internal summit meetings on union premisses at Bishops Stortford (ASTMS) and Woodstock (GMWU) in the hope that 'peace deals' might be struck between the left and the right. However, as Taylor explains, there were those on the left who were suspicious of the TULV's role in this period, regarding it as a right wing plot to undermine the advance of the CLPD, an impression that those involved in TULV sought to dispel. This did not prevent the NUM from withdrawing as early as 1980.

By the time of the 1983 election the TULV was running on a well established basis; unions representing over 90% of the affiliated party membership were associated with the body, which was financed and staffed by the unions, had an annually elected executive of its own and held regular general meetings. A special levy fund had been established in 1981, with unions contributing 10p for each of their affiliated members, and this helped the general election effort in 1983 (see table 2.7). Labour officially assessed the TULV contribution to the 1983 election effort to be 'of enormous value', and went on to describe the main activities of its staff during the campaign:

> They cooperated in the training of key workers at regional level and in allocating trade union officers to work in the key marginals...they established an office at Walworth Road and their officers worked closely and in harmony with party officers at national and regional level (NEC Annual Report 1983: 7).

TULV claimed to have been responsible for organising a funding drive which raised more than £2,000,000 for the election, and to have instituted programmes of election work training, the recruitment of volunteer campaign workers, the allocation of union officers to work in key seats, the provision of speakers' notes and of election articles for union journals throughout the campaign. This last point touches on the issue of political education through the unions, which is worth reflecting upon.

It is interesting that the unions seem traditionally to have neglected to take responsibility for this task. This is not necessarily surprising when it is remembered that the British Labour Party has never been the kind to take on the task of building a distinctly radical working class sub-culture, to reiterate a point made earlier in this chapter. This seems to be reflected in the comparative ineffectiveness of traditional political communications between unions and their members. In the 1960s, for instance, Butler and Stokes reported a remarkably weak political impact made by union journals. For instance, although nearly two-thirds of union members reported reading their union journals, only 20% could recall having seen any articles on political matters subsequent to the 1964 election. Ironically, readers of union journals actually turned out to be slightly less inclined to vote Labour than non-readers. Moreover, less then 2% actually recalled any union representative approaching them and asking about their voting intentions. It was concluded that the evidence could hardly be reconciled with an image of the unions actively seeking to 'shape their members votes' (Butler and Stokes 1969: 201-202). However, the advent of the TULV and the sort of thinking that it has inspired about the need to sell the Labour Party's cause more directly to ordinary union members has produced some effects in the area of political education. For instance, the party was able to report that prior to the 1983 general election:

> A series of courses on election campaign preparation was held jointly for full time union officers and Labour Party designated agents and key workers...(this provided) practical training on publicity, canvassing techniques, polling day organisation, absent voters and electoral law (NEC Annual Report 1983: 45).

Needless to say, these courses were hosted by the trade unions; the colleges of ASTMS, GMBATU, EETPU and TGWU were all used. Moreover, table 2.17 displays an evident upward trend in the deployment of party political education officers.

Table 2.17
Labour Party political education officers, 1976-83

Year	Number	Year	Number
1976	249	1980	498
1977	279	1981	579
1978	340	1982	696
1979	473	1983	641

Source: NEC Annual Report 1983: 45

Furthermore, the party took the step of establishing a Political Education Advisory Panel on which the TULV was represented; one of its earliest objectives was to encourage the editors of union journals to introduce more material on the Labour Party. It seems obvious enough that the party has got the message that political education is important in order to communicate with and mobilise the grass roots of the movement, and the unions have involved their own officials in this political education effort.

It is evident that in 1983 the TULV represented some sort of an organisational innovation in the traditional party-union relationship, but this was not enough to avert an electoral catastrophe for Labour, nor to avoid TULV becoming embroiled in problems of its own. For instance, Minkin has indicated that the underlying tension between many constituency activists and the TULV probably hindered the effectiveness of the latter (Minkin 1986). More generally though, it should be recognised that TULV was a victim of the internal party political tensions that constituted the environment in which it was born. These tensions always hindered its work. It was perhaps fortuitous in some respects that the political fund ballots absorbed the political energies of the party and the unions after 1984. Amongst other things, these campaigns provided the circumstances under which the formal demise of the TULV could take place, for in early 1986 the decision was taken to merge it with the TUCC. A new organisation was to be formed out of the ashes of the former two, and it was hoped that this would avoid the weaknesses and build upon the strengths of these precursors. This new body was to be TUFL.

7. Trade Unions For Labour (TUFL)

TUFL is in many ways a variation on the theme of TULV, and in 1987 it usurped the role played by TULV at the previous election. It was launched in February 1986 as a body with an electoral purpose rather than a policy one. The SOGAT'82 leader Bill Keys, who had been so active with TUCC during the political fund campaigns, now took over at the helm of TUFL, working from an office in Walworth Road. The NEC was to be represented on TUFL's executive and financial committees by experienced men like Larry Whitty (the party general secretary) and Sam McCluskie of the NUS. 'Intensive' consultation quickly developed at this level over matters of membership, affiliation, finance, campaigning and organisation, with a particular emphasis on the grass roots level of the movement.

It was the aim of the new organisation to encompass as many unions as possible, and to avoid policy matters at all costs. This was regarded as essential if the problems faced by the TULV were to be avoided. In its constitution, TUFL laid particular emphasis on:

i. The need to build on the momentum provided by the political fund campaigns by enhancing political education efforts within the unions' rank and file memberships.
ii. The need to maximise party membership and levy payment among union members.
iii. The need to maximise political activity by union members within the party.

Writing during the early days of TUFL's development, Derek Fatchett summarised the philosophy and hopes which underpin it in the following terms:

> TUFL, it would seem, is not designed as an organisation which will provide the Labour Party with a financial drip feed, or which will come to life at general elections in the, judging by past experience, forlorn hope of suddenly persuading their (ie, trade unions') members to vote Labour. TUFL is regarded as an organisation which will campaign amongst rank and file members before, during and beyond the next general election (Fatchett 1987: 97).

Consequently, we are bound to ask how significant a role TUFL played in the 1987 general election campaign. As in the case of TULV before them, TUFL officers provided campaign workers and speakers, arranged meetings and produced literature for dissemination; thus, for example, all regions received material on issues like defence, low pay and workers' rights as well as more general electoral briefings. In 1987, however, TUFL was to concentrate on providing union resources and expertise for specially targeted constituencies that the party hoped to win. The expert input was channelled largely through the medium of *Trade Union Liaison Officers (TULOs)*; it is the intention that these remain permanent positions, and by the end of 1988 some 70% of all CLPs had a TULO (table 2.17). Consequently, there are now more TULOs in the Labour Party than any other type of rule book position. 28% of all constituencies had one full time trade union official working for them on a full time basis in the 1987 election campaign, 21% had two, 22% had three and 18% had four or more. In addition, 10% of CLPs benefited from the part time services of a union official, 20% from two part timers, 9% from three and 38% from four or more. 10% of seats had no full timers, 17% no part timers. Understandably, the bigger unions were more inclined to be involved in constituency work during the election, although it is interesting how few seats one or two of the traditional bastions of the labour movement were involved with. Thus, while the TGWU sent its officers into 67 constituencies, GMBATU to 49 and NUPE to 46, the NUR only supplied workers to 5 local campaigns, and the NUM to 3 (TUFL Annual Report 1986-87: 3-7).

Table 2.18
TULOs active in the Labour Party as of August 1988

Region	Number of TULOs	Number of constituencies	Percentage with TULOs
Scotland	82	72	72
Wales	23	38	61
North	20	36	56
Yorks	41	51	80
North West	57	74	77
East Midlands	31	44	70
West Midlands	46	58	79
East	30	51	53
London	58	84	69
South	53	77	69
South West	30	48	63
	441	633	70

Source: NEC Annual Report 1987: 25

It appears that officials and ordinary union members involved at grass roots level were largely consumed by the traditional activities of British parliamentary constituency campaigning - canvassing, organising meetings, leafleting and arranging transport. These are no doubt worthy activities, but they do seem rather to miss the central point of TUFL's original rationale, which was specifically to reactivate Labour's support within the trade union movement. Nonetheless, subsequent to the election fully three-quarters of the special target seat coordinators that the party had appointed during the campaign claimed that union officials had been employed 'effectively'; moreover, virtually all of them had used the good offices of TUFL to contact union members. This notwithstanding, certain problems do seem to have arisen in union-constituency relations during the election campaign. One-third of target seat coordinators reported that there had been 'very little' union participation, and had found it difficult to obtain direct access to union memberships. This was most frequently due to a lack of interest or cooperation on the part of union officials; for instance, union officials were occasionally apt to refuse to provide lists of their members, and other times they simply failed to circulate election material that had been provided.

Nevertheless, the party was sufficiently enthusiastic about the work of TUFL in 1987 to claim that it had a positive effect on, firstly, the levels at which unions affiliated to constituency parties, and secondly, the actual voting behaviour of union members.

> There is some evidence that the union vote did rise as a result of unions and local parties campaigning among trade union members. Although the overall union vote rose only a disappointing 3%, this hides large changes in overall union membership since 1983, changes towards more white collar service jobs which we would not expect to favour Labour. However, within the overall 3% increase there was a very substantial rise in the manual unionist vote. This, of course, is where much of the campaigning effort was directed (NEC Annual Report 1987: 8).

This claim is based on essentially circumstantial evidence and is backed up by the view that techniques such as the use of target letters, localised literature and an emphasis on employment rights issues (unfair dismissal, a statutory minimum wage and health and safety legislation) were what impressed the manual unionsists, of whom half voted for Labour (NEC Annual Report 1987: 14). It is contended by the party that this approach was especially appealing to women; thus, the most significant swings to Labour since 1983 seem to have occurred among working class women in general (where Labour's lead over the Conservatives has advanced by 17 percentage points), and among unionised women in particular (12 points). There may be something in this, since it is well established that both these groups of women are highly likely to be concentrated among the ranks of the poorly paid and the unskilled; the attractions of minimum wage and health and safety provisions are obvious. Moreover, Labour go on to add that, whilst the evidence may not be conclusive, they feel that trade union assistance has had a marked effect on voting in some local authority elections, such as those held in parts of

Birmingham and Scotland in 1987 (NEC Annual Report 1987: 26). However, it is hard to be sure how far these effects are attributable to the specific impact of TUFL.

Since the 1987 general election the work of TUFL and the TULOs has broadened. Joint regional campaign training sessions for constituency party and union officials have been established by TUFL, and a monthly bulletin of news and facts concerned with employment and union issues is now circulated to all TULOs, CLP secretaries and party branches. Further evidence of collaboration between TULOs and constituencies has been made manifest in some of the campaigns that have been run on issues such as the poll tax, the National Health Service and local industrial disputes. In addition, TULOs were encouraged to communicate their views about the way the party's major policy review was developing. This latter fact has provoked some to argue that TUFL is bound to take on more of a policy role as time goes by, something which may well provoke the sort of suspicions on the left that became apparent in the case of TULV. Whatever, it is clear that despite any misgivings the left may feel, TUFL is here to stay for the present. In the most general terms, the notion of drawing the unions ever closer to the institutional heart of the party in the name of reactivating party organisation and membership is unlikely to attract strong disapproval from the grass roots party activists; any input of resources is a help, obviously. More importantly, though, the internal balance of power within the party is now such that, grumble as they might, the far left are no longer in a position to prevent the progress of the moderate reformism of the leadership's policy review - and the unions are regarded as important to this. The policy review, in the thinking of the party leadership, needs to be complemented by the dilution of the influence of the militant CLP activists through an influx of new 'ordinary' members; TUFL can play a role in this, so TUFL is likely to be around for some time to come.

Conclusion

The discussion of the development of TUFL concludes our examination of the organisational links between the party and the unions. In the opening chapter it was suggested that there were three possible sources of explanatory influence on the electoral behaviour of trade unionists - organisational factors, social factors and political factors. From what we have uncovered in the course of this chapter it seems evident that purely organisational sources of electoral change can be discounted. Stated simply, there has been no substantial weakening in the organisational linkage between Labour and its affiliated unions since the early 1960s. Individual membership has declined over the past

25 years, and affiliated membership is correspondingly more important to the party rather than less, even though it is regarded in some quarters as 'mythical' membership. It follows almost as a matter of course that the party is more than ever dependent on the unions for financial solvency, and there is no evidence that the unions are shirking these responsibilities; they pay most of the day to day general expenses involved in sustaining the party organisation, they have provided new and better premises and facilities when called upon, and they foot most of the bill for the increasingly sophisticated and expensive election campaigns the party runs. They remain crucial to the party's policy making process at present, with their presence heavily apparent in committees and at conference. Thus, they were central to the (in retrospect) somewhat brief ascendancy of the left on constitutional matters in the early 1980s, just as they have been to the resurgence of the moderates during the progress of the post-1987 policy review. This is true despite the virtual demise of that institutional device without any clear definition within the party rules, the TUC-PLP Liaison Committee; and even though the conference role of the unions may be modified through the proposed reform of the block vote, this can only have an impact on the future. It cannot account for the changing electoral behaviour of union members between 1964 and 1987. During this period the power of the unions at conference was in no way diminished. The unions remain, for a variety of instrumental and sentimental reasons, wedded to the system of sponsoring parliamentary candidates, moreover. And through the medium of TULV and TUFL, they have even managed to extend the nature of their organisational connection with Labour, so that the coordination of grass roots links is more effective. In short, it seems inconceivable that trade unionists are less inclined to identify with the Labour Party simply because they perceive a growing disinclination on the part of their organisations to contribute to and participate in the running of the party. If the party and the affiliated unions have 'grown apart' in any meaningful way since the 1960s, then, it must be in the political and/or sociological senses of the phrase rather than in the organisational one. Whether this has in fact been so is the question to which we now turn.

Notes

1. Table 2.1n illustrates that there exists a host of small trade unions who remain outside the structure of the TUC. Nonetheless, roughly 90% of Britain's entire union membership is affiliated to the TUC.

Table 2.1n
The comprehensiveness of TUC organisation, selected years

Year	Total no. of unions	Number in TUC	% in TUC	Total union membership	TUC membership	% in TUC
1976	473	113	23.9	12,386,000	11,036,326	89.1
1979	453	112	24.7	13,289,000	11,865,390	89.3
1983	394	102	25.9	11,236,000	10,510,157	93.5
1985	370	91	24.6	10,821,000	9,855,204	91.1

Sources: Labour Research Department Fact Service 51/19; Labour Party Annual Report 1987.

2. To take one minor but illustrative instance, on the opening day of the 1989 Congress Bill Brett of the IPMS displayed his clear irritation at the fraternal address presented by Dennis Skinner, then chairman of the Labour Party; Skinner's speech 'verged on the rude', according to Brett, in so far as it implicitly assumed that everyone at the Congress was a card-carrying member of the Labour Party. Brett's comments were made during the course of an interview broadcast on BBC 2's coverage of the TUC (4th October 1989).

3. More specifically, the 1913 Act legalised political action in so far as the following activities were concerned:

i. Paying the election expenses of candidates for public office.
ii. Holding and publicising election meetings.
iii. Financially maintaining elected public officials.
iv. Registering electors.
v. Selecting candidates for elective public office.
vi. Holding public meetings or distributing political literature.

In addition, it was considered legally permissible for a union to spend money from General Funds on political objects outside the terms of the 1913 Act, so long as the purpose of such spending was not specifically *electoral.*

4. Of the shadow spokesmen elected to the PLP in 1987, only Bryan Gould, Jo Richardson, Jack Straw and Denzil Davies were not sponsored by trade unions. The remaining spokesmen and their sponsors were:

N. Kinnock	(TGWU)	J. Cunningham	(GMBATU)
R. Hattersley	(USDAW)	D. Dewar	(NUR)
D. Foster	(USDAW)	F. Dobson	(NUR)
S. Orme	(AEU)	R. Hughes	(AEU)
G. Brown	(TGWU)	G. Kaufman	(GMBATU)
D. Clark	(NUPE)	M. Meacher	(COHSE)
R. Cook	(NUR)	J. Prescott	(NUS)
J. Smith	(GMBATU)		

5. A good impression of the scope and extent of TULV's activities and its value to Labour is provided by its pattern of expenditure during the period leading up to the 1983 general election:

Table 2.2n
Labour's general election expenditure, 1983 (£)

Direct Labour Party spending	1981/82	1982/83
Campaigns	95,000	
General Election Fund		100,000
Constituency parties	4,450	6,000
Fund raising		40,500
Head Office Study/Finance Department		45,000
TULV activity		
Regional activity		36,894
General election campaign		47,252
Membership drive		10,486
Election training		4,077
Conferences	2,593	5,383
Legal and accounting	1,375	1,041
Clerical and administration	2,088	7,296
TOTAL	105,706	263,448

3 Party-union Linkages Since 1964: The Political and Social Dimensions

It is the contention of this book that both social and political factors offer an insight into the nature of change in trade unionist voting behaviour. In particular, the political relationship between the party and the unions is critical to our understanding, but it cannot be entirely distinguished from the domain of social change. As we shall be seeing in this chapter, party-union relations have been considerably complicated by the social changes that have affected trade union memberships.

The story of the political relationship between the party and the unions since the 1960s revolves largely around the well rehearsed issue of incomes policy; though much has been written and said of this subject, we cannot overlook its major features since these will be central to the explanation of electoral change that will be developed.

1964-1970: Trouble brewing

Incomes policies first emerged during the post war era under the Labour government of Clement Attlee; it was Chancellor Sir Stafford Cripps who introduced a voluntary policy of pay restraint which was sustained by the loyalty of major union leaders like Arthur Deakin of the TGWU, Tom Williamson of the NUGMW and Will Lawther of the NUM. Ironically, there was little in the way of formal pressure for wage restraint throughout most of the 'thirteen wasted years' of Conservative government that followed - until the severe sterling crisis of July 1961 provoked Selwyn Lloyd's decision to institute his infamous 'pay pause'. The government imposed this wage freeze upon the TUC, but attempted to sweeten the medicine somewhat through the introduction of the National Economic Development Council (NEDC). Though the TUC welcomed this move towards more permanent and formally institutionalised consultation with the government, it tried to insist from the outset that a permanent incomes policy was to remain off the NEDC agenda (Panitch 1976: 49). Although voluntarism was the essence of the labour movement's understanding of pay restraint, there were signs - even prior to its return to power - that the party was considering seriously the need for a more regularly instituted pay policy, however. This flowed, in part, from the general attraction of economic planning for European social democratic parties during the period. There was a widespread perception that planning had worked in France in the 1950s, and even the Conservatives under Macmillan, and the Federation of British Industries (FBI) had shown some interest (Blackaby 1979: 402). Prior to his untimely death, Hugh Gaitskell had indicated that an incomes policy could be an important element of a planned economy, so long as it fulfilled certain conditions. Such a step was regarded as central to controlling inflation during a period of planned growth, but any such policy had to be seen to be applied broadly and fairly to the income of both capital and labour (Panitch 1976: 56).

In office, the Labour Party's problems began, almost literally, on day one; the new government of 1964 was shocked by the size of the current trade deficit it inherited, and pressure on sterling was exacerbated by a run on the pound (Stewart 1977). It is now a commonplace observation that a most significant decision taken by this government - and one that undermined its entire planning strategy, condemning it to years of tension with the unions - was the early refusal to countenance any devaluation of the pound. The only logical alternative to enhancing the attractiveness of exports by cutting the cost of the pound is to stem the flow of imports and simulataneously cheapen exports by deflating the economy. This reduces domestic aggregate demand and, it is hoped, curbs inflation. It also undermines any pretensions about promoting growth or industrial planning at a stroke. This is why it forms the central element of the depressing 'stop-go' cycle that characterised British macro-economic management for much of the post war period. Furthermore, the deflationary process can obviously be developed by the adoption of a plan for incomes restraint - and this is the direction that was taken by the Labour governments of 1964-70.

In December 1964 the general principles of an incomes policy were embodied in the tripartite *Joint Statement of Intent on Productivity, Prices and Incomes*; this envisaged a basically voluntary policy in which wage increases would be linked in some way to productivity. The government white paper *Machinery of Prices and Incomes Policy* (Cmnd. 2577, 1965) which was issued in February 1965, established the broad institutional basis for a further, and more detailed, white paper published two months later (Cmnd. 2808, 1965). Together, these papers proposed a voluntary policy of restraining wage rises to 3.5%, to be administered and vetted by the new *National Board For Prices And Incomes (NBPI)*. This wage norm was founded on the assumption that planning would engender a growth rate of around 4%. Exceptions were to be countenanced only where productivity deals or relativity claims could be established.

In fact, the policy achieved little; the TUC was unhappy about the 'unrealistic' level of the 3.5% norm - especially since there was no corresponding price control, and since the new National Plan unveiled by George Brown's Department of Economic Affairs was swiftly undermined by a package of deflationary measures introduced by the Government in July 1965. The one advantage the government had during this period was that it still retained much of the goodwill that unions wished to extend to it after thirteen years of Conservative government. Thus, when Harold Wilson's ministers harangued the TUC about lack of compliance with the new incomes policy, chairman George Woodcock prevailed successfully upon the General Council to accept the responsibility of 'vetting' all claims by individual unions. Quite how this vetting procedure was expected to be effective given the TUC's relative lack of resources or central authority within the union movement was never clearly elucidated. With the benefit of hindsight it is perhaps all too easy to see, therefore, that the next stage of the government's strategy would breach the ramparts of the voluntarist consensus within the Labour movement.

As part of a new package of deflationary measures announced in July 1966, the Wilson government introduced a compulsory six-month wage freeze, which was to be succeeded by a further six months of 'severe restraint'. This would, it was explained, enable the economy to take a 'breathing space' of twelve months during which productivity would catch up with the 'excessive' increases in incomes which had been awarded (Cmnd. 3073, 1966: 7). But it was becoming increasingly evident that incomes policy was now a short term crisis measure rather than a Gaitskellite device of coherent and equitable long term planning (Blackaby 1979: 371). Although the TUC General Council formally supported the move, the political loyalty of the unions was being severely tested; it was at this point, for instance, that former TGWU general secretary Frank Cousins resigned from the cabinet in order to oppose the incomes policy. Within the cabinet some resentment of the 'no devaluation' strategy was beginning to emerge, emanating chiefly - and not surprisingly - from George Brown whose National Plan had been rendered a non-starter. The deflationary package even produced Brown's resignation during one of the famous histrionic outbursts to which he was periodically given, but Wilson assuaged his cantakerous Minister for Economic Affairs and the resignation was withdrawn (Crossman 1979: 222-230). The logic of the government's strategy was clearly likely to provoke conflict with the unions in the (not particularly) long run, moreover. Consider the government's position in the following terms:

i. It insisted that incomes could only increase in line with output.
ii. The deflationary measures that it introduced ensured that output would struggle to grow at all.
iii. It therefore followed that incomes could not be allowed to grow.

The logic of this straightforward syllogism and the apparent success of the period of frozen wages and severe restraint (in terms of wage increases and industrial disputes) encouraged the government to urge continued restraint on the TUC after the middle of 1967. In the new white paper published in March of that year, therefore, it refrained from explicitly mentioning an acceptable level of wage increases for the future - but it was clear that the expectation was of a continuation of the zero norm (Cmnd. 3235: 1967). The vein of political loyalty that the government had been mining within the TUC was beginning to run very thin, however. The unions were particularly resentful of the fact that income restraint seemed to be directed more at the wages sector than the profits sector, for one thing; and for another, although some union leaders still recommended continuing support for the government's policy, the rank and file memberships were becoming increasingly restive. The TUC therefore ignored the new white paper and proposed an alternative economic approach of its own, consisting largely of price controls and import quotas (Panitch 1976: 145).

Commentators have often recognised 1968 as a critical year in the relationship between the Labour Government and the unions (see, for example, Middlemas 1979: 439-440). In November of the previous year Callaghan and Wilson had finally admitted defeat in their battle to protect sterling at all costs and the pound had been devalued by 14%. Nonetheless, they were keen to maintain controls over wage rises and demand in order that devaluation would be fully successful. Accordingly, the government urged unions to accept the continuation of a zero norm and conferred statutory powers upon the NBPI to delay price and wage rises for up to eighteen months. Real wage rises were lower than in other OECD nations and the unions' rank and files were increasingly disinclined to acknowledge further exhortations for restraint on their part. The public sector and skilled manual employees were especially disgruntled at the compression of their relative positions within the income pecking order - an exact foreshadowing of developments a decade later. Industrial disputes multiplied suddenly and dramatically (see table 3.1).

Table 3.1
Industrial dispute statistics for Britain 1966-1970

Year	Number of strikes	Number of workers involved	Strike days
1966	1937	530,000	2,400,000
1967	2116	731,000	2,800,000
1968	2378	2,255,000	4,700,000
1969	3116	1,654,000	6,800,000
1970	3906	1,793,000	11,000,000

Source: Coates and Topham 1986: 198

The ordinary union members became increasingly militant during this period as bargaining became more decentralised; in reality, wage and price rises drifted well beyond the implicit zero norm the government professed to have in mind. This situation continued into 1969, by which time it had become obvious to the government that incomes policy under the prevailing conditions was simply not working; moreover, the political costs were high, but the Labour government's next move seemed to belie any sensitivity to this fact.

At the end of 1968 it announced that it would not renew that year's Prices and Incomes Act, but instead it proposed a short bill aimed at regulating the practice of industrial disputes. This legislation was to be based upon the White Paper *In Place Of Strife*. The union response was one of incredulous rage to the main provisions of this paper, which were threefold. Firstly, it was proposed that all strikes be preceded by compulsory ballots of all members, secondly, that a 'cooling-off period' be imposed before unofficial strikes could start, and finally that restrictions be placed on certain forms of inter-union dispute. The unions reacted as a single unit against the thrust of these proposals and mobilised support within parliament, the constituency parties and ultimately even the Cabinet against their implementation. When it finally became clear that Wilson and his Employment Secretary Barbara Castle were isolated within the Cabinet the bill was withdrawn. A face-saving device of sorts was concocted when the TUC General Council signed a 'solemn and binding' undertaking to take responsibility for shepherding inter-union disputes, but much damage was already done. The conflict divided not only the party and union elites, but also provoked bitter divisions within the party itself, at all levels. Furthermore, it probably had the effect of emphasising the destructive power of the shop floor - the last thing the government had wanted to achieve. Incomes policy was now virtually redundant throughout the remainder of the Labour Party's period in office.

1970-1974: Party-union relations retrieved

The nation was subject to two distinct, but profound, shocks during the week beginning June 14th 1970; firstly, the English national football team was knocked out of the Mexican World Cup, and then later in the week the Labour government was soundly and surprisingly beaten in the general election of the day. There were disappointed men in high places who hinted darkly that the two events may not have been entirely unconnected[1]; certainly, it seemed that there was at least one parallel between the vanquished teams, in that both seemed to have succeeded in grasping defeat from the very jaws of victory. England's perspiring soccer stars squandered a healthy enough looking advantage that had been established over their West German nemesis, while the Labour government had entered the final stages of the electoral campaign with most of the opinion polls predicting a comfortable victory. Unhappily for Labour and the embarrassed pollsters, these predictions proved utterly misleading (Butler and Pinto-Duschinsky 1971: Ch. 8). The real trauma for the Labour movement was only just beginning, however.

Heath's new government set out to embody the principles of 'Selsdon Man', a characterisation invented by the press to describe the rightward shift the Conservative Party appeared to have undergone since the days of Butler, Macmillan and Douglas-Home. The initial postures of the Heath government were echoed by the approach adopted by the Thatcher government at the end of the decade, although Heath's cabinet probably lacked the conviction of its Conservative successor, and most certainly lacked its political good fortune. Heath and his acolytes were committed to reducing direct taxation and public expenditure, to trimming welfare budgets and withdrawing subsidies to nationalised industry, and to reform of industrial relations. It was this latter aspect of the new government's programme which - along with its approach to incomes policy - had the most profound ramifications for the labour movement in the country.

In December 1970 an industrial relations bill was tabled by the government setting out its strategy. The new bill envisaged various measures designed to curb traditional union rights and to enhance state control over industrial relations. In the first place, the closed shop was to be outlawed, and all unions were to register with a new body to be known as the *Commission On Industrial Relations (CIR)*. This CIR would have the right to define and recognise legitimate representative labour organisations; unions failing to register with, or be recognised by, the CIR would not qualify for immunities from prosecution extended by the Trade Disputes Act of 1906. Moreover, the government was to have the power to request either a cooling-off period of sixty days or a secret ballot of all members over all strike calls considered a threat to the public interest; a special *National Industrial Relations Court (NIRC)* was established to consider such cases. In addition, it was proposed that, unless expressly stating the contrary, collective agreements were to become legally binding. Finally, there were to be restrictions upon sympathetic and secondary industrial action.

This new threat to the position of organised labour provided a common rallying theme around which the party and the unions could unite. The TUC-PLP Liaison Committee was established in January 1971 in order to develop a common strategy against the proposed legislation. Two months later the party agreed to back an initiative emerging from a special TUC congress at which it was decided to boycott the new law. All member unions were ordered not to register with the CIR, nor cooperate in any way with the CIR and the NIRC. Unions had to take care to stipulate that all collective agreements lacked a legally binding status. In the face of effective solidaristic opposition to it, the legislation lacked impact. Unions failing to de-register from the CIR were suspended from the TUC, while attempts to apply the new law's sanctions met telling resistance in many cases. For instance, the TGWU ignored fines that the NIRC imposed upon it for refusing to cooperate with the court.[2] Most notorious perhaps was the case of the 'Pentonville Five' - five Dock union shop stewards who the president of the NIRC, Sir John Donaldson, sent to jail in July 1972 for organising an illegal picket. With the country on the point of a national general strike, the prisoners were released as the House of Lords decided that it was the union as a whole, rather than the individuals concerned, that should be held responsible for the official activities of its shop stewards (Freyman 1980: 130). Elsewhere the government discovered that the imposition of 'cooling-off' periods and strike ballots could not be relied upon to dissuade unionists from striking.[3] On occasion it clearly decided that discretion was the better part of valour and did not even seek to employ the provisions of the act - for example in the case of the NUM's national strike of 1972.[4]

The second aspect of the labour movement's troubles with the Conservative government during this period concerned the question of incomes policy. The Heath government initially declared its intention of eschewing a formal incomes policy in the private sector (Dorfman 1979: 51). But by establishing a pattern of continually reduced wage increases in the public sector (the famous 'N-1' formula), it was hoped that the private sector to follow suit. However, by the end of 1972 the government felt obliged to rethink its strategy as unemployment and wage settlements rose and signs of cooperation were not forthcoming from the unions. As talks with the TUC broke down the government imposed a ninety day wage and price freeze as the first part of a three stage strategy starting in November 1972. Stage Two ran from March to November of 1973 and consisted of a limit of £1 per week plus 4% up to a maximum of £250 per year. This was followed by the third stage of governmental policy which allowed for a 7% wage increase up to a maximum of £350 per year; the so-called 'threshold clause' in the policy meant that extra money was available if inflation exceeded 7%, and there was further scope for flexiblilty over relativities (Barnes and Reid 1980: 177). The unions had already done much to achieve a strategic victory over the government in the case of the Industrial Relations Act, however; some were now ready to move onto the attack over wage restraint.

On the day after stage three began the NUM executive announced an overtime ban as it rejected a National Coal Board offer of 16%. The government responded by immediately declaring a state of national emergency and imposing restrictions on the use of electricity and energy supplies. By the new year, a three day working week was curtailing the use of resources in manufacturing. At this point the government signalled its intention of meeting fire with fire. After the NUM membership overwhelmingly approved a national strike beginning on February 10th, Heath intervened to call a snap General Election to be held at the earliest possible date (February 28th). The clear question placed before the electorate was 'who governs - the government or the unions?' At the time the election was called the polls suggested that the Conservatives held a lead over Labour, and that at least a third of the electorate saw prices and strikes as the most urgent problems facing Britain (Butler and Kavanagh 1974: 178). However, aided not a little by the iniquities of the British electoral system, Labour emerged as the largest single party in the Commons, though without any overall majority. Evidence suggests that perceptions of Labour's competence in handling industrial disputes and union affairs helped sway the voters (Butler and Kavanagh 1974: 140).

1974-1979: The corporatist failure

Following the triumph of their resolute and united strategy, there was much sweetness and light in the relationship between the unions and the Labour Party during 1974. The miners' dispute was swiftly resolved, there was close collaboration in designing new legislation to replace the Industrial Relations Act and the TUC agreed to keep wage demands in line with inflation, rather than ahead of it. Labour's new strategy was based on the notion of a 'social contract' that had been established with the unions prior to the February 1974 election. The basis of this lay essentially in the hope that social democratic corporatism along Scandinavian lines could be introduced in Britain. In itself, this was a perfectly reasonable strategy from Labour's point of view, since studies have indicated how such union-party cooperation is central to the longevity and programmatic success of social democratic parties (Stephens 1979). However, the conditions for the effective deployment of a corporatist strategy usually include the presence of a centralised union movement - a condition that has been singularly absent in the British case. Ultimately, this proved too great a handicap for the British Labour movement in the 1970s.

The basis of the Social Contract lay in a document published by the Liaison Committee early in 1973; *Economic Policy and the Cost of Living* promised to trade wage restraint by the unions for various measures of social and political action by a future Labour government - for instance, price and rent control, food subsidies, industrial democracy and workers' rights (TUC 1974: 312-315). At the outset the strategy seemed promising; measures of this sort were put in place, major union leaders reiterated their willingness to exercise restraint in wage demands and the Labour Party managed to improve its parliamentary position a little in a new election held in October of 1974. In general the unions could look forward to a period of augmented influence via their political contacts with the government and their involvement in tripartite industrial planning. However, the eighteen months or so following the return to power of the Labour Party also witnessed developments which boded less well for the future. Pressure for higher wage settlements was building up at shop floor level; the public sector in particular had suffered from the Heath government's policies, and the inflationary impact of OPEC oil price increases tended to exacerbate difficulties. Under pressure, the government agreed to refer a series of claims by public sector unions to pay review bodies; these reviews generally recommended large wage rises which the government somewhat reluctantly agreed to implement. As a result, there was a change in the ratio of public to private sector income in favour of the former for the first time in some while. Consumer demand and inflation, inevitably, rose quickly and export sales were hit. Before too long Labour was playing its customary governmental role of having to defend a shaky pound.

By early 1975 ministers were appealing for restraint on the part of the unions, and these appeals were backed up by a mildly deflationary budget in the spring. The message was not lost on the union bosses; some sort of a voluntary incomes policy would have to be cobbled together or the government would be obliged to respond with further and more drastic bouts of economic rigour. The government published the white paper *The Attack On Inflation* in July, the main elements of which consisted of a flat rate £6 maximum increase with a freeze on incomes above £8500 per year. Jack Jones of the TGWU had lobbied for a flat rate policy in the name of equality and managed to persuade the majority of General Council delegates to accept this. Profits were subject to a 10% limit and the onus was placed upon employers to ensure that wage settlements did not surpass the stipulated limits; transgressors would be likely to find selective industrial assistance and/or contracts issued by the government withdrawn. It was also emphasised that the government was prepared to back these provisions with statutory powers if necessary.

The stated aim of the government was to reduce inflation to 10%, and in many ways the first year of the new policy proved a success. The number of days lost in industrial disputes was virtually halved in 1976 (falling from 6,000,000 to 3,300,000) as was the level of inflation (declining from 30% to 16%). These developments greatly helped in the fight to control the trade deficit. Nonetheless, inflation remained higher than for most of Britain's OECD competitiors, and the pressure on sterling remained; despite growing doubts within the unions and the left wing of the party, the government (now under the helmsmanship of Jim Callaghan) therefore pressed for another round of 'the attack on inflation'. A special TUC in June 1976 endorsed this second stage of the policy which basically comprised an 'average' 4.5% increase staggered over three different income groups - that is, a flat rate £2.50 per week limit for the lowest paid, a 5% limit for those on or near average earnings, and a £4.00 flat rate maximum for the highest paid (Cmnd. 6507 1976: 6).

Although wage drift did not exceed these limits by more than two or three percent, the basis for continued restraint on the part of the unions was undermined in two ways. In the first place, the real living standards of the rank and file members were declining; in particular, the public sector employees and skilled workers felt frustrated by the relative compression of their earning capacities (Coates and Topham 1986: 42). In the second place, union leaders were increasingly dismayed at the government's inability to deliver its side of the bargain. In mid-1976 Chancellor Denis Healey felt constrained to request a major loan from the International Monetary Fund (IMF) in order to contain the effects of a severe run on the pound. The IMF stipulated that this loan was to be contingent upon the government restricting the size of the public sector borrowing requirement, and as a direct consequence Healey announced a package of deflationary measures in December 1976. (The government's economic strategy was in any case already moving in this direction - consider, for instance, the deflationary package of

July 1976.) By the late summer, the TUC was endorsing motions for an 'orderly return to free collective bargaining'. Thus, when a new white paper was issued in July 1977 stipulating a 10% wage norm, the government was unable to obtain any formal backing from the TUC beyond an agreement to urge members not to seek major pay settlements more than once a year. By now the government was committed to an incomes policy, given that the parliamentary understanding entered into with David Steel's Liberals (the 'Lib-Lab pact') was conditional upon its retention. For a while the government was afforded some moderate help from the prevailing economic circumstances; the developed economies of the world were to some extent recovering from the first OPEC shock and, helped by North Sea oil, the pound had appreciated in value. The governmment even found room for some tax cutting exercises in 1977. Aided by these factors, perhaps, wage drift only mounted to around 4% on average in the year leading up to August 1978.

By this stage there was no realistic prospect of the unions agreeing to an incomes policy for the forthcoming twelve months. Union leaders were unlikely to be able to deliver their members' compliance even if they wanted to. Nevertheless, with an expected autumn general election pending, it was decided to maintain the unilateral imposition of a non-statutory policy, this time with a 5% norm. Callaghan made a brave but foolhardy decision to postpone the election in the wake of the TUC's categorical rejection of the incomes policy. His entertaining rendition of a comic music hall act might have stirred and amused delegates at the Labour Party conference in October, but it did little to sway them, as conference also dismissed the idea of a further round of wage restraint. Early in the wage round the Ford Motor Company decided to ignore the threat of government sanctions by settling a 17% pay increase on its employees. A wave of highly publicised and unpopular public sector strikes followed - the notorious 'winter of discontent' (Taylor 1987a: 104-105). The number of strikes did not actually increase over the previous year - but both the number of workers involved and the number of working days lost in strike activity did, and dramatically so (Coates and Topham 1986: 198). Callaghan's brittle parliamentary majority finally shattered in the spring, and the subsequent electoral defeat at the hands of Margaret Thatcher's brash and determined new generation of Conservatives was hardly a major surprise.

1979-1983: 'The battle for the Labour Party'

Superficially, the return to opposition might have been expected to generate something of a re-run of the experience undergone during the years of the Heath government. After all, there were clearly certain parallels; the problems of constructing and maintaining an effective incomes policy had contributed much to the defeat of the Labour government, and had embittered party-union relations to a significant extent. Yet faced with an apparently uncompromising Conservative nemesis intent upon clipping the wings of organised labour in Britain, there was obvious motivation for the re-establishment of a united front. Thus far, there would seem to have been an evident similarity with the situation in which the party and the unions had found themselves in 1974. Yet it would be odd indeed for history to repeat itself with total precision, and there were to be greater problems for the movement this time.

For one thing, it is possible that the depth of bitterness felt on both sides of the labour movement ran deeper. Significantly, the ambience of mutual recrimination coincided with the rise of internal pressure for democratisation of the Labour Party. This pressure came from various bodies on the party's left wing, chief amongst which was the *Campaign For Labour Party Democracy (CLPD)*. This was important in so far as the unions found it difficult to avoid being drawn into the factional conflict that this provoked; consequently, the chances of establishing a coherent and unified opposition to the newly vaunted Thatcherite alternative were seriously undermined. Even more crucially, the involvement of the unions in questions of internal Labour Party reform led directly to the secession of what was to become the Social Democratic Party and given the idiosyncracies of the British electoral system, this virtually precluded any prospect of replacing the Conservative government in forthcoming general elections. Under circumstances such as these, there was considerably less electoral pressure on Margaret Thatcher and her ministers to deviate from their stated industrial relations strategy than there had been upon their Conservative predecessors in the early 1970s. It was essentially for these reasons that the period following the 1979 election turned out rather differently to that between 1970 and 1974.

As a result of the failure of the neo-corporatist experiment and the 'gradual and insistent spread of shop-floor power' in Britain (Crouch 1990: 326), the Conservative strategy for dealing with the unions in the 1980s was characterised by a rejection of the search for compromise in industrial relations. Instead, emphasis was placed upon the need to alter the environment within which the unions operated. This showed itself in various features of government policy after the 1979 election. In the first place, it soon became clear that there was a willingness to accept - or rather, to impose - a macro-economic climate that was broadly unfavourable to the way in which unions function. The adoption of monetarist financial policy produced (or at the very least exacerbated) an economic downswing; the unemployment associated with this affected union membership and discouraged militant action. This much is clearly revealed in Table 3.2.

Table 3.2
Industrial dispute statistics, 1979-1983

Year	Number of strikes	Number of workers involved	Strike days
1979	2080	4,580,000	29,500,000
1980	1330	830,000	12,000,000
1981	1338	1,499,000	4,300,000
1982	1528	2,101,000	5,300,000
1983	1352	571,000	3,800,000

Source: Coates and Topham 1986: 198.

This apart, probably the most distinctive feature of Conservative industrial relations strategy was the determination to impose a tough new legal framework upon trade unions. During the first Thatcher government, the first two in a series of pieces of relevant legislation were guided through parliament by Conservative Employment ministers. James Prior's 1980 Employment Act was notable mainly for the constraints that it placed upon secondary picketing and the closed shop, and for the provision of state funds to support union postal ballots in matters of choosing officials and deciding whether to strike.

Notwithstanding the observation that government legislation did not go as far as it might have done under the circumstances (MacInnes 1987: 55), the party and the unions reacted with predictable horror. The government had no great reason to be unduly concerned about the unions' reaction this time, however; the latter were in no position to respond in the way they had to the 1972 Industrial Relations Act. For one thing, unemployment was rising rapidly and few union members would be coaxed into 'political' action under such circumstances. For another, the new Employment Act was no Industrial Relations Bill; indeed, it was a far more modest project. An important lesson had been learnt by those who had observed the experience of the Heath government. This time, it was decided that legislative progress would be made in a series of comparatively unambitious, but nonetheless significant stages. Accordingly, a further Employment Bill was introduced in 1982 by Prior's successor, Norman Tebbit. This concentrated on reducing some of the unions' traditional immunities - for example, it was to become permissible for employers to dismiss strikers selectively in the future. Moreover, closed shops would henceforward only be legally ratified following a rigorously conducted ballot of all workers concerned. For the labour movement, there was no grand legislative edifice such as the 1972 Industrial Relations Act against which to mobilise this time. Instead of TUC-versus-government battles, the sort of conflict that typified the 1980s involved legal battles between individual unions and employers. These confrontations were conducted through the ordinary courts. Furthermore, the unions were faced with the virtually inescapable fact that parts of the new legislation were popular with their rank and file members (especially those sections concerning strike ballots).

Crouch has pointed out that, quite apart from exploiting the effects of legislation and unemployment, there were at least two other notable aspects of the Conservative strategy for dealing with the trade unions. In the first place, an attempt was made to reduce what he calls the 'institutional regulation of conflict' so as to expose industrial relations more directly to the effects of the market (Crouch 1990: 331). This was revealed partly in the willingness of the government to abolish institutional constraints on the labour market such as the public sector pay research units established in the 1950s, certain low pay minima, and the negotiating mechanisms for public sector pay and conditions such as those that the teaching profession lost in 1987. Furthermore, the imposition of public sector cash limits on wage increases had a similar effect. Employers and employees knew in advance the sum of money that the government made available for pay rises within a sector, which meant that any rise exceeding this level could only be accomodated through the shedding of labour or an increase in productivity. The Conservatives saw this as an effective substitute for an incomes policy in that the unions were obliged to recognise the direct consequences of their wage bargaining in the labour market, without the government actually having to intervene.

The other notable aspect of policy introduced by the first Thatcher government consisted of the attempt to weaken the legitimacy of trade unions as participants in national political life. Crouch argues that the government sought to exclude the unions from involvement on public bodies of general interest, although they could, of course, still be consulted about affairs which directly affected them (Crouch 1990: 332). For example, in 1987 union representation on the Manpower Services Commission was halved relative to employer representation, and the following year the Commission was abolished, to be replaced by a new training agency which is not obliged to coopt union representatives at all. (It might be added that the unions themselves have occasionally exacerbated the problem by actions such as the boycotting of the National Economic Development Council over the Cheltenham GCHQ affair, although they would undoubtedly have responded that the NEDC had been largely emasculated anyway since 1979.)

So how did the party and the unions respond to this onslaught on the position of organised labour? TUC and Labour Party policy was initially 'grounded on the assumption that the Conservative victory was temporary' (Taylor 1987a: 116); accordingly, it was supposed by many that party-union cooperation would render life problematic for the new government. But there were others who wished to seize the opportunity to alter the balance of power within the Labour Party itself, almost as a prerequisite of effective resistance to the Tories. We shall turn to this presently, but first, what of party-union cooperation on economic and industrial policy?

In the wake of the traumatic experience of 1978-1979, it was hardly surprising that neither the unions nor the party were openly enthusiastic about the notion of incomes policy. In 1981 both the TUC and the Labour Party conference formally rejected the idea. The official taboo that was placed on incomes policy within the movement required that it yield to some new formula; this substitute was to become known as the *National Economic Assessment (NEA)*. However, the NEA was in many ways a thin disguise; implicit within it was some notion of incomes planning, although Labour's front bench politicians were unwilling to emphasise this until after the 1983 general election. Initially, the NEA was regarded as a means by which economic priorities and strategies could be developed in tripartite councils without threatening free collective bargaining in any sense. This was the position adumbrated in the document *Partners In Rebuilding Britain* which was issued by the Liaison Committee in early 1983 (TUC-PLP Liaison Committee 1983). The central idea was that NEA would strive to formulate a mutually acceptable division of resources between wages, profits and investment; the compliance of the unions would be secured by two things - the ideal situation of growth allied with low inflation that the NEA should engender, and the willingness of government to bestow national political responsibility upon the unions. Crouch has noted that British unions have habitually concentrated on the industrial domain, whilst neglecting the political. The very decentralisation of the unions which has made them aggressive industrial bargainers has precluded their developing an overall strategic perspective of their position within the national economy. Essentially, unions have tended to see themselves first and foremost as a means of institutionalisating *private* interests, rather than as participants in national policy making. The latter role would imply:

> ..a union leadership capable of making strategic decisions and taking macroeconomic considerations into account when formulating wage policy. This is forestalled by union decentralisation (Crouch 1982: 183).

The point of the NEA is that it stands to offer the unions a new strategic influence in economic management in exchange for their traditional clout in local industrial bargaining. Naturally enough, strategic power demands a sense of strategic responsiblity; the unions would not be expected to continue acting as purely private interest representatives while exercising public policy responsibilities. Essentially, this is a reiteration of the corporatist message; the unions can expect greater long term benefits if they are able to widen their perspective beyond the constraints of shop floor bargaining. But in a very real sense incomes policy - in some guise or other - must underlie any corporatist strategy. The politicians, however, were wary of shouting this message loud and clear in the direct aftermath of the 1979 general election.

Between 1979 and 1983 the party and union elites actually expended much of their political and intellectual energy in internal battles concerned with the balance and structure of power within the Labour Party itself. This is a subject that has been dealt with in detail elsewhere (see, for instance, Kogan and Kogan 1982), but its impact may have been critical for union members, indeed for the British electorate as a whole. Something, therefore, needs to be said of this episode.

The CLPD was an internal party grouping formed in the aftermath of the 1974 general elections. Although the party had fared relatively well in these elections, there were those on the left who felt uneasy with the way they had been won. In particular, there was considerable disgruntlement at the apparently cavalier manner in which Harold Wilson had overlooked many radical elements of the party's programme in drafting the election manifestos. The party programme was an amalgam of resolutions passed by the annual conference; however, the party leadership was not obliged to include all such provisions in the final election manifesto. Left wing activists, convinced that Wilson and his governments were 'betraying' the movement, decided to mobilise in order to challenge the balance of power within the party (Hatfield 1978). Subsequent to May 1979, grass roots party activists were not the only ones bearing a sense of betrayal. Many trade union activists felt similarly about the party leadership. This was a fortunate turn of events for the CLPD, who now made effective overtures to the leaders of several major unions. (For some while, they had already been forging links with rank and file unionists and lay officials.) One of the aims of the CLPD was to ensure that the party manifesto would be drafted by the NEC in future, an organ on which the right wing of the party could by no means be assured of a majority. The CLPD were, therefore, now able to argue that it was in the interests of unions to support the 'democratisation' of the party, for NEC control of the manifesto was the only way of ensuring that incomes policy would not be reintroduced by the party leadership in the future (Taylor 1987a: 133). In addition, it was proposed that the party leader no longer be elected solely by Labour MPs, but by an electoral college incorporating parliamentary, union and constituency delegates.

Some union leaderships were clearly interested in having greater influence within the party; however, in retrospect it may have been naïve of CLPD activists to expect the majority of unions to be seduced by the prospect. For a start, the flirtation of the major unions with the left was a relatively new thing; for many years, there had been a tradition of support for the party leadership against opposition from the left. Things had only begun to change during the late 1950s, and was exemplified by the internal conflict over Gaitskell's attempt to alter clause four of the party constitution in 1960. The political rift between the major unions and the PLP leadership was widened in the 1960s, with the emerging influence of Jack Jones of the TGWU and Hugh Scanlon of the AUEW. Left wing pressure on the PLP leadership was maintained during the early 1970s, but the main sympathies of most trade union leaderships lay neither with the right nor the left, as such, but rather with the need for party stability and credibility. Consequently, the extent to which the major unions were willing to be drawn into factional strife within the party was limited. It was crucial that the Labour Party was not so damaged that it forfeited all electoral viability, and the battles over inner party democracy did little to improve its image amongst the general public. Indeed, with the trend towards the exclusion of the unions from public consultation procedures, their reliance upon the electoral success of the Labour Party became even greater.

The decision of the 'Gang of Four' front bench politicians to leave the party over the question of its growing left wing bias and the elevated influence of the unions only served to undermine further the electoral position of the Labour Party, however. With great public interest in the formation of the Alliance and the possibilities of centre party politics, the Conservatives were handed a major slice of political good fortune. Given the vagaries of the electoral system in Britain and the vulnerability of Labour's support to Alliance incursion, they became virtually irreplaceable at the polls. This fact was not lost upon the unions. By early 1982, they had taken the initiative of calling a special joint meeting between the party NEC and the TULV at the headquarters of ASTMS in the Hertfordshire town of Bishops Stortford. At Bishops Stortford a compromise was worked out between the left and the right whereby the former would present no more challenges to the annual re-election of party leaders at Conference, whilst the latter would not seek to overturn the constitutional changes already wrought on the party by CLPD prior to the next general election. An uneasy peace held throughout the next year or so, but to little avail; in June 1983 the Labour Party produced its worst national electoral result for more than half a century, only narrowly avoiding the ignominy of returning a lower proportion of the vote than the Alliance.

1983-1987: The emergence of 'the new realism'

In the run up to the 1974 general election, the Labour Party was able to promise that it would repeal the industrial relations legislation introduced by the Heath government. This was a strategy designed to appeal to both the trade union rank and file and the electorate as a whole, since it could be argued that the Tory legislation had provoked an unprecedented level of industrial conflict from which all members of society had suffered; the legislation lacked effectiveness and legitimacy in the eyes of many who were directly touched by it, and should be swept away. Only a Labour government could placate the unions and restore order to industry. The aftermath of the 1983 election was entirely different, however. The Labour Party was in no position to make credible and alluring promises about the abolition of Conservative industrial relations legislation, since the acts of 1980, 1982 and 1984 were in many ways popular - and not only with the non-unionised sections of society. In the 1980s surveys of trade union respondents revealed high levels of support for various aspects of the Conservatives' legislation affecting trade unions, and in particular for the democratising of certain union procedures such as the initiation of strike action or the recruitment of leaders (Marplan 1984; MORI 1985). Table 3.3 highlights how far the labour movement needed to adapt its traditional responses; even among blue collar trade unionists, only a minority were willing to accept the view that, overall, the government had 'gone too far' in the legal restrictions it had sought to place upon the unions.

Table 3.3
Union members' views on how far Conservative legislation affecting unions had gone, 1984

	Blue Collar Members	White Collar Members
Too far	42	29
Not far enough	12	18
About right	36	45
Don't know	10	7

Source: Marplan 1984

Thus, by 1984 there were those in the Labour movement who doubted the possibility of returning to trade unions the old 'immunities' from legal action that they had formerly enjoyed. It was in this year that the outgoing General Secretary of the Labour Party, Jim Mortimer, suggested to the Liaison Committee the alternative strategy of a future Labour government replacing the Conservative legislation with laws of its own. These would be designed to guarantee unions a set of 'positive rights' to organise, bargain and initiate action on behalf of their members. Amongst other things, it became clear that these 'rights' would very likely include certain provisions already laid down by the Conservatives, notably those relating to strike and leadership ballots (MacIntyre 1985). This formula provided a fairly neat means by which to offer the unions and their members something positive without forfeiting the popular aspects of Tory reforms. Consequently, it would not be so easy for Labour's adversaries to accuse them of simply reintroducing the days of untrammelled union power. This is not an insignificant point; the provisions on strike ballots in particular may well have been of considerable benefit to the unions, ironically enough, in terms of enhancing the legitimacy of their actions among the wider public. Although the legislation has probably contributed to the falling incidence of official strike activity, when it does occur it must be clear to all and sundry that it is at least duly and democratically constituted action. This is, arguably, one of the few advantages that the Conservatives have conferred upon the labour movement since 1979, and from the latter's point of view it is not one that ought to be squandered. Accordingly, the 1987 election manifesto issued by Labour included proposals to replace the Conservative legislation with a new set of laws which would, amongst other things, provide for:

> ..a right for union members to have a secret ballot on decisions relating to strikes, and for the method of election of union executives to be based on a system of secret ballots (Labour Party 1987: 13).

In addition, the manifesto promised to establish the right to belong to unions and for unions to organise and bargain; the other major elements of the new 'positive rights' package that Labour offered the electorate in 1987 included statutory protection of part time workers' employment, health and safety protection, the restoration of fair pay resolutions and the wages councils, the strengthening of ACAS and the appointment of a new independent complaints tribunal.

The 1987 election manifesto also made considerable play of the notion of a national economic summit - to 'assess fully the condition of the economy' - as the first stage of the NEA. It was seen as the means of establishing a priority programme of:

> ..concerted action that will need to be taken by government, employers in the private and public sectors, and trade unions to increase investment, contain inflation and achieve sustained recovery (Labour Party 1987: 4).

The party claimed that a million new jobs could be created in two years through a series of public works recovery and improvement programmes, industrial training and job release schemes. In addition, it planned for the introduction of a British Industrial Investment Bank, Regional Development Agencies and a new Ministry of Science and Technology; all these measures would form part of the five year project for the industrial and economic regeneration of Britain. Not one word was uttered about incomes policy, however.

There seem to be three reasons why it was supposed the unions could be relied upon to exercise restraint. In the first place, the party was still pinning its hopes on boosted productivity which would deliver inflation-free growth. The unions, it was argued, would not need to demand exorbitant wage rises in order to protect their members' real incomes. Secondly, it was presumed that 'responsible' trade unionism - that is, restrained trade unionism - had to be preferable to five more years of Thatcherism, from the unions' point of view. Finally, the unions were being offered greater strategic responsibility and involvement in the running of the economy - they were being invited back into Whitehall.

The acceptance by many within the unions that certain features of Conservative legislation were here to stay came to be known as the 'new realism'. The new realism essentially consisted of a mood of resignation about the way that the political and social context in which trade unions had to operate was changing. A notable manifestation of this mood was provided by the willingness of some unions to recruit and operate on the basis of new, comprehensive deals agreed with certain employers - most controversially those which stipulated single-union and 'no-strike' conditions. The most newsworthy example of such a deal during the 1980s was probably supplied by EETPU's combative general secretary, Eric Hammond. The deal he signed with press publisher Eddie Shah in 1985 enraged the traditional print union, the NGA, which was effectively excluded from operating in Shah's companies (Hackett 1985: 9). The new realism was also revealed in the attitude that new industrial legislation should not be challenged by extra-legal means and that industrial muscle should not be flexed for overtly political motives. There were even unions who felt justified in seeking to make elements of the legislation work to their own pecuniary benefit; thus, although it provoked considerable internal TUC ructions, both EETPU and the AUEW chose to accept the government cash available to them under the terms of the new Employment Acts in order to pay for the conduct of postal ballots. This flew in the face of the TUC's decision to minimise compliance with the legislation while acting within the law. Despite the apparent threat to the unity of the TUC, and the clear feeling of many activists and officials that the government's offer of cash was 'a case of Greeks bearing gifts', the AUEW and EETPU challenged the TUC to do its worst (McIlroy 1985: 8).

Clearly, this was a sharply different response to that evinced by the Industrial Relations Act of 1971, and it reflected the relative sophistication of the Conservatives' approach to 'the union problem' in the 1980s. Yet it was a response that was resented in certain parts of the union movement. Some union leaders might have warned the TUC that their members were not interested in fighting the government, and that such a strategy risked further divorcing the rank and file from the leaderships, yet others were convinced that the unions had to go on the offensive. Thus, attempts were made to ignore the legal provisions concerning secondary and mass picketing (as in the disputes involving the Warrington Messenger or the Times Group of Newspapers at Wapping); most spectacular, of course, was the year-long strike initiated by the NUM without a preliminary ballot of members in 1984. The result was probably decisive for the future strategy adopted by the TUC; the failure of the miners led by Arthur Scargill, a confirmed class warrior sure that his was as much a political mission as an industrial one, tipped the balance in favour of the new realists within the movement. The balance, moreover, remained solidly in their favour after the 1987 election, with the TUC affirming its continuing acceptance of key elements of Conservative legislation into the 1990s (Maguire 1991).

Labour and the unions since the 1960s: The development of a mobilisational problem

Since 1964 the task of mobilising support among ordinary trade union members has become an increasingly arduous and depressing one for the Labour Party. The 1966 pay freeze was the initial step on a path which led towards a more complex and in some ways more distant relationship with the unions. This was the first time that a Labour government had introduced a statutory incomes policy and it represented a serious violation of the principle of voluntarism, which had been central to trade union thinking in Britain. Voluntarism encompasses the view that the state should keep a relatively low profile in the field of industrial relations, while taking centre stage in other economic and social affairs. As such it leaves the way clear for unions to adopt a free collective bargaining approach in the labour market. As Anthony Fenley has said of the undermining of voluntarism:

> Trade union *political* activity must be seen in terms of the defence of the doctrine of voluntarism...when governments have no longer been prepared to accommodate the voluntarist ideology..unions have extended their political activity both in scope and content (Fenley 1980: 51).

In itself the breach of this principle ultimately forced the unions to contest the government's handling of industrial relations matters in the political sphere. Moreover, the unions were additionally disappointed by the failure of Labour administrations in the 1960s and 1970s to provide the optimal economic environment within which voluntarism could be sustained, that of expansion and full employment. By the late 1960s there is evidence that many in the unions were realising that they had put too much trust in a Labour government's capacity to hand down reform from above. To quote one contemporary example:

> It has really needed this last three years of Labour government for them (the unions) to grasp that they cannot just assume that the government will identify the needs of the working class of this country and then strive to meet those needs. It has taken a large part of those three years to recognise that the trade unions must identify their own priorities and must make their own independent analyses of the situation (Hughes 1968: 81).

Allied to the unions' attempt to shift themselves 'out of Trafalgar Square and into Whitehall' during the 1960s and 1970s, this realisation amounted to a certain distancing in the political relationship between the Labour Party and the unions. Notwithstanding the way in which a hostile Conservative government has virtually ousted the unions from Whitehall once again, it is perhaps true that the party and the unions regard each other a little more circumspectly than they did in 1960. Mutual support clearly exists, yet seems now more contingent upon the right political bargain being struck. Neither side is likely to make an over-simplistic assumption about an identity of interest and ethos shared with the other. Such a condition tends to make the mobilisation of electoral support for Labour amongst union members more problematic than it once was.

However, we can be still more specific about the process by which the political relationship between Labour and the unions has been modified. Two developments have complicated this relationship, and both have made the joint task of mobilising political support for Labour among trade unionists more difficult. The first is the growing social heterogeneity of union membership, and the second is the altered balance of power between different levels of the trade union organisation.

The unions since the 1960s: Growing social diversity

The most obvious way in which the social profile of trade unions has altered over the past twenty years or more lies in the growth of white collar and professional unionism. Indeed, the onset of this process precedes the period on which we are concentrating, though it most certainly developed significantly after the middle of the 1960s, as table 3.4 reveals.

Table 3.4
Changing levels of white collar union membership, selected years

Year	Total union membership	White collar membership	White collar percentage of total
1920	8,348,000	1,129,200	13.5
1948	9,363,000	2,062,000	22.0
1968	10,200,000	3,056,000	30.0
1973	11,456,000	3,966,300	34.6
1979	13,447,000	5,124,700	38.1
1989	8,478,000	4,325,000	51.0

Note: No figures are readily available for the 1980s, although the 1989 Labour Force Survey provides data from which the relevant figures can be calculated. This means that the 1989 figure should only be regarded as an estimate.

Sources: Bain 1983: 5; Department of Employment Gazette, August 1990.

Many of the fastest growing unions in the 1970s and 1980s were white collar, moreover; for example, of the TUC's twenty biggest unions in 1986, just nine had grown bigger during the previous decade, and of these, only two (COHSE and SOGAT) were not primarily white collar or professional. The top five growth unions (TASS, NAS-UWT, BIFU, NCU and NALGO) were all white collar or professional (Labour Research 1987: 14). Interestingly, the growth of white collar unionism accelerated from the late 1960s onwards precisely because of the impact of incomes policies. Bain and Price have pointed out that white collar earnings generally kept up with, and even exceeded, manual workers' wages between 1945 and to 1968, but that this situation was reversed in the ensuing decade:

> The white collar/manual earnings differential was severely squeezed, primarily as a result of the flat rate characteristics of a series of incomes policies...Hence, there can be little doubt that the behaviour of prices and earnings encouraged large numbers of workers, particularly those in white collar jobs, to unionise in an attempt to defend or improve their standards of living (Bain 1983: 16).

Table 3.5 provides an indication of this. A brief glance at the figures reveals that the considerable increase in manual density during the years between 1968 and 1979 owed much to the decrease of potential membership (that is, to the loss of 866,400 manual jobs in the manufacturing sector). By contrast, the vast increase in white collar density owes very little to the loss of potential - just 33,700 white collar jobs were lost in net terms - and rather more to an increased propensity to join unions. In particular, the public sector white collar

Table 3.5

Union membership and density in manual, white collar and public employment sectors, 1968 and 1979

	1968			1979		
Sector	Mem'ship	Potential	Density	Mem'ship	Potential	Density
Manual	3,808,100	6,139,900	62.0%	4,234,600	5,273,500	80.3%
W/Collar	330,300	2,146,000	15.4%	922,800	2,112,300	43.7%
Public	3,661,000	5,536,900	66.1%	5,189,900	6,297,200	82.4%

Source: Bain 1983: 11

employees who stood to lose most from pay policies (these policies being really enforceable only where the government was the actual employer) showed a markedly greater inclination to join.

Elsewhere, the same writers have calculated that there was an 18.7% increase in white collar unionism just between 1970 and 1974 (with a 4.2% increase in union density), compared to a 1.3% decline for manuals (and a 1.9% drop in density) for the corresponding period (Price and Bain 1976: 347). The ethos of unions who wish to appeal to such a clientele is bound to be different to that of the old bodies who were sure of their working class identity. In a sense, one is put in mind of the new sort of interest group that Otto Kirchheimer identified as becoming more prevalent in Europe during the 1960s. His impression was of an independent, non-ideological group which tempered its partisan links in order to recruit from a broad social basis and to nurture contacts with all potential governing parties. The old ethos borne out of a 'joint strategy towards a common (ideological) goal' is transformed in such a group (Kirchheimer 1969: 364). Certainly, this changed political and social ethos is typical of many white collar unions. Indeed, in analysing the different outlook and goals of white collar unions, Robin Blackburn once argued that many were barely unions at all, but merely 'professional associations' when examined against traditional criteria which truly indicated 'unionateness'. These criteria included a commitment to collective bargaining and the protection of members' interests, willingness to use the strike sanction and affiliation to the TUC and the Labour Party (Blackburn 1967). As M.P. Jackson has said, Blackburn,

> ..clearly has a view of a trade union as being something more than simply an expression of cooperation between employees in the same industry or trade; he views a union as being part of a social movement (Jackson 1982: 38).

The relative growth of white collar trade unionism has been accompanied by the wider geographical and occupational dispersion of unionism in general. In the 1980s, the gradual process of industrial decline was particularly accelerated in the traditional heartlands of British unionism. This in turn affected many of the historical bastions of industrial unionism; the unionisation of the workforce instead began to spread out of the major conurbations to peripheral areas and smaller towns. In particular, the skilled manual and craft unions have lost members through these processes, and the non-manualisation of union membership has been accompanied by its de-skilling, feminisation and growing public sector character (Massey and Miles 1984: 19-22). Taken together, these processes mean that the traditional model upon which British industrial unionism was built have been modified considerably, if not to say altered out of recognition in many instances.

Amongst other things, it especially means that the nature of the union movement as a 'working class institution' has been diluted; for instance, there are few remaining cases of immobile communities which are founded largely upon a single industry and a heavily unionised working class culture. It is obvious that the memberships of unions such as BIFU or IRSF do not regard their organisations as part of such a milieu. At the beginning of the period that we are studying, in 1964, about 65% of all white collar unions were affiliated to the TUC, and they represented a little more than 20% of total TUC membership; already by 1979, however, 85% of white collar unionists were affiliated to the TUC, and they comprised around 36% of TUC membership. What is more, in 1982 the TUC finally adopted contentious proposals to introduce automatic representation on the General Council for all unions with a membership of more than 100,000, a move which 'almost certainly means a larger say for the civil service and white collar unions in the affairs of the TUC than hitherto', according to Rod Hague (Hague 1983: 141).

What is the significance of all this for the political relationship the unions enjoy with the Labour Party? On the face of it, it might appear to suggest that an organisational divorce between Labour and the TUC has taken place with the growing importance of non-affiliated white collar unions in the latter. But it is not simply true that fewer trade unionists now vote Labour because less of them are members of organisations affiliated to the party. As we shall see in chapter 5, it is not white collar, but *manual* trade unionists who have been most inclined to desert Labour at the polls. Yet we know that they belong to unions which continue to affiliate to, and provide resources for, the Labour Party. In simple terms the organisational linkage remains, but the inflow of white collar members has increased political tension between the party and unions in a way that affects all unionists, including manuals.

White collar growth, as we have already said, means that the character of the union movement as a working class institution has been diluted. The easy assumption that the party and the TUC are all part of a social movement sharing broadly homogeneous values and identities can no longer be made. Partly because of this, the party cannot hope to adopt a straightforward class-based electoral strategy. Rather, it creates general problems of response for the Labour Party in relation to union demands. The interests and ethos of the union movement have become so diverse and heterogeneous that it has become very difficult for the party to identify and respond to those interests effectively. To take one example, it has become increasingly problematic for the party to construct incomes and taxation policies which universally represent the best interests of all trade unionists. Rather, policies are bound to favour some members over others. Flat rate incomes policies suppress differentials, frustrating skilled manual and white collar workers; progressive taxation and benefit policies can have similar effects. On the other hand, these redistributive effects are in the interest of lower paid manual trade unionists. Differentiation within British trade unionism is by no means a novel phenomenon, it should be emphasised, but it has been exacerbated by the growth of non-manual employment.

Quite apart from the impact of white collar growth, there are other sources of union conflict in modern Britain. For instance, there is the potential problem of the often divergent interests that public and private sector members have. And what of the 'no strike' or 'single union' deals that some unions controversially signed with employers in the 1980s? Should a future Labour government look to intervene and legislate against such deals? To reiterate, the potential for a coherent party-union political relationship has been undermined by the increasing structural heterogeneity of the latter.

The changed balance of power within the unions

It is important to bear in mind that relationships between party-union elites and the grass roots of their organisations can vary within the context of political mobilisation. Elites can either find themselves in a situation of relative control over their mass base (that is, a situation in which they are able to exert *downward control*), or they may find themselves largely constrained by that base (a more *interactive* relationship). To some extent, demands will flow upwards in any elite-mass relationship, but an interactive relationship is one in which we find a greater degree of grass roots intiative in exerting institutional control, defining interests and formulating campaigns of action. Within many union organisations since the 1960s the mobilisational nexus has become more interactive. For instance, Geoffrey Hodgson has said that:

> Since the 1960s a democratic ethos has developed within the trade union movement..Whilst..leaderships may be formally in control, their power is constrained and checked on a number of issues (Hodgson 1981: 135).

This applies to political as much as industrial issues. It is questionable whether union elites have ever had unchallenged downward control over their rank and file on industrial matters that have remained outside the political arena. Since the 1960s industrial affairs have frequently found their way into this arena, however, and it is clear that this has served to heighten the political consciousness of many union activists. Moreover, a direct consequence of the pay policies of the 1960s was a sudden and massive upsurge in the levels of union recruitment, as we have seen. In many unions, this was accompanied by a parallel development of devolved shop steward power. Unions were not always able to meet the organisational requirements necessitated by this sudden growth without recourse to the stewards. The role of full time union employees had increasingly to be delegated to lay officials (convenors, shop stewards, branch secretaries and the like, who are paid by their employers, but who spend part or most of their time concentrating on union responsibilities). This was not necessarily true of all unions - for instance, the POEU and UCATT both maintained central control to an effective degree - but it certainly characterised some major unions like the TGWU, NUPE, ASTMS, AUEW (Engineering section) and NALGO. All this emerges from an exhaustive study of union change conducted over several years and published at the beginning of the decade by Undy and his colleagues. It is worth quoting their findings on the TGWU in detail:

> In the case of union government we noted two distinct forms of change. The first was towards decentralisation and diffusion. This happened in both non-bargaining and bargaining channels of internal decision making in some unions. The process was taken furthest in the TGWU, where regional secretaries were encouraged to expand their influence at the expense of national officers and an additional layer of government was introduced at the district level. At the same time greater reliance was placed on lay representation and the development of workplace-based forms of participation. This resulted in a shift of the balance of influence from full-time officers to lay activists - especially shop stewards - at the district and local level (Undy, Ellis, McCarthy and Halmos 1981: 314).

It is clear, moreover, that these lay officials have not always been disposed to accept directives from national union elites very easily. As Hague has observed:

> To union leaders, the incomes policy was at best a necessary evil, but could also be used as a bargaining counter in negotiations with government about a wider range of issues. To shop stewards the pay off from such high level encounters

> was remote and largely irrelevant, whereas incomes policy was a straitjacket on their activities and a chafing frustration (Hague 1983: 137).

This was amply illustrated by the outburst of unofficial union activity that occurred during the late 1960s. In our terms, this phenomenon of the 'wildcat strike' confirms that the elites were losing their 'downward' control over the rank and file. A perfect illustration is provided by the London Dustmen's dispute that took place in the autumn of 1969, a dispute that Leo Panitch has referred to as 'trend setting' (Panitch 1976: 218). Although the TGWU, NUPE and GMWU leaderships were all claiming a fifteen shillings a week rise, they were eventually obliged to 'chase their memberships' by making the lay officials' demand for a 14.5% increase official - or risk the formation of a breakaway union.

Where it has developed in major labour organisations, this growing shop steward power has made the nature of the mobilisational relationship within unions preponderantly interactive. However, it ought to be stressed that the trend towards interactiveness in the relationship between union leaders and lay officials was underpinned by greater rank and file autonomy. It would be misleading, therefore, to regard the rank and file membership as simply being under the control of a new breed of lay militant. That these ordinary members were not easily manipulated even by lay officials was illustrated by incidents like the notorious Thornett Affair that took place at British Leyland's Cowley plant in 1974. An avowedly Trotskyite steward, Alan Thornett was stripped of his responsibilities after losing the confidence of management and workers alike through his activities (Taylor 1978: 141-143). What was significant about the growth of lay officials in numerical and political terms is that it provided a vehicle for the upward transmission of the dissatisfaction felt by ordinary members at some of the industrial and political events of the 1960s and 1970s.

The importance of this in mobilisational terms is that, once again, it makes Labour's job potentially harder. One of the clear lessons of the 1960s and 1970s was that even if union leaders were inclined to be loyal to the party when it was in government, they were in reality frequently constrained by the desires of the rank and file. They had to remain union men first and Labour's allies second. Ultimately this forced the hands even of union leaders who might have wished to hold their fire. This was evidently a contributory factor to the collapse of Labour's incomes policies in 1968 and 1978-79. Equally evidently, this message was not lost on the party leadership, since an important element of *In Place Of Strife* was the proposal to bolster the central authority of the trade union movement over its own periphery; the government of the day would have liked to introduce new powers for the TUC to discipline recalcitrant member unions.

All this makes it clear that Labour could not presume the union elites would be able to inspire automatic loyalty towards the party and its policies. When we recall that constructing policies with a universal appeal for members of unions was becoming increasingly fraught, it is obvious that Labour was entering an era of perplexing strategic complexity. These factors have complicated the political relationship between the party and the unions, and have made the task of creating a basic appeal to union members an onerous one; inspiring an enduring loyalty is correspondingly more difficult.

Conclusion

We have now completed our initial consideration of the possible sources of electoral change among trade unionists. In chapter 2 it became clear that the organisational linkage between the party and the affiliated unions remains substantially undamaged and therefore its putative erosion can be dismissed as an effective explanation. In this chapter, however, we have revealed the pattern of volatile political relationships and social flux which constitutes a far more promising line of enquiry. Before attempting to examine directly the evidence of electoral change among trade unionists, it is necessary to paint a broad picture of electoral behaviour in Britain since the early 1960s, for this is the general context in which the phenomenon that interests us is located. We need to understand the changing union electorate as part of this context, and to formulate an appropriate research strategy.

Notes

1. It is remarkable to reflect upon how these sorts of consideration exercised the minds of members of the 1964-1970 governments. Crossman provides a particularly astonishing piece of political analysis in speculating on the effects of England's World Cup victory of July 1966. This, of course, took place shortly after the introduction of the government's deflationary package, yet he ebulliently asserts that England's success on the soccer field could in some way 'change Wilson's luck'. Even more amazingly, perhaps, he goes on to eulogise the 'tremendously gutsy' performance of the English players at Wembley, and feels sure that this would influence foreign bankers in a positive way! (Crossman 1979: 234) More recently, Denis Healey has revealed that the

coincidence of timing between the 1970 general election and the World Cup held in Mexico that year was a factor that concerned Harold Wilson (Healey 1989: 344).

2. In the middle of 1972 the TGWU was fined £5,000 for refusing to attend a session convened by the NIRC to deal with the blacking of container lorries at Liverpool. This was later increased when the union refused to pay.

3. For example, in April and May 1972 the government employed both tactics against the rail unions, but a national strike ensued regardless.

4. The government decided to ignore the provisions of the Industrial Relations Act and instead appointed a special Court of Inquiry headed by Lord Wilberforce. This recommended that the miners be considered a 'special case' and the NUM wage claim was virtually conceded.

4 Electoral Change in Modern Britain

The contention that trade unions have in some ways affected British electoral behaviour since the 1960s seems inherently plausible, but in seeking to establish the truth of this proposition, one is faced with the problem of eliciting persuasive evidence. What sort of questions should we be asking, and which variables selecting for examination? The broad answer to these questions is that existing electoral research can guide us. Such research provides a cue for the approach to adopt. As with many areas of academic inquiry, the study of voting behaviour is characterised by alternative theoretical perspectives and by variations within broad theoretical schools. We are bound to engage in some attempt at a critical review of the field of electoral research in order that we may settle upon a specifically useful approach to the study of union voting behaviour. This is the prime purpose of this chapter. In addition, a review of the literature on voting in Britain will provide a broad impression of the major themes of electoral change; this will serve as a wider context within which to set our understanding of the role and effect of trade unions.

Until the middle of the 1970s, it was something of a cliché in political science that electorates - and consequently, party systems - throughout western Europe were remarkable for the stability which they displayed. There are one or two frequently cited observations that demonstrate the mood which predominated in electoral studies at that time:

> ...the party systems of the 1960s reflect, with few but significant exceptions, the cleavage structures of the 1920s (Lipset and Rokkan, 1967: 50).

> ...the first priority of social scientists concerned with the development of parties and party systems since 1945 is to explain the *absence of change* in a far from static period in political history (Rose and Urwin, 1970: 295).

Yet since the time these words were written, the attention of political scientists has been grabbed by electoral change, not stability. Given the perception that change has started to occur in some political systems, analysts have turned to the question of how general such a phenomenon might be. Britain in particular has been the subject of many studies concerned with understanding if there has been greater electoral instability, and if so, to what extent.

Measurements and indicators of electoral change

The literature on voting behaviour seems to have thrown up three main ways of measuring electoral change - by looking at the stability of a party's aggregate vote (Rose and Urwin 1970; Maguire 1983), by focusing on electoral volatility in the party system as a whole (Pedersen 1979; Pedersen 1983; Crewe and Denver 1985; Lane and Ersson 1987) and by identifying changing rates of partisan identification (Crewe 1977; Crewe 1983; Mair 1984).

For instance, Maria Maguire, in updating work initially conducted by Rose and Urwin, made two important discoveries about the *stability of aggregate party support* in western Europe; firstly, during the years between 1960-1979, an increasing proportion of parties experienced a significant trend in their level of electoral support.[1] In the second place, Maguire noticed that the parties most vulnerable to instability tended to be older parties in general, and the Social Democratic parties in particular (Maguire 1983: 85). In the case of Britain, if we take the period from 1945-1987, it transpires that the Conservative Party's support remained virtually stable, by the criteria employed in the Rose/Urwin and Maguire studies, whereas the Labour Party suffered a significant decline.[2]

There have been two broad approaches to the concept of *electoral volatility*. In the first place, *gross volatility* can be taken to refer to the total amount of vote switching by individuals from one election to another. Panel study evidence suggests that this increased somewhat in Britain during the 1970s, until '...only half the electors who were eligible to vote at any two successive elections cast the same vote twice' (Miller et al 1990: 9). The bulk of these switchers chose to abstain at the second election, it should be noted (Crewe and Denver 1985: 110). *Net volatility* measures the relative change in the various parties' share of the vote across a pair of elections. It is net volatility which has tended to exercise the interest of political scientists (partly, no doubt, because it is considerably easier to identify), and it has commonly been measured by the *Pedersen Index*. This is most easily explained by saying, as Pippa Norris does, that the index is calculated by 'summing the percentage point changes in each party's share of the vote compared with the previous election, and dividing by two' (Norris 1990: 122-123). On reflection, it becomes clear that this is equal to the sum of the cumulative gains of all winning parties (or obversely, the sum of cumulative losses of all losing parties) at an election. Thus, for example, in a three-party system where party A lost 10% in an election, party B gained 7% and party C gained 3%, total net volatility would be:

$$(10 + 7 + 3)/2 = 10.$$

The Pedersen Index has a range running from 0-100, and most western European party systems have tended to produce a score of between 5 and 15 throughout the twentieth century; this, it should be said, demonstrates the *limits* of electoral change in the region as much as anything else.

In general, levels of net volatility often seem to have fluctuated - notably in countries like Italy, West Germany, Austria and Switzerland. Studies have tended to show up both countries where electoral net volatility has increased notably since 1970 (Denmark, Finland, the Netherlands, Norway and Sweden) and others where it has declined in an equally significant manner (France, West Germany and Ireland - see Lane and Ersson 1987: 178; Pedersen 1983: 39). However, taking western Europe as a whole, it has been pointed out that, firstly, average net volatility does appear to be increasing (specifically, from 6.5% in the early 1960s to 9.3% twenty years later, according to one study. [See Mair 1984: 170]), and secondly, that the number of 'low volatility' elections has declined - from about one-third of all elections held during the twenty years immediately subsequent to the second world war, down to around one-eighth of all elections that took place during the following decade (Pedersen 1983: 42).[3]

Compared to the rest of western Europe, Great Britain is in fact a country characterised by a relatively *low* level of net volatility; since 1945, only Austria, Sweden and Switzerland have experienced lower levels of volatility, and both of the latter two countries have undergone significant increases since 1970 (Lane and Ersson 1991: 189). In terms of its own history, Britain does not present a neat secular trend. Throughout, there is a fluctuating pattern of low and high volatility (see table 4.1). However, if we divide the twelve post war general elections into two chronological groups, it becomes clear that average net volatility is higher for the later period. The 1970s and 1980s have seen some relatively high volatility elections; in particular, it would seem that the elections of 1974 represent something of a turning point for contemporary Britain (although 1987 saw a notable decline in net volatility once again).

Table 4.1
Net volatility in Britain since 1945

1945-1966		1966-1987	
1945-50	3.9	1966-70	6.0
1950-51	6.8	1970-Feb.74	13.3
1951-55	1.7	Feb.74-Oct.74	3.1
1955-59	3.2	Oct.74-1979	8.2
1959-64	5.9	1979-83	11.8
1964-66	4.4	1983-87	3.2
Average	4.3	Average	7.6

The third major way in which electoral analysts have attempted to trace patterns of change is by focusing their attention upon rates of *partisan identification*. Although it has sometimes been argued that this concept has little genuine relevance in the context of non-American party systems, it does have the value of demonstrating the depth of enduring loyalty that parties maintain within the electorate. By concentrating upon rates of partisan identification it is possible to obtain an impression of the underlying trend of party support undistorted by the effects of short term factors that may be relevant only to specific election campaigns (such as candidate images, marketing approaches and special issues).

If we exclude countries where democratic party competition has only been established comparatively recently - and where, consequently, there has been little opportunity for the establishment of long-standing party attachments - there is evidence to suggest that rates of partisan loyalty are falling in many parts of western Europe. For instance, in the late 1970s the proportion of electors who claimed to maintain a general party attachment appeared to increase only in the case of Belgium; in at least eight other nations the contrary turned out to be the case. Indeed, Britain was among four countries where the

Table 4.2
The decline of party identification, 1964-1987

	Partisans	'Very Strong' Partisans
1964	93	44
1966	92	44
1970	91	42
1974 (February)	90	30
1974 (October)	90	27
1979	87	22
1983	87	21
1987	86	19
Net Change 1964-87	-7	-25

Source: Norris 1990: 127.

fall in the rate of partisan alignment was especially notable (that is, between 4.5% and 10%) during a period of just six years (Mair 1984: 176-9).[4] However, of possibly greater significance than the fall in the *proportion* of electors claiming a general partisan allegiance has been the change in the *strength* with which that allegiance has been maintained. After all, in the case of Britain some 86% of electors do still claim such a loyalty, but there has been a marked decline in the numbers willing to call this a 'very strong' loyalty. They used to amount to more than two-fifths of all electors; now, it seems, they comprise less than one-fifth (see table 4.2).

Realignment or dealignment?

So much for the indicators; Britain appears to be a country of comparatively low, but nonetheless growing, electoral instability, particularly in so far as the Labour Party is concerned. The extent to which these general patterns of electoral change and instability are reflected in the behaviour of trade union members will be considered in the course of the next chapter. But how is this instability to be interpreted? It has become standard to regard electoral change as evidence of one or the other of two types of process - either *realignment or dealignment*.

These terms were coined by the American political scientist V.O. Key (Key 1955). *Realignment* refers to the process of transition that party systems undergo periodically when new ties between social and political structures are formed. That is to say, in the wake of a period of realignment, there exist clear links between certain social or ideological communities and party organisations, but these are not the same links that preceded the transition. New cleavages come to structure the party system and patterns of electoral support. By contrast, the process of *dealignment* is one whereby established patterns of connection between party and society break down, but are not replaced by new structural associations. The party system comes to float increasingly free of its social moorings. Moreover, the long term scenario for dealignment suggests that a relatively small proportion of the electorate will maintain any general partisan loyalty; consequently, short term factors such as candidate and issue assessments are likely to have a permanently enhanced bearing upon the way that people decide to vote.

Are unstable systems, such as the British one, realigning or dealigning? Unfortunately, there is little that is really conclusive in the evidence as yet available. This is because the initial symptoms of both phenomena are likely to be similar - for instance, weakening partisan identification, declining electoral turnout and increasing volatility. Only time will really tell whether these phenomena herald the onset of a realignment of parties in line with new social or ideological cleavages or a radically different phase of enduring partisan dealignment. However, it has been argued that the view that one takes of the *causes* of electoral change may well guide one's interpretation (Flanagan and Dalton 1985: 8). Crudely, it is possible to collapse many of the possible explanations of electoral change into two broad categories - those which emphasise the decomposition of social cleavages, and those which stress the declining functional relevance of political parties.

Emphasis on the *decomposition of social cleavages* is often indicative of the view that party systems are undergoing processes of *realignment*. This follows from the perception that certain cleavages 'age' and become gradually obsolete.

> Any given set of issues that provokes a particular pattern of social cleavage and party alignment will inevitably wane in salience over time...voters who are two or three generations removed from the issue conflicts which precipitated the

> original alignments should show little further commitment to these issues as they are resolved or lose their relevance (Flanagan and Dalton 1985: 10).

This, it is suggested in some quarters, is the fundamental reason underlying the electoral decline of west European parties which have traditionally depended upon specific clienteles; Christian inspired political parties which have suffered from the decline of the religious cleavage present an obvious example.[5] Similarly - and more pertinently for us - the aforementioned instability of social democratic party support might conceivably be a consequence of the decline of the class cleavage in some western societies. The view that realignment is a consequence of the ageing of the class cleavage has often been proposed, albeit in various forms, to explain electoral change in Britain (see below for a more detailed review of the debate over class voting in Britain). From this perspective it is generally argued that class is of diminishing relevance to electoral and political mobilisation as a result of one or more, possibly interconnected, trends. These include:

i. The impact of social mobility on the class structure

Thus, an ever larger proportion of the electorate is coming to share similar occupational, material and cultural characteristics as the growth of the tertiary sector and widespread affluence become the norm. In terms of class characteristics, this group is somewhat 'cross-pressured', and it is typically less partisan than other social formations. Rose and McAllister, for instance, have spoken of 'a block of voters who are caught in the middle by conflicting pressures', and they go on to elaborate:

> The ideal-type manual worker, who left school at the minimum age, thought of himself or herself as working class, belonged to a trade union, and was a tenant, is a small minority of the working class today...The ideal-type middle-class person, who has some further education, owns a home, thinks of himself or herself as middle class, and would not belong to a trade union, is also very much in a minority. More than five-sixths of the British electorate today is mixed in social position, having some stereotype working class and stereotype middle class characteristics (Rose and McAllister 1986: 99).

Marshall and his colleagues have discovered that the attitudinal distributions of cross-class couples on a series of questions relating to inequality, distributional justice and partisanship differ perceptibly from those of class-homogeneous couples (Marshall, Newby, Rose and Vogler 1988: 134). Marshall also admits that liberal social theorists like Daniel Bell would find support for their views about the end of class politics in countries like Britain where the level of upward social mobility has been great. Nonetheless, they take pains to point out that evidence on relative mobility rates reveals that 'the association between an individual's class of origin and his or her eventual destination has proved remarkably stable' (Ibid: 271-272). Therefore, many clearly remain locked within class boundaries.

ii. Weaker community integration

Advanced industrial societies are associated with high levels of urbanisation and residential mobility, both of which serve to break down the narrow homogeneity and social solidarity of small, single-class communities. Therefore, there exist fewer communities which effectively propagate and reinforce clear-cut class identities and values. This is a phenomenon that, in the opinion of some sociologists, has produced an excessively 'privatist' outlook by many within the working class. For instance, Eric Hobsbawm has written of the replacement of solidaristic forms of community consciousness by 'the values of consumer-society individualism and the search for private and personal satisfactions above all else' (Hobsbawm 1981).

iii. The presence of new cleavages that cross-cut the class cleavage

In this respect, there are perhaps two particular types of 'new cleavage' that, it is sometimes suggested, exert pressure upon established patterns of alignment in countries like Great Britain. Firstly, there is the 'post-materialist' or 'new politics' cleavage which is particularly associated with the name of Ronald Inglehart (Inglehart 1971; Inglehart 1977). By altering the agenda and strategic partisan options of politics, new politics activists promise to disrupt the established patterns of links between party and elector.[6] Secondly, it has been suggested - particularly in the case of Great Britain - that sectoral cleavages may be developing. Especially associated with the work of Patrick Dunleavy, sectoral arguments assert that divisions between people who consume and/or work predominantly within either the public or the private sector are of increasing political significance. These sectoral alignments cross-cut class alignments and offer a potential explanation of the apparent weakening of the latter in Britain. We shall be looking at Dunleavy's general model of voting behaviour in more detail later in the chapter, but for now it is worth observing that the sectoral argument potentially offers an especially relevant account of the political proclivities of trade union members in Britain, and consequently our data analysis in subsequent chapters will devote itself in part to the specific question of sectoral effects and unionism.

It might be appropriate at this juncture to make the point that if a notion such as the 'ageing of the class cleavage' is to be of any help to us, it is important to appreciate that the waning of certain social cleavages is not a simple matter of unmediated social processes alone. As Peter Mair has said, 'issues and conflicts become relevant to politics partly, if not largely, because parties make them so' (Mair 1983: 420). Traditional European parties based upon religious and class appeals may well survive widespread social change if they are able to sustain the position of religious issues and class issues on the political agenda, and/or to keep 'new' issues or demands off this agenda, or in the last resort to adopt new appeals that fit the changing situation. In Britain, one of Labour's problems has been how to adapt to the demands of new groups of trade unionists without disillusioning traditional supporters from other parts of the movement. The tension between public and private sector union members in the late 1970s is one example of this problem. Realignment due to the erosion of socio-political cleavages can be a matter of some detail, therefore, and one which encompasses party and union strategy, as well as social change per se. All these factors play a part in notions like the 'ageing' of the class cleavage.

So electoral change might, to some extent, be a result of the erosion of cleavages. An alternative view is that political parties are gradually losing their functional relevance for modern political systems, a perspective that coincides with the notion of permanent *dealignment*. The thrust of the argument is that voters now rely less and less upon party leaders and their own habitual loyalties to provide cues about issues and voting decisions. Rather, such voters are characterised by increasing interest in, knowledge of, and sophistication about modern politics and are therefore more prepared to make independent judgements about its complexities (Barnes and Kaase 1979). Parties themselves are, in various ways, being superceded by new institutions. For example, input functions like interest articulation are falling increasingly within the remit of single issue groups and the mass media, whereas output functions such as policy-making are being usurped by bureaucrats and interest groups in technocratic and/or corporatist style political systems.

Indeed, some of these points may be of relevance for the case of British trade unionists; as we have seen, evidence suggests that a majority of union members in Britain would like to see the end of the exclusive organic link between the unions and the Labour Party, although they are quite happy to countenance a continuing role for unions in political affairs. Such political involvement would centre around the representation of members' interests in single issue campaigns, or perhaps direct participation in public policy-making (see table 2.8; see also Webb 1987: 20; Taylor 1987b: 12; Torode 1984). The growth of non-partisan, but political, unionism seems to exemplify the developing independence of groups of electors from political parties. Union members prefer to see their unions either as single-issue interest organisations or corporatist policy actors, but they no longer perceive an advantage in maintaining exclusive partisan connections or identities. This may or may not signify the growing obsolescence of parties per se.

Electoral change and models of voting behaviour

Much of the debate about partisan dealignment and realignment in Britain has been conducted in terms of which theoretical model of voting behaviour is most appropriate. It is neither easy, nor desirable, to circumvent this question in surveying the literature. In attempting this, it is useful to concentrate upon three broad model types - the partisan identification model, attitudinal models and the so-called 'radical model'. Such a review, it should be noted, necessarily incorporates a consideration of the debate over class dealignment.

The partisan identification model

The partisan identification model of voting behaviour was developed in the 1950s by a team of scholars based at the University of Michigan in the U.S.A. It draws largely upon two important concepts derived from psychology and sociology. Firstly, *identification* itself refers to a persistently held affective attachment to some group-object in the social environment - such as a political party. The group-object acts as a reference point by which other objects in the social and political environment may be evaluated; in short, it becomes a source of cues for interpreting the political world. Hence, for the authors of *The American Voter* political parties structured an 'individual's cognitive and affective map of politics' (Campbell et al, 1960). As the most enduring objects in the political environment, political parties offer a comparatively stable guide to the evaluation of other political 'objects' (for example, policy issues or candidates). Partisan identification leads to selective perception of the voter's political environment, and so tends to be self-reinforcing. Since the voter depends so much upon party cues, therefore, his or her perception of issues is such that it always confirms initial partisan commitment.

The second important concept introduced into political science with the partisan identification model is that of *socialisation*. Mark Franklin has pointed out that the notion of socialisation lies in the 'deep-seated human desire for conformity' (Franklin 1985: 50). Face to face contact, it is suggested, is inclined to produce a mimicry of attitudes and values, just as it does of patterns of speech and dress. Thus, people are first induced to adopt a partisan identification during childhood, before they have any well-developed cognitive understanding of politics. This initial family socialisation experience may be reinforced by other primary and secondary group links so that partisan identification actually tends to harden with age.

When the partisan identification model was first adapted to the British case by Butler and Stokes in the 1960s social class location was also seen as being important; in a sense, partisan identification theory was married with a social group model. Thus, the political values and identifications that new generations learn were seen as going hand in hand with class values and identifications. Indeed, the latter were very often the basis of the former. However, Butler and Stokes also discovered that British voters were more inclined to switch partisan identification along with changes that they made in their actual voting choices - unlike most of their American counterparts. They were forced to concede that:

> British voters are less likely than the Americans to make distinctions between their current electoral choices and more general partisan dispositions. The majority of voters do in fact have general dispositions toward a party which give continuity to their behaviour in a succession of specific choices. But in transferring their vote from one party to another they are less likely to retain a conscious identification with a party other than the one they currently support (Butler and Stokes, 1974: 44).

The partisan identification model has been criticised on various grounds. Not surprisingly, perhaps, one criticism concerns the theoretical usefulness of a concept which is not easily disentangled from the act of voting itself. Can we really speak of voters having a partisan identity which is independent of, and prior to, voting choice in Britain? Doubts about this have stirred some to argue that it would be best to dispense with the partisan identity variable and to concentrate upon other likely independent causal factors such as issue preferences or social background.

A second line of attack questions the continuing relevance of notions of partisan loyalty for voting behaviour. The strength of the model clearly lies in its ability to account for electoral *stability*, rather than *change*. It explains the continuity of voting patterns and the entrenchment of cleavages into patterns of political alignment *once they have been initially mobilised*. Put simply, it helps us to understand the half of the electorate in Britain that always votes in the same 'habitual' way. However, the model has limitations when it comes to accounting for electoral change; this tends to be accounted for within the model by emphasising the breakdown of socialisation processes due to social group (for instance, class) decomposition.

It is worth reiterating that levels of partisan identification appear to have been falling in many western European electorates, especially Britain's. In this context, it is not so easy to remain convinced of the centrality of partisan loyalty to the voting decision. Moreover, there are commentators who clearly doubt the notion that partisan attachment continues to harden with age. Rose and McAllister, for instance, have discovered that pre-adult primary socialisation explained less of the vote in 1983 than it did in 1964.

> The weakness of the traditional closed-class model of political socialisation is just that it is traditional. It assumes that people do not think for themselves, or that learning stops as soon as a person is old enough to be independent of parents. Moreover, the model is static in its assumptions about old parties. It is assumed that parties salient in the parents' lifetime will always remain salient...The recurrence of multi-party competition in Britain demonstrates the limits of political socialisation in determining the vote...In place of the dead hand of the past, contemporary circumstances gain influence (Rose and McAllister 1986: 114).

Those who are sceptical about the influence of the 'dead hand of the past', often supplement their criticisms of the Michigan model with a new-found confidence in the growing sophistication and cognitive wisdom of electors. Electoral change for these writers is often, therefore, a question of dealignment borne of the growing independence of voters from parties. Those who retain some sympathy for the partisan identification perspective, however, may remain sceptical about the alleged sophistication of voters; for them, electoral change has more to do with a fundamental realignment that results from the decomposition of the class cleavage. It is to this central theme of British electoral research that we now turn.

The partisan identification model and class dealignment in Britain

The debate over class dealignment in Britain is distinguished by the quantity of literature that it has generated, if not necessarily for having produced any conclusive arguments. In attempting to review the major features of this debate, our approach will concentrate upon two broad questions that seem to lie at its heart: Has class dealignment really occurred? And if so, why?

Those who incline to the view that class dealignment has indeed occurred point to some striking evidence. For instance, relative class allegiance to the major parties has changed; whereas the proportion of the working class voting for Labour was 2.7 times greater than the proportion of the middle class doing so in 1964, it was just 2.3 times greater in 1983 (Harrop 1986: 40). Relative class voting can also be measured by the odds ratio (see footnote 8), and this fell from 6.4 to 3.9 between 1964 and 1983. Moreover, the overall proportion of electors voting according to their occupational class has fallen from 63% in 1964 to just 47% in 1983 (Heath et al 1985: 30).

But not all commentators have been readily persuaded that such findings constitute evidence of the existence of genuine class dealignment (see, for instance, Barton 1986, Heath et al 1985, and Marshall et al 1988). Arguments have, inter alia, ranged over methodological issues (for example, how should we measure class voting?), theoretical questions (how should we define 'class'?) and empirical questions - which may well depend, in part, upon methodological and theoretical positions (for example, is Britain a less class divided society than it once was?) Illustrative of some of these points is the work of Anthony Heath and his colleagues. They are broadly inclined to reject the view that class dealignment has taken place since the 1960s, on at least four different counts.

In the first place, they claim that the apparent fall in class voting that occurred between 1979 and 1983 'is in fact almost wholly spurious, an artefact of the inadequate manual /non-manual dichotomy.' These authors insist that such a crude distinction, whilst valuable 'as a rough first approximation...is wholly inadequate for studying the social bases of politics since it ignores important divisions which have little to do with the colour of a man's or woman's collar'. Consequently, they prefer a more complex five-fold class scheme comprising a salariat, routine non-manual workers, petit bourgoisie, foremen/technicians and the working class.[7] However, it is not clear that such a class model produces a notably less dramatic picture of decline in class voting between 1964-1983 (Heath et al, 1985: 30-34) .

Writers like Ivor Crewe have maintained that there remain certain advantages to employing the simple manual/non-manual distinction, morover; he insists that the working class is an 'ideologically laden' term for a certain section of manual employees who mount to barely one-third of the workforce. Moreover, there are practical difficulties for researchers who isolate the salariat. For instance, in constructing measures of class voting which compare the behaviour of the middle and working classes, using the salariat as an indicator of the former may mean ignoring fully 40% of the sample (that is, the petit bourgoisie, routine non-manual employees and foremen). By contrast, the manual/non-manual dichotomy enables one to base one's findings on the entire sample which divides neatly in half (Crewe 1986: 623-4).

The second, and perhaps most important, point raised by Heath is that it is misleading to concentrate, as many commentators have done, upon levels of 'absolute class voting'; rather, it is better to focus upon 'relative class voting'.

> ...while the overall proportion of the electorate voting for its natural class party can be thought of as a measure of *absolute* class voting, what we are really interested in is a measure of *relative* class voting. (Heath et al: 31)

The advantage of measuring cross-class voting with the odds ratio - and thereby focusing upon relative class voting - is that it avoids the pitfall of attributing too much of the Labour Party's electoral difficulties to the decline in class voting. For example, Heath points out that Labour's losses in the 1983 election were far from specific to the working class. However, while accepting the general validity of this argument, it has been suggested that Heath's interpretation and construction of the odds ratio is misleading.[8]

Table 4.3
Class composition of the electorate, 1964 and 1983

	1964	1983
Salariat	18	27
Routine Non-Manual	18	24
Petit Bourgoisie	7	8
Foremen/Technicians	10	7
Working Class	47	34
	100	100

Source: Heath et al 1986: 36.

The third objection raised by Heath to the notion of class dealignment is that commentators have often falsely attributed electoral change to it when much is really down to the changing relative size of different classes. Table 4.3 illustrates how the salariat has grown relative to the size of the working class since 1964. Heath suggests that too many observers are quick to regard Labour's electoral slump in the decade following 1974 as a result of class dealignment, which leaves the simple, but highly significant fact of the shrinking of the working class out of the argument.

Finally, Heath and his collaborators contest that arguments in favour of the existence of class dealignment have frequently been a product of the specific time period under scrutiny. This reflects the fact that detailed academic election surveying only commenced in Britain in 1964.

> In general, the period from 1945 to 1974 shows no consistent trend. There are certainly ups and downs, but we would see these as having more to do with changing political events - the nature of parties' programmes, their success in office, etc. - than with any underlying evolution of the classes. The mistake of recent commentators is that they have taken 1964 as their baseline. As we now see, this was a rather unfortunate choice since it marked a peak in relative class voting (as measured by the odds ratio). The adoption of a longer time perspective clearly calls into question claims about any secular trend towards class dealignment (Heath et al: 34).[9]

An interesting variation on the theme of class dealignment has been suggested by William Miller. For Miller, class dealignment has both occurred and it has not, depending upon the level at which one conducts analysis. The paradox of class voting is that whilst it appears to have weakened at the level of the individual, quite the opposite has proved to be the case at constituency level. People, apparently, are pulled towards voting in line with their 'class environment'; thus, in predominantly working class constituencies, non-manual groups of electors are more likely to vote Labour than the national norm, whilst in middle class areas, manual groups are more Conservative than normal (Miller 1978). Partisan identification theorists refer to socialisation in emphasising, as Miller does, that this is because 'those who talk together, vote together'; other writers prefer to place greater stress upon more purely economic interest factors that might underlie this pattern of behaviour. Dunleavy and Husbands, for example, argue that manual workers in inner city areas are more likely to rely on public services, to live in poorly-maintained council housing or to be unemployed, all of which might incline a voter to choose the Labour Party in the polling booth. Their manual counterparts in the leafy suburbs stand a far greater chance of owning their own homes, driving their own transport and being reasonably well-paid. Thus, political and economic interests, not social contact mechanisms, could in fact underlie 'constituency effects' (Dunleavy and Husbands 1985: 21-25, 137).

Notwithstanding Miller's intervention in the debate, the main concern has been with dealignment at the individual level. If we accept that to some extent class dealignment has occurred at the individual level - and bearing in mind Scarbrough's comments about the odds ratio (see footnote 8) and our own findings in chapter 5, the evidence is quite persuasive - then we are confronted with the question of why this should have been so. Partisan identification theorists have been challenged about this, especially by attitudinal (or *issue voting*) theorists.

The partisan identification school inclines to the view that class alignment is weakening as the class cleavage ages - possibly making way for a long term realignment of the electorate. Thus, the generation growing up in the 1920s and 1930s was class mobilised, and its successor generation of the 1940s and 1950s inherited strong class and partisan identifications; subsequent generations have been less responsive to class appeals, however. Butler and Stokes themselves initially suggested that the class cleavage was likely to weaken as the basis of British electoral support for at least three reasons: firstly, the ideological erosion of the Labour Party's distinctive class appeal following the establishment of a Butskellite two-party consensus; secondly, growing working class affluence (but see Goldthorpe et al 1969, and Westergaard and Anderson 1965 for various criticisms of this view); and thirdly, the increasingly middle class nature of the Labour Party's leadership. In retrospect, none of these seem to offer highly persuasive reasons for the quite sudden growth of class dealignment *after 1974*.

Issue voting theorists (whose models we shall be considering shortly) generally prefer to regard class dealignment as a *consequence* of partisan dealignment rather than as a *cause* of it. For partisan identification writers, partisanship is based upon class identity; therefore, when class consciousness fades, it follows that partisan consciousness is likely to, also. However, issue voting theorists perceive a gradually widening rift between traditional party supporters and their parties over certain key political issues, and this is regarded as central to any explanation of weakening partisan loyalty. Since party support in Britain has traditionally been about class support it follows that this too is undermined. Ivor Crewe is probably the best known exponent of this line of interpretation; he has produced much evidence of the growing attitudinal divergence between parties and their (erstwhile) supporters. For example, he has drawn particular attention to the

> ...quite exceptional movement of opinion away from Labour's traditional positions amongst Labour supporters over the last twenty or thirty years. There has been a spectacular decline in support for the collectivist trinity of public ownership, trade union power and social welfare (Crewe 1985: 138).

The Michigan model of voting behaviour, embodying a British scenario in which class and partisan values are learnt by new generations, has been criticised heavily since the middle of the 1970s, largely because it fails to offer an adequate explanation of electoral change. Electoral change has been too sudden and too great for the breakdown of socialisation mechanisms to offer anything like a comprehensive or convincing explanation. Within the partisan identification perspective trade unions were typically regarded as 'secondary socialisation variables' which served to reinforce class and partisan values; in the following chapter we shall see that such a conception of the role of trade unions in influencing electoral choice is no longer feasible. This obliges us to consider the interpretation of union effects in terms of other models of voting behaviour, models that developed with the growing criticism levelled at the Michigan model in the 1970s.

The attack on partisan identification theory

It is a basic tenet of democratic theory that public policy should in some meaningful sense be subject to popular control. In practical terms, the 'popular will' has commonly been understood to be indicated by the majority of citizens' individual preferences about a public issue or programme of policies. The act of voting is therefore regarded, at least implicitly, as a coherent assessment of the programmatic alternatives on offer at election time. Those who would take this to be a realistic account of the relationship between democracy and electoral processes, base their credulity upon certain important assumptions; for a start, voters are regarded as relatively sophisticated and rational political actors. This means that they have a set of crystallised public policy preferences, that they clearly and correctly understand the positions of the various parties or candidates on these issues, and they then vote accordingly. None of these things can be freely and easily assumed, however.

And even if voters do appear to have definite attitudinal preferences, how can we be sure that such preferences actually shape electoral choice? Might voters not simply use a partisan loyalty as a cue for the attitude they 'should' take on a given issue, as the partisan identification theorists suggest? Doubts about the validity of these assumptions helped produce the Michigan model in the first place, but by the 1970s the tide was turning within political science. Nevertheless, the foundations of the Michigan model were well established.

In some ways we might plausibly trace doubts about voter rationality back to Schumpeter's classic mid-twentieth century critique of modern democracy. His scepticism was clear. For instance, he questioned how far it was possible to seriously attribute a rational and independent political will to the citizenry. This will, he suggested,

> ...would have to be implemented by the ability to observe and interpret correctly the facts that are directly accessible to everyone, and to sift critically the information about the facts that are not...And all this the model citizen would have to perform for himself and independently of party groups and propaganda, for volitions and inferences that are imposed upon the electorate obviously do not qualify for the ultimate data of the democratic process (Schumpeter 1952: 253-254).

Schumpeter recognised that many citizens remain essentially detached from politics: 'Without the initiative that comes from immediate responsibility, ignorance will persist in the face of masses of information, however complete and correct.' Consequently, he argues that:

> ...the typical citizen drops down to a lower level of mental performance as soon as he enters the political field. He argues and analyses in a way that he would readily recognise as infantile within the sphere of his real interests. He becomes a primitive again. His thinking becomes associative and affective (Ibid: 262).

Later, Campbell and his associates discovered that, across a range of foreign and domestic policy issues, only around one-half to two-thirds of American electors actually seemed to have clearly crystallised attitudes about issues they were familiar with. Still less did these people actually perceive any party difference on such issues - and where they did, there was no guarantee that this would be the *correct* perception. For these reasons, no more than 20-30% of electors could be regarded in a prima facie sense as being potentially rational *issue voters*.

Moreover, even where a link between issues and voting was found, Campbell pointed out that party loyalty itself might be a *cause*, not a consequence, of attitudinal formation. 'The identifier who sees his party take up new issues is likely to be influenced thereby' (Campbell et al 1960: 97). For partisan identification writers, short term issue effects may well be apparent, but issues tend to be interpreted in the light of prior partisanship. In the 1960s, writers suggested that this could happen in one of two ways. Firstly, a voter might be *persuaded* to alter his or her own issue position in order that it be congruent with that of a party or candidate with whom there was a prior identification. Such would not represent a case of genuine issue voting. Secondly, voters who favourably identify with a given party or candidate might even *project* their own issue positions on to that party or candidate, regardless of the latter's actual attitudes. An illustration of this could be found in the way that Republican identifiers who were 'hawks' on the question of the Vietnam war regarded Nixon as a hawk at the time of the 1968 presidential election, whereas Republican 'doves' perceived him to be a dove (Page and Brody 1972: 988-9).

The first detailed consideration of these types of argument in relation to Britain was undertaken by Butler and Stokes in the 1960s. Notwithstanding the widespread view that British politics was then - and still is in all probability - more programmatic and ideological than American politics (see, for example, Epstein 1967), they were sceptical about issue voting in Britain. In the first place, they pointed out that British voters held issue positions in a random manner over a relatively short period of time (Butler and Stokes 1974: 280-1). Thus, as in America, voters' attitudes were seldom crystallised. Moreover, the electorate as a whole appeared to display a remarkable lack of consistency across related issues - a point that was to be reiterated by commentators in the 1980s like Patrick Dunleavy, as we shall see. Butler and Stokes seem to have been indicating that the cognitive development of the British electorate was too limited for us to countenance seriously the notion of issue voting (Ibid: 320).

However, a defence of the issue voting model did eventually emerge. The first writers clearly to challenge Butler and Stokes' view were Alt, Sarlvik and Crewe in an important article published in 1976. These writers claimed that where partisan identification conflicts with issue preferences, the latter are at least as likely to determine voting choice as the former. Moreover, they met the problems of 'persuasion' and 'projection' head on. Firstly, they demonstrated that about 95% of the sample that they worked with was correctly able to identify the various party positions on a range of issues, thus suggesting that projection was not likely to have greatly distorted perceptions of party positions:

> ...most people appear to display a considerable grasp of the issues and where the parties stand on each...it appears that, the conventional wisdom notwithstanding, the great majority of the British electorate have both partisan preferences and realistic perceptions of the parties' policies (Alt et al 1976: 284).

With regard to the problem of persuasion they pointed out that, even though very strong partisans continued to support their own party when an alternative was closer to them on the issues, such was not the case for *weaker* partisans. This, they argued, constituted evidence that perhaps people *did* recognise differences between themselves and 'their' parties over issues, and were even inclined to withdraw their support if those differences were considered significant enough. Indeed, even among 'very strong' partisans, only 57% continued to prefer their party when they acknowledged themselves to be closer to an alternative party on the issues, compared to fully 87% of those who saw themselves as closer to their own party on the issues. It might be countered that this begs the question of why 57% voted 'irrationally' (that is, voted in spite of, rather than because of, their issue preferences), but Alt, Crewe and Sarlvik argued strongly that many people 'who disagree with their party are to a large extent aware that they are doing so' (ibid: 289).

Allied to growing evidence of the partisan dealignment and volatility of the British electorate, the arguments of Alt, Crewe and Sarlvik encouraged a widespread reappraisal of Butler and Stokes' view of voting behaviour this side of the Atlantic. Over the ensuing decade or more, publications with titles such as *Party Identification And Beyond* (Ian Budge et al), *The Rise Of Issue Voting In British Elections* and *The Decline Of Class Voting In Britain* (Mark Franklin), *Class Does Not Equal Party* (Richard Rose) and *Voters Begin To Choose* (Rose and Ian McAllister) all indicated the progression of British psephological study. Partisan dealignment and volatility have meant that the focus of contemporary studies has shifted to the question of explaining electoral *change*. This is precisely where attitudinal models are most helpful; they offer an insight into the comparatively short term shifts in electoral choice that confront political scientists. For instance, Budge and Farlie have tried to demonstrate how useful an understanding of issue preferences can be in 'explaining and predicting elections' (Budge and Farlie 1983). However, there is nothing conclusive about issue models, and the debate has been a lively one.

Heath and his associates, for example, have pointed out that the clear victor of the 1983 general election, the Conservative Party, actually held no clear lead over the Labour Party on any of the five issues that electors felt were most important during the campaign (Heath et al: 91-96). Attitudinal models, it should be said, are far from monolithic; various models have been developed, and it is instructive to consider briefly one or two of the most influential examples.

Attitudinal models

The earliest of attitudinal models was that proposed by Anthony Downs in his seminal book *An Economic Theory Of Democracy* (1957). The Downsian model was strictly rationalistic, instrumental and individualistic. His work really represents the transposition of the simplified rationality of economic models into the domain of political science.

Downs assumes that voters are able to calculate their personal 'incomes' in terms of the amounts of utility that they would individually derive from the implementation of alternative party programmes. They would then vote accordingly in order to maximise their utility. In practice this is, of course, a highly simplistic account of reality. In particular, the pure Downsian model has been criticised for assuming an unlikely level of political knowledge and calculation on the part of the ordinary voter; the benefit to be gained from a rational vote might well be outweighed by the cost of executing it in terms of time and effort. Moreover, writers like McLean (1982) have pointed out that the chances of a particular individual vote having any decisive bearing upon the outcome of a national election are so infinitesimally small that strictly rational individuals would probably not bother visiting the polling booth at all. Nonetheless, whilst it may not constitute an entirely convincing account of reality, Downs' model has the merit of representing a serious attempt to work out how voters would vote if they *were* rational. As such it amounts to an important step along the path towards the development of attitudinal models.

Hilde Himmelweit's 'consumer model' of voting focuses not directly upon individual utility maximisation as such, but upon personal policy preferences (Himmelweit et al 1981: 11-16). It is assumed that the voter knows his or her own mind with respect to a range of potential policy alternatives, and that he or she then seeks out the party programme that best matches these preferences. Like a shopper in the market place, the voter may develop partisan 'brand loyalties' to some extent, but this does not mount to partisan identification in the sense of the Michigan model. Loyalties are rarely as deeply rooted as the Michigan model suggests since voters approach each election like shoppers returning to the market place on the look-out for fresh ideas and bargains.

Himmelweit's model is more realistic than its Downsian counterpart, and its focus upon policy preferences per se rather than personal self-interest complements work which indicates that people rarely vote with their own wallets in mind. For instance, Alt (1979) and Mosley (1984) have both suggested that individual economic circumstances probably matter less to a person's vote than perceptions of overall national performance. In the jargon, people are more inclined to vote in a *sociotropic* way than an *egocentric* one.

Nonetheless, the consumer model has met criticism on several counts. One of these criticisms might be levelled at rational choice models in general; this concerns the question of whether voters genuinely do hold 'political attitudes'. As we have seen, the work of writers like Brody and Page, and Butler and Stokes, in the 1960s suggested that they do not. In a variety of ways this message has been confirmed by Converse (1964), Scarbrough (1986) and Dunleavy and Husbands (1985), who have shown up logical inconsistencies in voters' attitudes in related policy areas (the problem of low attitudinal 'constraint'), whilst Lievesley and Waterton (1985) have demonstrated that many voters change their policy preferences over a comparatively short period of time. These criticisms, if accurate, threaten to render the consumer model - along with other issue models - inherently implausible, since they imply that it is is unlikely that many voters are ever in a position to match up party programmes to their crystallised policy attitudes. In many ways, this question goes to the heart of the debate over issue voting. Crewe has maintained that examples of coherent and consistent trends in electors' attitudes are to be found (witness, for instance, the growing disapproval of Labour's 'collectivist trinity' referred to above), and these are indicative of 'real views'. Nevertheless, even Crewe admits that a certain amount of equivocation was evident in the voters' views on several party issues in 1979 (Crewe 1985: 138-140). One can avoid these criticisms to some extent by redefining voter rationality. For instance, Budge and Farlie have argued that most voters have a limited, but meaningful sense of issue awareness; they tend to understand the broad issue stances of parties in given issue areas. Often, issue areas are 'owned' by parties in that there is longstanding and widespread voter acceptance of their views in these areas. Thus, welfare policy is generally an electorally positive issue area for socialist parties, as law and order is for conservative parties. This voter awareness becomes significant as different issue areas become salient in given election campaigns. Some areas remain almost permanently salient (for instance, economic performance) whereas others are far less frequently so. Moreover, it is possible that they are not so bad at explaining *stable* behaviour as has been sometimes contended. Budge and Farlie argue that the key to explaining individual electoral stability may lie with certain issues upon which voters have 'abiding fixations', rather than with the partisan identification variable. If true, this provides an issue based account of long term partisan predispositions, rather than a socialisation based one (Budge and Farlie 1983: 36,41). These are effective ways of making issue models realistic and workable, since perceptions of an issue's importance count for more than detailed policy preferences. A degree of rationality emerges in voter behaviour, although this argument does not necessarily satisfy the stringent conditions of citizen sophistication and knowledge laid down by Schumpeter. Moreover, to reiterate a point made already, doubt has been cast on the notion that even salient issues are all that decisive for the outcome of elections (Heath et al 1985: 91-96).

In addition, Himmelweit's model has drawn criticism on methodological grounds relating to the small and allegedly biased nature of the sample that it has been tested against (Kuchler 1984: 2; Dunleavy 1983: 3-7). It has also been alleged that, in common with other issue voting models, Himmelweit's approach neglects the sources of voters' attitudes (Scarbrough 1986). However, there is logically no need for this to weaken attitudinal models per se; various writers have, for instance, shown how such models may allow for the influence of social background upon attitudinal formation (Farlie, Budge and Laver 1983; Robertson 1984; Heath et al 1985: 174).

Leaving aside the models of Downs and Himmelweit, there is a third attitudinal approach which, it has been suggested, is 'analytically sharper, less demanding of the voter and intuitively more plausible...' (Harrop and Miller 1987: 153). This is Fiorina's 'retrospective performance' model. According to Fiorina, ordinary citizens seldom have clear preferences about political issues. Instead of attempting to compare crystallised policy preferences with party programmes, Fiorina suggests that most voters probably undertake an intellectually less ambitious and time consuming task; namely, the evaluation of how effectively the government of the day has performed in pursuing certain broad and uncontroversial policy objectives - low unemployment, stable prices, industrial calm and so on. Thus, their vote becomes a retrospective judgement on the government's managerial record, rather than an evaluation of its philosophical attributes or policy proposals, and electors are likely to punish any government that they regard as a disappointment. Fiorina is faced with the problem of all rational choice theorists - how to explain the large numbers of electors who rarely change their partisan inclinations. This he does by conceding that many do in fact develop a form of party loyalty, but it is not one built upon affective attachments, as the Michigan theorists suggested. Instead, voters develop a view of the overall historical performance of parties, and this view will be modified in the light of the most recent party performance. Established partisanship will only be rejected when the most recent performance is radically different to those of the past (Fiorina 1977).

Writers like Whiteley and Miller have applied models of retrospective assessment to the British case (Whiteley 1983; Miller 1984; Miller et al 1990). One might add that since performance in economic management is the most salient of retrospective judgements, the growing body of literature on 'political business cycles' is of relevance (Alt and Chrystal 1983: Paldam 1981.) That is, retrospective evaluations may well reflect media-influenced perceptions of the government's recent economic performance. Because of the empirical value and sheer plausibility of retrospective performance models, we shall incorporate one such model into our analysis of the behaviour of union members in Britain (chapter 6). It is worth emphasising that, regardless of one's view of issue models, it would be unwise to reject them altogether; even partisan identification models allow for some influence by short term issue assessments. Whatever, many now believe, like Mark Franklin, that the decline of class voting in Britain has 'opened the way to choice between parties based on issue preferences rather than class loyalty' (Franklin 1985: 176). For this reason alone, some consideration of issue effects is desirable.

There remains one further category of voting model that might broadly be classified as 'attitudinal', and which we have yet to consider; these are the models that concern themselves with *ideological voting*. As we have already mentioned, Butler and Stokes were quick to reject the notion that ordinary voters were governed by coherent ideological systems of belief; it was parties, rather than principles, that provided the focus for the way in which voters viewed politics:

> The assumption that voters see themselves or the parties on a left-right dimension at all is contradicted by our evidence on the slightness of the role that the words left and right played in the political thought of the British mass public. A thin layer of the most ideologically aware did seem to use left and right to organise their views about where the parties stood on current issues. But such people were vastly outnumbered by those who had more impoverished and static interpretations of the concepts. A large majority of the electorate apparently gave left and right no political meaning at all (Butler and Stokes 1974: 336-337).

Nonetheless, in recent years more commentators have been willing to contend that ideological thinking of a sort does underlie partisan choice. Indeed, if short term issue preferences are important to electoral choice, the question of the origins of such preferences arises; one possible source of these preferences might be the general and enduring principles or beliefs by which people abide. (What is more, these ideological values, if we can properly so call them, may in turn derive from factors connected with social location and family influence, as suggested in Figure 4.1.) On the other hand, underlying values and short term assessments might each influence vote quite discreetly of one another.

What is 'ideology' in the context of voting behaviour? By ideology - sometimes more blandly referred to as 'belief system' - we mean a set of underlying normative and cognitive attitudes that (some) people adhere to, and which are broadly consistent internally, and not easily modified or shed. Ideological imperatives go beyond the narrow rationality of self-interest or retrospective assessment. Cognitive strands are intermingled with non-bargainable moral sentiments which, ultimately, might not be justified in purely rationalistic terms. People with clearly defined principles and commitments may well continue to vote for a given party or candidate as an act of moral affirmation or expression, *regardless* of particular policy shortcomings or demonstrable managerial incompetence that the party or candidate in question might display.

Figure 4.1

Possible connections between vote, basic principles, short term attitudes and social background

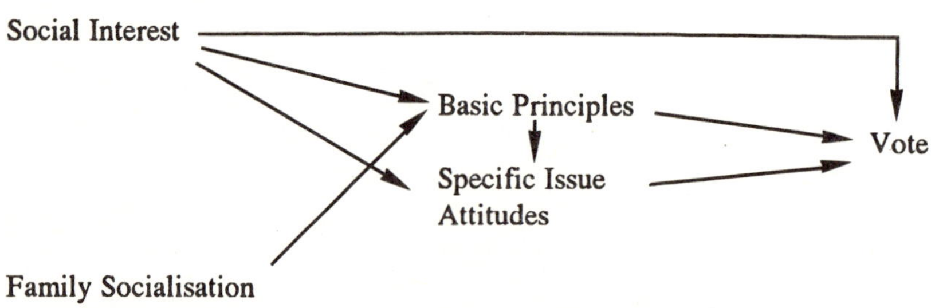

The place of ideology in voting decisions has been considered by several authors over the past few years, most thoroughly perhaps in the book-length treatment accorded the subject by Elinor Scarbrough (1984). She tested a 'preliminary' model based upon four ideal-type ideologies which derive from historical political forces. In addition, Rose and McAllister have argued that general political principles are the most important of all influences at work in their preferred model of voting (Rose and McAllister 1986: 129-131, 135). Interestingly, several researchers - most notably, perhaps, Robertson (1983) and Heath et al (1985) - have claimed that such principles can be reduced to two underlying ideological dimensions; firstly, there is a left-right dimension concerned with questions of economic redistribution and social ownership that are typical of class and status politics, and secondly, there is a 'north-south' dimension which focuses upon issues connected with social liberalism or authoritarianism (see Robertson 1983, Figure 6.1., or Heath et al 1985, table 8.6). Heath's 'interactionist model' concerns itself with very broad principles; eschewing the roles of habitual loyalty, narrow instrumentality or careful and close consideration of specific policies, it contends that voters are inclined to vote in accordance with broad or 'synoptic' evaluations of what parties stand for: 'It is the fit between the general character of the party and the voter's own general ideology which...best accounts for electoral choice' (Heath et al 1985: 99). To some extent, this puts one in mind of Budge and Farlie's claim that citizens understand party appeals in terms of broad, rather than detailed, issue stances.

There exist two kinds of criticism that are of notable importance with regard to ideological models. In the first place, we have seen that researchers like Butler and Stokes questioned the ability of voters to employ abstract ideological concepts. Subsequently, Hans Klingemann confirmed that around four-fifths of the British electorate appeared unable or unwilling to spontaneously evaluate political parties in terms of concepts of 'left' and 'right' (Klingemann 1979). The second main line of criticism concerns the question of how far electors can be regarded as having coherent and enduring belief systems. Converse (1964) issued the classic pioneering study of American electors in this vein. Butler and Stokes found a similar pattern of substantial attitudinal instability (on questions of nationalisation and nuclear disarmament) over time during the 1960s (Butler and Stokes 1974: 315-316). More recently, Dunleavy and Husbands have reiterated an essentially similar message. Their approach consisted of an attempt to focus on the degree of logical inter-connection between different questions on the same subject . Thus, for instance, they claimed that between 2% and 8% of the voters of the various parties in 1983 offered strongly inconsistent responses to a series of questions on nuclear disarmament. This, one might contend, hardly amounts to overwhelming evidence of the incoherence of electors' belief systems. Furthermore, the authors themselves admit that the question of precisely what constitutes a 'consistent' position over some attitudes is a little 'esoteric' - perhaps even 'casuistical' (Dunleavy and Husbands 1985: 177-180). Therefore, whilst Dunleavy and Husbands focus upon something significant for the question of ideology and voting behaviour, their case is not entirely conclusive. In addition, it should be emphasised that electors are unlikely to be static in terms of their attitudinal and ideological development; for example,

American writers like Nie and his colleagues have made the interesting point that 'ideological' candidates or party programmes can stimulate a more ideological response from voters (Nie et al 1976).

In conclusion, whilst the evidence for the existence of deeply-rooted and well-developed ideological voting in Britain may be far from compelling, there is enough that is suggestive to encourage electoral researchers in this direction. Therefore, it is interesting and informative to look at the underlying political values held by union members in Britain, and we shall be doing this in chapter 6 by applying Heath's simple, but useful, concept of synoptic values.

Before concluding our review of electoral research, there is one final model of voting behaviour that is worth consideration; this is the so-called 'radical model' that emerged in the 1980s, and which claimed to stand somewhat outside the established lines of electoral interpretation.

Dunleavy and Husbands' radical model

This model of electoral behaviour in Britain has developed as an outgrowth of Patrick Dunleavy's work on 'sectoral cleavages' in politics (Dunleavy 1980). In collaboration with Chris Husbands, Dunleavy developed the radical model as a rather self-conscious alternative to the debates of the 1970s. In precisely what sense Dunleavy's model is actually 'radical' is never quite clear; but it is evident that sociology remains very close to the heart of the model since the fundamental influences upon electoral choice are regarded as being the socio-economic interests that people have as members of various social groups. Dunleavy and Husbands explain that:

> People will not necessarily (and perhaps not often) articulate the influence of their social location in structuring their votes - the phenomenon may be objectively apparent to an analyst without being explicitly recognised by voters as involved in their decisions (Dunleavy and Husbands 1985: 19).

However, while people always vote to 'promote the collective interests of their social location', it is important to recognise that certain ideological agents - chiefly the media and the political parties - can affect the way in which these interests are perceived. One gets the feeling that Dunleavy and Husbands find the interminable detail of the partisan identification-versus-issue voting debate somewhat trying; hence, in their 'radical' way, they cut through it all to reassert the overwhelming importance of the real sources of political behaviour - social interest and ideological hegemony.

We have already referred to Dunleavy and Husbands' views regarding the (lack of) logical coherence in people's political beliefs. Not surprisingly, in view of this, they profess scepticism about attitudinal models. Thus, they insist that social interests and ideological conditioning operate in some manner that bears *directly* upon the voting decision - *not* via the prior mechanism of issue assessment. However, the argument does not always seem crystal-clear at this point:

> They (issue attitudes) do not constitute important causal factors in structuring the way in which people vote, however closely voting and attitudes may be associated. *Even if shifts in attitudes predate shifts in alignments, these leads and lags demonstrate only that a change in people's overall orientations shows itself first in more finely graduated responses to issue questions, and only later becomes evident as a switch in the relatively crude indicator provided by actual behaviour* (Ibid: 20, my emphasis).

So, it is contended that people change their attitudes about political issues (due to changing interests or changing receptiveness to ideological messages presumably); later, they might realise that the time has come to alter their partisan allegiance, given these new circumstances. Yet in a certain sense, we are asked to regard the two occurrences as causally unconnected. At least, Dunleavy and Husbands assure us that it would be quite erroneous to infer that people actually change their vote as a result of their new attitudes about the political world. Yet surely there is nothing so implausible about the suggestion that attitudes might operate as some kind of intermediary mechanism linking social location and vote. Perhaps their real point is to indicate how issue voting writers have often ignored the social sources of attitudinal change; in this sense, the *ultimate* source of electoral change may be social location and/or ideological agents, but there seems to be little point in rejecting the place of attitudes altogether, even if only as an intervening variable. Indeed, even the Michigan model allows a place for short term issue assessments. Moreover, as I have pointed out elsewhere about Dunleavy and Husbands' work on the 1983 general election:

> Given the accompanying exposition of the shortcomings of the issue voting approach...the ensuing emphasis on the role of issues at the 1983 general election is a little confusing; refer, for example, to statements to the effect that, 'In the 1983 general election, Labour lost the issue battle' (p. 180),

> and that it '...was unable to push to prominence one issue - public services - where it might have been able to gain votes' (Webb 1986: 348).

So do Dunleavy and Husbands regard issues as significant in determining electoral behaviour or not? It sometimes appears that they are not altogether sure. They make a serious and strongly worded attack on the issue voting school, yet then go on to infer that issues might be of some importance after all.

How does the radical model deal with the question of the actual mechanism by which electoral decisions are made? Some sort of rationalistic or instrumental assessment on the part of the voter would seem to be implicit - although, as we have seen, this apparently does not actually involve consideration of any of the issues. Dunleavy and Husbands seek to deny that issue assessment is important. However, they also seem intent upon rejecting the arguments of the partisan identification theorists; socialisation - 'social contagion' - of values and identities is not considered by them to offer a serious explanation of why people living and working in close proximity should vote similarly. Rather, they insist upon the direct impact of social location. This is where they introduce the notion of 'sectoral' cleavages.

It is evident that one of the most significant socio-political divisions in modern Britain, we are told, lies between those who largely work and/or consume in either the public or private sector. These divisions cross-cut lines of class conflict; for instance, manual workers who own their own homes and rarely depend upon public transport may well consider themselves to have different social and political interests to their council house-dwelling, non car-owning counterparts. Stated thus, the consumption sectors theory sounds perhaps uncomfortably like a reformulation of the embourgeoisement thesis for the 1980s. Nevertheless, since the 1960s evidence has quite strongly suggested that housing, at least, is one of the most powerful structural influences on voting in Britain. Indeed, in chapter 5 my own data reveals something of the impact of housing upon voting, but table 4.4 indicates how research traced the growing influence of housing through the 1960s and 1970s.

The production sector effect is particularly interesting from our point of view since it provides a potentially direct explanation of the changes in the voting behaviour of trade union members. One could envisage the pattern of trade unionists' voting behaviour changing because of an ever more critical divide between those who work in the public and private sectors. Unions remaining importance as political agents may even be for the role thay play in mobilising the production sector cleavage rather than class cleavage. For this reason we shall be taking a particular look at trade unionists and the production sectors argument in the course of chapter 6. However, for now it is worthwhile noting that little evidence has yet been produced to suggest production sector effects are anything more than negligible.

Table 4.4

The influence of housing and other structural variables upon voting in Britain 1959 - 1979

Year	Occupation	Housing	Union	Education	Religion	Sex
1959	15.0	-	3.7	0.6	-	0.5
1964	13.5	-	3.8	0.5	0.6	-
1966	9.7	5.8	3.1	0.5	-	-
1970	4.1	7.1	2.1	-	-	-
1974 (Feb.)	9.6	3.1	4.1	-	-	-
1974 (Oct.)	3.1	11.9	3.9	-	-	-
1979	0.7	8.4	2.5	-	0.5	-

Note: All figures are percentages derived from an AID tree analysis (see Morgan and Sonquist 1964).

Source: Rose 1982: 152.

For these reasons, some commentators are rather sceptical about Dunleavy and Husbands' sectoral theories and about the criticism that they level at socialisation or 'social contagion' (see, for example, Franklin 1985: 50-55). Moreover, the sectoral arguments are also open to some doubt on grounds of causal inference; for instance, are graduates in public sector jobs and council housing left wing because of their sectoral locations, or do they choose to live and work in the public sector because of their political convictions? (Harrop 1986: 45) However, the radical model does have the virtue of forcing political scientists to re-think certain matters. For example, Harrop - otherwise largely critical of Dunleavy's work - has conceded that it may have been easily assumed in the past, but 'rarely demonstrated', that trade unions do indeed have some sort of a socialisation effect upon their members. In fact, writers like Verba and Nie have reported that political discussions within American labour union milieux are comparatively rare (Verba and Nie 1972: 176-179), and similarly, Butler and Stokes discovered that, at the time of the 1964 general election:

> ...there is remarkably little evidence to suggest that the ethos of the workplace, and still less the persuasive efforts of the unions themselves, have much impact on the direction of the worker's party allegiance (Butler and Stokes 1969: 208).

In short, Dunleavy and Husbands' radical model is a stimulating alternative in many ways - the sectoral arguments are clearly of potential usefulness - but overall the model seems to have too many shortcomings to be really convincing. In a sense, it is perhaps something of a structural anachronism in electoral studies at a time when voting behaviour appears to be floating freer of social anchors than in the past.

Conclusion

It has been the purpose of this chapter to review critically the literature on electoral change in modern Britain. This is prerequisite to establishing the line of analysis to adopt in the case of trade union members. Thus, for example, the literature review started with a consideration of definitions and measurements of electoral change; this provides a cue to examine the electoral volatility and dealignment patterns of trade unionists between 1964 and 1987. Time has also been spent considering the arguments about models of voting behaviour, and this should be of use for the analysis of union members in Britain. But what can be extracted from the confusing detail of the debates? Some observers have commented upon a certain sterility that has attached itself to aspects of the argument. For instance, Heath, Jowell and Curtice have suggested that the voting act comprises both expressive and and instrumental elements:

> We believe that this antithesis between expressive and instrumental theories of voting behaviour is a false one. We doubt if voters were ever quite so loyal and unthinking in their voting decisions as the old orthodoxy maintained...Programmes and policies have always been important. But it is equally evident that on its own the new orthodoxy of instrumental voting will not do either. If people voted purely on the basis of rational calculation about the benefits the rival parties would bring them, they would never vote at all. The individual vote can make so little difference to the outcome of an election that the rational, instrumental elector would never waste his or her time in going to the

> ballot box. We have to introduce an expressive or moral element to explain the act of voting itself (Heath et al 1985: 9).

In a similar vein, Martin Harrop and William Miller have argued that empirical reality is obliging a certain inevitable convergence between partisan identification and issue models.

> ...both models portray a voter who pays relatively little attention to politics, who develops a standing commitment to a particular party but is also susceptible to influence by major government successes or failures (Harrop and Miller 1987: 162).

They also make the not unreasonable point that 'we will increasingly ask *when* particular models are useful rather than *whether* one particular model has the edge.' That is, in periods of stable alignment the partisan identification model is clearly instructive; during times of dealignment and instability, however, issue models offer a useful guide to the sources of change.

If there is a simple way of summarising the outcome of these debates to date, it is perhaps this; modern accounts of electoral behaviour all tend to agree that it comprises both long term partisan predispositions, and the influence of short term cues. The long term element may be regarded as partisan identification in the sense of the Michigan school, as synoptic values (Heath et al), as critical issues upon which voters 'fixate' (Budge and Farlie), or as accumulated historical evaluations of party performance (Fiorina); whatever, it is a tangible phenomenon. No less significant, however, is the effect of short term factors such as issues that are salient in the context of particular elections. The evidence of issue and retrospective voting models is testament to this, as is more recent work on the short term individual change that occurs during the period of an election campaign (Miller et al 1989, Miller et al 1990). Thus, it is important to focus upon both the long term predispositions of trade unionists and their responses to short term cues.

Therefore, our analysis must start by considering the changing pattern of partisan identification and the social basis of electoral alignment found among union members. Equally important is some examination of their attitudinal profiles - both their underlying principles and the retrospective assessments they make. In chapter 5 we concentrate on what has happened to the old relationship between unionisation, partisanship and class since the 1960s. In chapter 6 we move beyond party and class to consider the impact of possible alternative cues for electoral behaviour - attitudes and sectoral location. In this way we can attempt to provide a rigorous and informative analysis of the changing electoral behaviour of British trade unionists.

Notes

1. A 'significant' trend was considered in both the Rose and Urwin and the Maguire studies to be constituted by a net change equal to at least 0.25% per year.

2. Maguire also considers developments before and after 1960. Interestingly, if we do the same, it transpires that both the Conservative and Labour parties experienced significant trends prior to 1960 and after. Thus, between 1945 and 1959, the Labour Party experienced a significant downward trend, and the Conservative Party a significant upward trend; between 1959 and 1987, both parties sustained significant losses - an especially heavy haemorrhage in the case of Labour (see Table 4.1n).

Table 4.1n
Significant trends in British party support, 1945-1987

	Conservative	Labour
1945	39.6	48.0
1959	49.4	43.8
1987	42.3	30.8

	Minimum net significant change (at 0.25% per year)	Actual net change Conservative	Actual net change Labour
1945-87	Plus or minus 10.5%	+2.7%	-17.2%
1945-59	Plus or minus 3.5%	+9.8%	-4.2%
1959-87	Plus or minus 7.0%	-7.1%	-13.0%

3. Mair has pointed out that it is perhaps possible to obtain an exaggerated impression of electoral change from these figures on volatility. He suggests that it may be more interesting to concentrate upon 'inter-block' volatility than straightforward inter-party volatility. For instance, in Scandinavian countries (some of which include the most volatile electorates of recent years) inter-block volatility (involving a shift of support between parties of the left

and the right) amounted to just one-quarter of total net volatility during the 1970s. That is, 75% of all volatility involved a shift of electoral support from one right wing party to another, or from one left wing party to another.

4. The other three countries were Denmark, Ireland and Luxembourg. Less marked decreases in the rate of partisan identification were registered in France, the Federal German Republic, the Netherlands and Italy between 1975 and 1981. Interestingly, perhaps, Mair noted that declining rates of partisan identification seem to have afflicted social democratic parties the most - a similar pattern to that discovered by Maguire in her study of party support.

5. An example of a party system suffering electoral instability due to the decline of religion, it has been suggested, is provided by the case of the Netherlands. It should be noted that the theory of cleavage development in modern European politics was elaborated in a seminal work by Stein Rokkan and Seymour Martin Lipset. Briefly, they envisaged the development of modern socio-political cleavage structures out of the impact of two broad historical processes - the 'national revolution' and the 'industrial revolution'. The former was associated with one of two major historical periods in most countries, the Reformation or the 'democratic' revolution that followed the socio-political earthquake of 1789. Both involved a challenge to the authority of the Roman church, and provoked conflicts based on religious identity. The industrial revolution provided the basis for two other types of cleavage in modern politics - urban-rural conflicts, and employer-worker conflicts. This latter class division has been given a further historical twist by the advent of the Bolshevik revolution, which served to fragment many of the working class movements of western Europe (Lipset and Rokkan 1967: chapter 1).

6. Inglehart's interest in the idea of post-materialism in politics arises from the contention that advanced industrial society is less and less characterised by conflict based upon class interest and ideology (Bell 1960; Lipset 1964). His idea of post-materialism starts from the notion that men have a clear hierarchy of needs - with 'materialist' needs (associated with physical and economic security) uppermost in this hierarchy; however, generations born into conditions of relative material security will be less concerned with such 'basic' goals. He proposes that materially secure post-war generations will be characterised by particular concern with 'post-material' political issues (or 'quality of life' issues, as they are sometimes called). These issues place emphasis on objectives associated with, amongst other things, personal 'self-actualisation' (for example, minority rights and fully participatory forms of democracy), unilateral military disarmament, support for under-developed nations, and - above all, perhaps - a concern for the environment. The implications of the irruption of post-materialist issues onto western political agendas - if such there be - could be of great significance. The concerns of the

'post-materialist left' do not always coincide with those of the traditional left; indeed, Inglehart has demonstrated that, by employing techniques of factor analysis, it is possible to distinguish two distinct and quite unrelated 'lefts' and 'rights' in terms of the attitudinal profiles of modern European electorates (Inglehart and Rabier 1986: 471). Post-materialist activists may pursue various strategies of political mobilisation; for instance, they might actually attempt to create a new political party that embodies all they claim to stand for. Alternatively, they may try to win influence within established parties (Poguntke 1987: 79-80). Either way, they wield some potential to disrupt established patterns of alignment.

7. The salariat comprises managers, supervisors of non-manual employees, professionals and semi-professionals. Such individuals all have some degree of authority over other workers, and have greater prospects of promotion, more job security and better fringe benefits than working class employees; since they are often less dispensable, and more likely to negotiate their own work and pay conditions, members of the salariat are also less given to collective action than other workers. The petit bourgoisie have different economic interests to both the salariat and the working class. It is a category that slices through the manual/non-manual distinction, but its members are directly exposed to the whims of the market being without the cushioning effects of either 'bureaucratic employment or trade union membership'. Foremen and technicians comprise a kind of 'blue collar elite' with authority over the mass of the workers, and for that reason they are set apart in Heath's scheme. Finally, routine non-manual employees include clerks, salesworkers and secretaries who have some of the advantages of bureaucratic and professional employment, but earn low wages and exert little authority. For practical purposes, Heath often collapses this five-class model into a simpler three-class one; this is effected by combining the routine non-manual, petit bourgeois and foremen categories into a single 'intermediate' class. This helps to maintain the size of frequencies in table cells and eases substantive interpretation, and is a practical step that I repeat in chapter 5 (Heath et al 1985: 13-16, 53).

8. The odds ratio is a useful technique for measuring *relative*, as opposed to *absolute*, class voting. Measures of absolute class voting (such as the Alford index) concentrate upon the aggregate of electors who vote according to their nominal social class. By contrast, the odds ratio focuses upon the question of the relative proportions of party support coming from different classes. If, for instance, Labour lost a similar proportion of votes within both the working class and the middle class, relative class voting would not decline, but if it lost more within the working class, then it would (Marshall et al 1988: 230). The potential weakness of relying upon measures of absolute class voting is that

they can encourage misleading impressions of class decomposition; absolute class voting may decline as a party adopts universally unpopular policies, but under such circumstances we can properly infer nothing about class cohesion.

The odds ratio compares the odds on a working class voter supporting Labour rather than the Conservatives with the odds on a middle class voter doing so. It is worthwhile noting the observations made by Elinor Scarbrough concerning this measure of class voting, however (Scarbrough 1986: 10-11). She makes two interesting comments, the first of which is really a criticism of the particular way in which Heath calculates the odds ratio, rather than a tilt at the odds ratio per se. Her argument here is that Heath's version of the odds ratio is useful only in the case of a two-party system. In this instance, a non-class vote is the same thing as a cross class vote. However, in a two-class, three (or more) party system, a non-class vote 'can be cast without engaging in cross-class voting' (Scarbrough 1986: 8). Scarbrough insists upon the importance of accounting properly for third-party voters. Thus, whereas Heath constructs an odds ratio in the following manner:

$$\frac{\text{Conservative vote/Labour vote within working class}}{\text{Conservative vote/Labour vote within middle class,}}$$

Scarbrough claims that it ought really to be constructed as:

$$\frac{\text{Labour vote/other party vote within working class}}{\text{Conservative vote/other party vote within middle class.}}$$

This substantially alters the picture that odds ratios present of the history of class voting in Britain. As table 4.2n illustrates the odds ratio now seems to confirm that class dealignment has taken place. Far from the pattern of 'trendless fluctuation' that Heath adamantly suggests we find, it would appear that the level of relative class voting did indeed fall between 1964 and 1983.

Scarbrough's second point is that the odds ratio can distort the overall picture by giving excessive weight to what is happening in one class. For example, if 80% of the working class voted for the Labour Party, and 10% Conservative, whereas 45% of the middle class voted Labour and another 45% Conservative, then this would produce an odds ratio of 8, indicating a high degree of class voting. Yet clearly, class voting would actually only be ocurring in one class, the working class. At the very least, reference to something like the Alford index would constitute a useful supplement in such a case.

Table 4.2n

The history of class voting 1964-1983: Comparing Heath's and Scarbrough's methods of constructing odds ratios

	Manual/Non-manual		Salariat/Working Class	
	Heath	Scarbrough	Heath	Scarbrough
1964	6.4	2.8	9.3	3.7
1966	6.4	3.3	7.3	3.5
1970	4.5	2.5	4.9	2.2
1974 (Feb.)	5.7	1.5	6.1	1.5
1974 (Oct.)	4.8	1.3	5.5	1.5
1979	3.7	1.5	4.9	1.7
1983	3.9	0.9	6.3	1.2

Source: Scarbrough 1986: 11.

9. Heath claims to be able to demonstrate his argument by presenting the following evidence on class voting (using the manual/non-manual dichotomy only) since 1945:

Table 4.3n
Class voting since 1945

	Non-manual Conservatives plus manual Labour voters as a percentage of electorate	Odds Ratios
1945	62	4.8
1950	62	5.5
1951	67	6.3
1955	65	5.9
1959	61	6.1
1964	63	6.4
1966	66	6.4
1970	60	4.5
1974 (February)	55	5.7
1974 (October)	54	4.8
1979	55	3.7
1983	47	3.9

Source: Heath et al 1985: 30

5 Trade Unionist Voting Behaviour Since 1964: Partisan and Class Dealignment

Having reviewed much of the literature on electoral behaviour in Britain, it is time to turn directly to the analysis of trade union members. We shall start in this chapter by considering the stability of union members' voting behaviour, their rate of partisan dealignment and their propensity to vote according to class location. In Chapter 6 we shall turn to the questions of how far, if at all, unions are able to mobilise the production sector cleavage and to affect members' political attitudes. The data comes from a series of election studies started by Butler and Stokes in the 1960s, before switching to the direction of research teams based at the Universities of Oxford and Essex.[1]

The changing vote

In this section, we shall commence our analysis by considering the basic pattern of electoral change among trade unionists, and the general impact of union membership on vote. We shall often concentrate upon net change across the years between 1964 and 1987, but table 5.1 permits us to look at the relationship between vote and union membership for every election during the period. This is a useful introduction, for it enables us to see two basic things that have happened; firstly, it is noticeable that Labour's vote changes in a way which suggests a prima facie connection with the estrangement of the party

Table 5.1
Vote by union membership, 1964-1987

	1964		1966		1970	
	Union	Non-union	Union	Non-union	Union	Non-union
Conservative	23.3	46.5	19.4	41.9	23.1	45.2
Labour	58.3	30.6	59.3	34.9	51.0	28.9
Other	8.1	13.4	8.1	8.1	5.6	7.9
Abstained	10.4	9.6	13.1	15.2	20.4	18.1
	100.1	100.1	99.9	100.1	100.1	100.1

	Feb. 1974		Oct. 1974		1979	
	Union	Non-union	Union	Non-union	Union	Non-union
Conservative	20.3	43.4	17.1	39.5	27.1	45.8
Labour	48.7	25.6	52.2	26.6	42.7	27.3
Other	19.4	18.1	16.1	18.6	15.5	12.2
Abstained	11.4	12.9	14.4	15.4	14.6	14.8
	99.8	100.0	99.8	100.1	99.9	100.1

	1983		1987	
	Union	Non-union	Union	Non-union
Conservative	27.3	40.9	27.5	41.5
Labour	33.0	20.8	37.1	23.3
Other	23.2	20.4	24.3	20.6
Abstained	16.3	17.8	11.2	14.6
	99.8	99.9	100.1	100.0

Note: Union member category for February 1974 includes 'household members', that is, respondents who are not actually unionists themselves, but who live in households which have members. *Throughout, all crosstabular relationships based on election survey data are statistically significant at the 1% level.*

Source for the figures for 1966-74, Freyman 1980: 145.

from the unions. In 1970, Labour lost support amongst members and non-members alike, recouping some of this loss among members, but *not among non-members*, by October 1974. (The detailed electoral consequences of party-union estrangement between 1964-1974 have been established in Freyman 1980.) In 1979, unionists turned away from Labour once more, whilst non-union alignment did not alter greatly. This picture of union dealignment has not changed much since.

Table 5.1a provides the second point of interest, which is that the overall impact of unionisation upon the two-party vote seems to have declined, at least since 1974. This is evident from the simple indices created by subtracting the percentage of non-members voting for a party from the percentage of members doing so. We can see in table 5.1a that this union/non-union difference has diminished since 1979. The nature and extent of change is demonstrated especially clearly by the odds ratios between unionists and non-unionists on two-party voting. The odds ratio was introduced in Chapter 4, and it is a simple technique that we shall be using again when we consider the question of class voting among trade unionists; but at this point it serves as a useful means of examining the general distinctiveness of trade unionist voting behaviour. There is, in fact, more than one set of odds ratios reported in table 5.1a; the different ratios are designed to take account of slightly different processes of electoral change that might conceivably have been occurring since 1964. The ratios reported in the top row are conceptually the simplest, and correspond to the classic assumption of two-party competition in Britain. Here, we simply take the odds on a trade union member voting Labour rather than Conservative, and divide them by the odds on a non-member doing so. An odds ratio of 1:1 would indicate that the relative strengths of the two parties were identical amongst unionists and non-unionists alike.

The odds ratios reported in the second row allow for the fact that more than two parties might be important for party competition and voting in Britain, however. Here trade unionists are contrasted with non-unionists in terms of the odds on them voting for Labour as against *any other party*, rather than just the Conservatives. In this way we account for flows of support away from Labour to third parties as well as to the Conservatives; this is an important consideration in view of the well recognised growth of minor party voting in Britain over the past twenty years. Thus, these measures might be referred to as *third-party* effect odds ratios, as opposed to the simple *two-party* effect odds ratios we considered first.

Finally, it is interesting to consider the possibility that trade unionists could be increasingly distinctive in terms of whom they do *not* support, rather than whom they *do* support. Modern unionists might not be as strongly pro-Labour as they once were, but they may well remain resolutely anti-Conservative given the well publicised onslaught of Conservative governments upon traditional union privileges and forms of action since 1979. Therefore, the odds ratios in the final row compare trade unionists and non-unionists in terms of the chances of them voting for *any party other than the Conservatives* rather than for the Conservatives. These can consequently be thought of as *anti-Conservative* odds ratios.

These ratios not only indicate the overall decline in trade unionist distinctiveness since 1964, but also have the added advantage of summarising very neatly the effect of the switches in alignment mentioned above. What is interesting is that all three different types of ratio are in fundamental concurrence with regard to the essential story they convey. Up to 1970, the odds on union members voting distinctly, however

Table 5.1a
The effect of union membership on vote, 1964 to 1987

	1964	1966	1970	Feb.1974
Conservative	-23.2	-22.5	-22.1	-23.1
Labour	+27.7	+24.4	+22.1	+23.1
Odds ratios				
Two-party	3.8	3.7	3.5	4.1
Third-party	3.2	2.7	2.5	2.8
Anti-Conservative	2.9	3.0	2.8	3.0
	Oct.1974	**1979**	**1983**	**1987**
Conservative	-22.4	-18.7	-13.6	-14.0
Labour	+25.6	+15.4	+12.2	+13.8
Odds ratios				
Two-party	4.6	2.6	2.4	2.4
Third-party	3.0	2.0	1.9	2.0
Anti-Conservative	3.2	2.3	1.9	1.9

Note: These figures for Conservative and Labour voting are simply the differences in rates of alignment between members and non-members, expressed in terms of percentage points. The odds ratios presented summarise the differing likelihoods of, alternatively, voting Labour instead of Conservative, or Labour instead of any other party, or non-Conservative rather than Conservative, for unionists and non-unionists (see text).

that is defined, fell slightly. That is, unionists moved closer to non-unionists in terms of the pattern of their two-party vote, their pro-Labour support and the degree of their anti-Conservatism. Interestingly, these changing odds ratios owe more to the vagaries of members' behaviour than to that of non-members. It tends to be trade unionists' odds which change more than those of non-unionists. By October 1974, the pattern reverses itself, however; no matter how it is defined, the odds ratio increases notably as trade unionists again swing back to Labour. And once more it is the shift of members' preferences - this time against Labour - that produces a sharp decline in the odds ratios in 1979; this decline continues in 1983 and is consolidated in 1987. To reiterate, throughout, the volatile factor is the behaviour of the trade unionists in our sample. Non-unionist voting odds are far less likely to alter significantly.[2] The only irregularity of any note in the message conveyed by the different types of odds ratio concerns their relative sizes. At all elections trade unionists are most sharply distinguished from non-unionists in terms of their two-party voting; between 1966 and 1979 the next criterion by which they differed was their anti-Conservatism, but in 1964, 1983 and 1987 the third-party ratio proved a slightly stronger basis for differentiation.

Table 5.2
Vote by union membership for manuals and non-manuals, 1964 and 1987

1964

	Manual		Non-manual	
	Union	Non-union	Union	Non-union
Conservative	20.5	35.6	40.3	60.9
Labour	65.5	37.6	27.3	18.5
Other	4.4	13.3	20.6	13.9
Abstained	9.7	13.5	11.7	6.7
	100.1	100.0	99.9	100.0

1987

	Manual		Non-manual	
	Union	Non-union	Union	Non-union
Conservative	22.8	31.0	33.2	49.8
Labour	43.6	34.5	28.9	14.1
Other	21.3	17.5	28.1	23.5
Abstained	12.3	17.0	9.7	12.6
	100.0	100.0	99.9	100.0

Table 5.2a
Union effect on vote for manuals and non-manuals, 1964 and 1987

	1964		1987	
	Manual	Non-manual	Manual	Non-manual
Conservative	-15.1	-20.6	-8.2	-16.6
Labour	+27.9	+8.8	+9.1	+14.8
Odds ratios				
Two-party	3.0	2.3	1.7	3.1
Third-party	3.2	1.7	1.5	2.6
Anti-Cons.	2.1	2.3	1.5	2.0

Tables 5.2 and 5.2a tell us something about the impact of occupational background on unionised voters. In fact, they suggest that the apparent weakening of the relationship between unionisation and vote may be more than a simple consequence of the changing occupational structure of union membership. For example, the growth of non-manual unionism (see table 3.4), could be responsible for spuriously suggesting a weaker correlation between unionisation and Labour support than hitherto. Stated crudely, unionism per se might be having as much effect as ever on the way people vote, but less unionists are voting for Labour because less of them are working class.[3] Indeed, others have demonstrated that such was the case in 1974; after controlling for the confounding influence of other social background variables (chief amongst which came occupational class), it was found that unionisation actually had a *greater* impact on voting choice than a decade before (Freyman 1980: 155-156; Franklin 1985: 119-120).

Our evidence may bring us to question whether this remained the case by 1987, however; as can be seen, there was a notable decline in the impact that membership had on both non-manuals and - indeed especially - on manual workers. Table 5.2a shows that the difference in electoral alignment between members and non-members diminished notably between 1964 and 1987, regardless of occupational category. This is confirmed by the substantial drop in the sizes of all the odds ratios for manual workers; moreover, it is interesting to discover that, once again, the odds ratio changes result largely from the altered behaviour of those manuals who are union members. For instance, whilst the two-party and third-party odds for non-members remained virtually unchanged between 1964 and 1987, they declined heavily for their unionised counterparts.[4] It is evident from table 5.2 that this owes much to the shift away from Labour by its 'core' Labour constituency of manual trade unionists. Being a member of a trade union was far less likely to make a manual worker pro-Labour, and somewhat less likely to make him or her anti-Conservative, in 1987 than it was in 1964.

It is worth observing at this point that, in one sense at least, the impact of social change upon manual workers can be discounted. By definition, they can not have been subjected to the effects of *upward mobility* to non-manual status, so the shift away from Labour cannot simply be attributed to this.[5] What other factors might account for Labour's heavy losses among unionised manuals? One is bound to consider the possibility that the political tensions between the party and the unions which have often emerged since 1964 have produced a particular disillusionment within this group. This line of speculation is supported by previous research; Freyman has argued that the behavioural trend between 1964 and 1974 followed a pattern which coincided with the state of political relations between the party and the unions. There was a shift from Labour amongst manual workers generally in 1970 - largely in the form of abstention rather than a vote for the Conservatives - followed by a switch back to Labour by October 1974 within the ranks of *unionised* manuals only. Thus, we have a clear indication that the working class trade unionist core was sensitive to the political events of the period.

It should be said that the overall net impact of union membership on voting choice can only really be assessed in the context of a broad range of factors that influence individuals. We have considered the role played by occupational status, but this is only one variable that might obscure the picture of the true relationship between trade union membership and vote. Though bivariate relationships are interesting and informative, the voting decision most certainly results from the interplay of a number of influences, both social and political. Therefore, it is important to construct a model of voting behaviour from which we can derive an impression of the particular importance of trade unionism in a wider social context. An appropriate way of doing this is to include unionisation and a series of other social background variables in a model of voting which is subjected to a *multiple classification analysis*. Using this technique, derived from a simple analysis of variance procedure, coefficients may be produced which summarise the relationship between unionisation and vote while controlling for the effects of other influences in the social background of individuals. In some ways these coefficients (based on the eta statistic) are analogous to the beta weights of regression analysis.[6]

Given that the essence of social background effects in Britain has generally been held to be that of social class, and that historically unionism has been closely bound up with class in the country, it follows that our model should basically be one of class voting. The variables selected for this model are those of unionisation, occupation, housing status, years in education, and the occupation of parents. Introducing these variables into a model of vote, we are able to extract a beta coefficient expressing the uncontaminated relationship between union membership and vote while holding constant the effects of all other independent variables. Whereas this coefficient stood at 0.16 in 1964, it had declined to just 0.11 by 1987. Thus it would seem that union membership lost some of its importance in determining vote over the period that concerns us, and this clearly reflects the decline in its capacity to make manual workers vote Labour.[7]

	Beta coefficient		Significance of effect	
	1964	1987	1964	1987
Occupation	0.19	0.15	0.00	0.00
Unionisation	0.16	0.11	0.00	0.00
Housing	0.16	0.22	0.00	0.00
Parental occupation	0.12	0.13	0.00	0.00
Education	0.04	0.03	0.00	0.19
Multiple R^2	0.18	0.15	0.00	0.00

Why should the unionisation effect have weakened? Three plausible reasons might be suggested. One concerns the development of the production sectors cleavage, an important effect of which might have been the cross-cutting of unionist alignment patterns as those in the private sector turned away from Labour. Of this, more anon (see chapter 6)[8]. A related, but not necessarily compatible, explanation is that the erosion of the class cleavage could have weakened the impact of trade union membership. Were it the case that the influence that unions once had stemmed from their capacity to mobilise class attitudes and behaviour, then it follows that social, political and organisational changes eroding this role would have left unions with no way of maintaining any impact on electoral behaviour for the present. The third possible explanation draws on an issue voting perspective. According to this, the reason that trade unions seemed to be growing in importance for voting choice in 1974 might very simply have been that industrial relations and the political role of unions were issues of central importance to the elections held that year (as they also were, of course, in May 1979.) By 1983, however, it is arguable that the question of industrial relations was not particularly contentious as an election issue which split union member from non-member. That is, it was not a salient issue *at election time* (see table 5.3n). We shall be examining these themes further throughout the course of this chapter and the next.

Indications of the extent of electoral change among union members

At the outset of chapter 4, we referred to three useful ways of measuring electoral change. It would be interesting at this juncture to expand our analysis by considering trade unionist behaviour in terms of these measures. For example, if we apply the criterion first used in the studies by Rose, Urwin and Maguire, it is possible to see that there has indeed been significant change in the levels of partisan support displayed by trade union members. Recalling that Rose and Urwin declared that a rate of change equal to at least 0.25% a year could reasonably be considered 'significant', we should need to find a minimum net change of plus or minus 5.75% in the support received by any given party over the twenty three years covering the period from 1964 to 1987. The changes that have actually been recorded are presented in table 5.3.

Table 5.3
Net changes in party support between 1964 and 1987

	Members	Non-members
Conservative	+4.2	-5.0
Labour	-21.2	-7.3
Other	+16.2	+7.2
Abstained	+0.8	+5.0

Note: All figures are percentage points.

As can be seen, changes in Labour and third-party support have reached the standard of significance laid down by Rose and Urwin. However, it is also obvious that overall electoral change has been greater among union members than it has been among non-members. (The average net change amongst members is 10.6, compared to 6.1 amongst non-members.) Indeed, this impression is confirmed when we turn to the second of the three measures that were introduced in chapter 4, that of *electoral volatility.* Figure 5.1 illustrates the changes in net volatility (Pedersen Index) displayed by members and non-members across every pair of elections between 1964 and 1987.

Figure 5.1
Net electoral volatility, 1964-1987

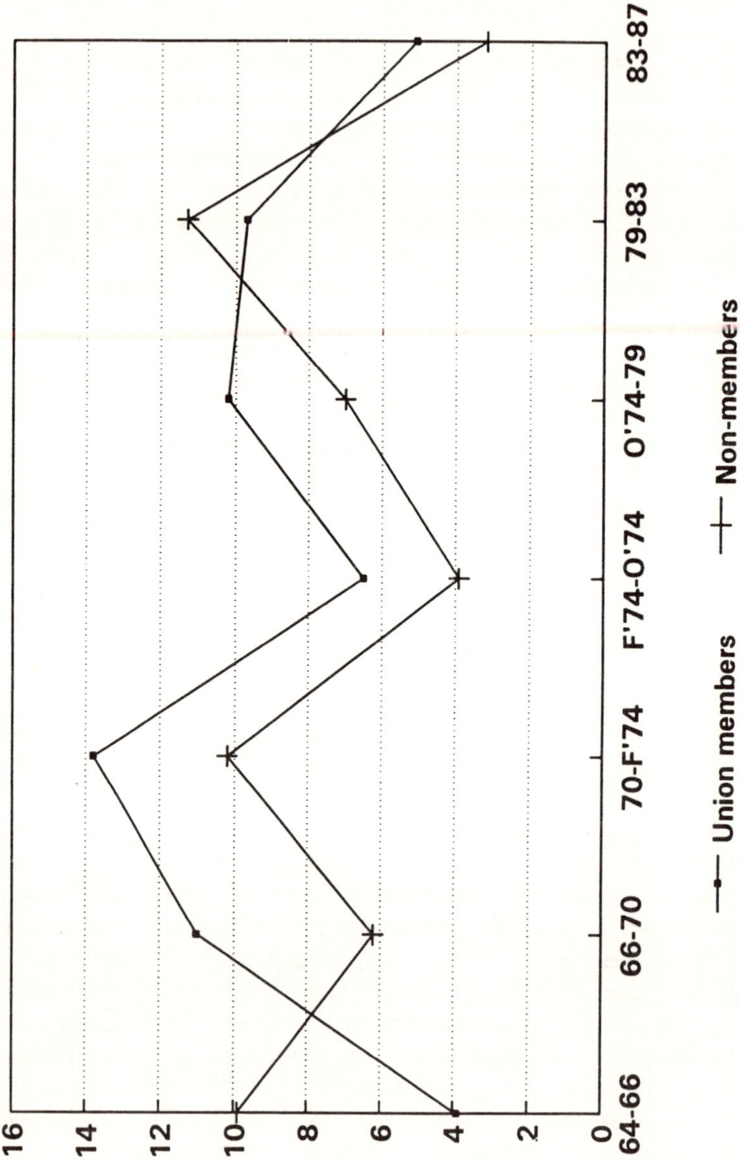

This graph reveals several interesting points. Firstly, we have confirmation that union members' behaviour has been somewhat more volatile than that of their non-union counterparts, over the period as a whole. *Aggregate* net volatility (based on overall change between the beginning and end of the period of study) for members was 21.2, compared to 12.2 for non-members; the *average* net volatility between any consecutive pair of elections within the period is not so very different, perhaps, standing at 8.6 and 7.4 for the two groups. But it is worth emphasising also that the net volatility of trade unionists is higher than it was at the start of the study, whereas that of non-unionists is now lower. This lends an impression of an upward trend in the level of volatility displayed by union members which is not apparent for non-members.

A further contrast between the patterns of volatility shown by members and non-members is revealed within the graph; union members manifested a quite distinct and sharp up-turn in volatility between the elections of 1966 and 1970. Clearly, events during the intervening period are likely to have done something to have disturbed the political loyalties of union memberships. Following this, the political history of the years between 1970 and 1974 shook up the electorate in general - but union members proved especially sensitive. The period between the two elections of 1974 was clearly too short to expect any great alterations in political alignment; in many ways, October served to consolidate the pattern emerging in February. Not surprisingly, therefore, we find a drop in net volatility by October 1974. But by 1979 the union question was once more to the fore in British politics, and this was reflected in the universal increase in electoral volatility; but again, it was union members who proved most volatile. By contrast, 1983 was probably the first election since 1966 in which union issues did not play a prominent role in the election, and this is reflected in the fact that, for the first time since 1966, trade unionists' net volatility falls below that of non-unionists.

The third of the indicators of electoral change that was introduced in the last chapter was the rate of partisan dealignment; this is revealed by the changing rate and strength of partisan identification displayed by various sections of the electorate. The details of partisanship and unionisation since 1964 are presented in tables 5.4 and 5.4a. As with vote, it seems that the effect of union membership dropped over the period. It is particularly interesting, perhaps, that the most notable fall in trade unionists' partisan affinity for Labour occurred in 1974, even though there was a slight increase in the proportion who actually voted for the party that year. This suggests that even though contemporary political circumstances obliged some union members to return to

Labour, this flow of support was contingent and short term. Events of the previous decade had undermined the loyalty that the party once had among a section of its core constituency.

Table 5.4
Partisanship by unionisation, 1964-1987

	1964		1966		1970	
	Union	Non-union	Union	Non-union	Union	Non-union
Conservative	24.6	49.2	20.2	47.4	26.0	48.7
Labour	62.7	34.2	61.8	35.0	60.7	33.7
Other*	12.7	16.5	18.1	17.6	13.4	17.4
	100.0	99.9	100.1	100.0	100.1	99.8
	Feb.1974		Oct.1974		1979	
	Union	Non-union	Union	Non-union	Union	Non-union
Conservative	23.1	47.1	22.5	44.0	25.0	45.5
Labour	53.9	31.5	52.6	31.0	49.6	32.0
Other*	23.0	21.4	24.8	24.9	25.4	22.5
	100.0	100.0	99.9	99.9	100.0	100.0
	1983		1987			
	Union	Non-union	Union	Non-union		
Conservative	29.0	46.1	30.4	48.0		
Labour	48.0	31.1	46.3	31.2		
Other*	23.0	22.6	23.3	20.8		
	100.0	99.8	100.0	100.0		

Note: * 'Other' figures include those without partisanship.

Again, odds ratios can be of help in conveying the story of changing partisan loyalty; such ratios can be calculated for partisanship in precisely the same way they were for reported vote (see table 5.4a). The two-party pattern resembles that found for vote in so far as the (rather slighter) decline of union impact in 1970 was recouped in February 1974, only to be followed by a more considerable decline in 1979. In general, the decline in distinctive partisan loyalty declared by trade unionists is probably smoother and more obviously linear than in their actual voting behaviour, but it is no less tangible for that. In one important regard there is concurrence between the various odds ratios, moreover; they are much smaller in 1987 than in 1964, no matter how they are constructed. The essential point is that trade union membership makes much less difference to partisan identification now than it did in 1964. Thus, union membership has less impact on both partisanship and vote. (This is confirmed by the percentage point differences between unionists and non-unionists, which are also reported in table 5.4a.) And once again, it would seem that the crucial element in these changes is the behaviour of trade unionists themselves rather than that of non-unionists.[9]

Table 5.4a
Union effect on partisanship, 1964-1987

	1964	1966	1970	Feb.1974
Conservative	-24.6	-27.2	-22.7	-24.0
Labour	+28.5	+26.8	+27.0	+22.4
Odds ratio				
Two-party	3.6	4.1	3.4	3.5
Third-party	3.2	3.0	3.0	2.5
Anti-Conservative	2.9	3.6	2.7	3.0

	Oct.1974	1979	1983	1987
Conservative	-21.5	-20.5	-17.1	-17.6
Labour	+21.6	+17.6	+16.9	+15.1
Odds ratio				
Two-party	3.3	2.9	2.5	2.3
Third-party	2.5	2.1	2.0	1.9
Anti-Conservative	2.3	2.5	2.1	2.1

Trends in the rate of partisan identification claimed by trade unionists can be further elaborated upon. Even the most cursory glance at table 5.5 reveals that net change in the rate of partisan identification between 1964 and 1987 was greater for members than it was for non-members.

Table 5.5
Net change in partisan identification between 1964 and 1987

	Members	Non-members
Conservative	+5.8	-1.2
Labour	-16.4	-3.0
Other	+10.6	+4.3

Note: All figures are percentage points.

A useful way of summarising these changes is to calculate rates of net volatility of partisan identification, as we did for reported vote. Aggregate volatility of partisan identity across the entire period works out to be 4.5 for trade union members, compared to 2.3 for non-members. As one would expect, these figures are considerably lower than the corresponding calculations for volatility of vote; (to recollect, for instance, aggregate net volatility of vote for members over the period as a whole was 21.2). Again, this tends to confirm that people do not necessarily change their underlying sense of partisan identity when they change their vote. Nevertheless, the pattern of change is substantially similar for partisan loyalty and vote. In particular, it is clear that the Labour Party suffered from a particularly acute haemorrhage of partisan loyalty amongst trade unionists (see figure 5.2).

However, it should be remembered that we are only looking at part of the picture in so far as partisan identification is concerned, for it is useful to consider not only the *direction* of partisanship, but also its *strength*. This is interesting since it is likely that some relationship exists between the strength of partisanship and the impact of short term issue effects on voting choice. For example, Freyman discovered that union membership only had an effect that was independent of partisan identification on those with weaker partisan affinities (Freyman 1980: 194-196). It is not unreasonable to presume that this may be an effect that works via people's assessments of short term factors.

Table 5.6 permits us to see that between 1964 and 1987 there was a definite shift from strong major party identification to weak major party identification, and towards minor party identification and no identification at all. This affected unionists and non-unionists alike, but especially the former. Overall, we see that there was a 16.6 percentage point drop in the number of Labour partisans amongst union members, compared with a 3.1 percentage drop among non-members. But in addition, it is clear that even of those who do claim to retain a basic affinity for Labour fewer are inclined to view this as a

Figure 5.2
Net partisan volatility, 1964-1987

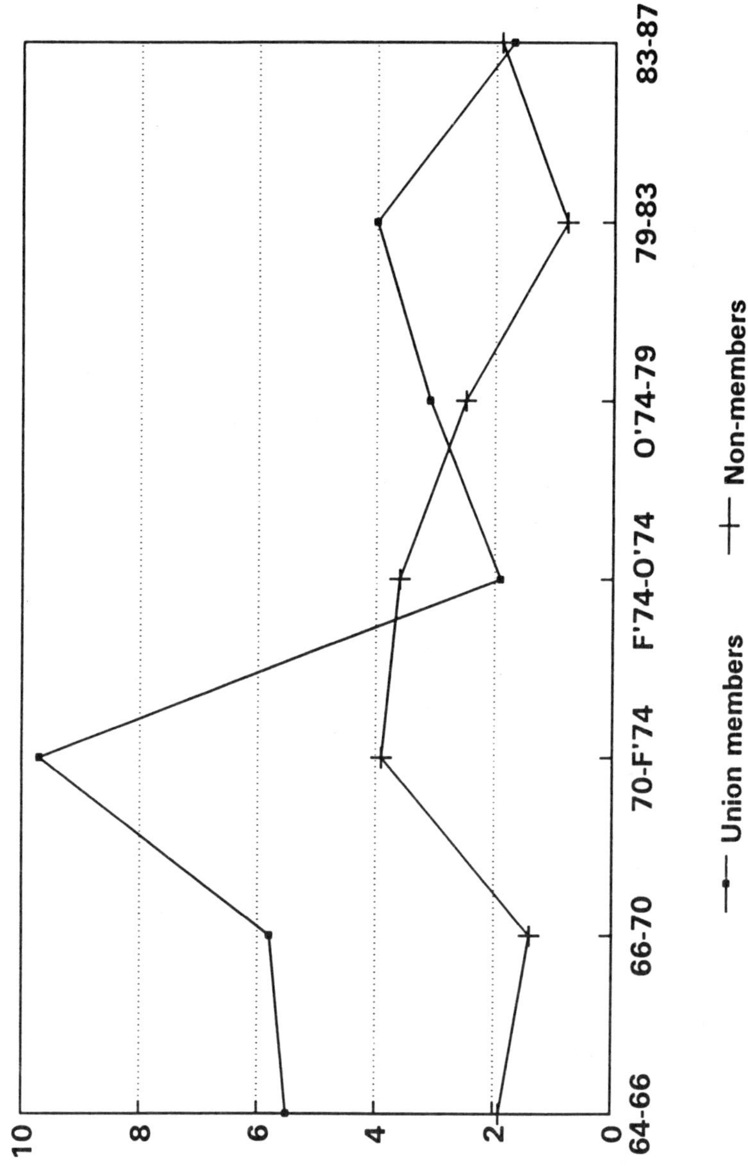

Table 5.6
Strength and direction of partisanship by unionisation, 1964 and 1987

	1964		1987	
	Union	Non-union	Union	Non-union
Very strong Labour	33.5	13.8	12.5	8.9
Fairly strong Labour	23.0	15.7	21.1	13.7
Not very strong Labour	6.2	4.7	12.5	8.6
Other partisanship	12.7	6.5	23.6	21.0
Not very strong Conservative	3.2	5.5	8.6	10.6
Fairly strong Conservative	10.5	20.9	17.3	24.8
Very strong Conservative	10.9	22.8	4.4	12.4
	100.0	99.9	100.0	100.0

reasonably strong attachment. Over half of all trade unionists who claimed a Labour partisanship in 1964 felt that it was 'very strong', compared to two-fifths of non-unionists; by 1987, just 27.1% of the former, and 28.5% of the latter, maintained such a firm sense of commitment to the party.

The overall changes in these tables are not easily absorbed at a glance; it is therefore helpful to calculate the lead that Labour has over the Conservatives in terms of a summary measure of partisanship that accounts for the strength as well as the direction of partisan feelings. This is done by simply weighting the proportion of the electorate in each of the groups of members and non-members holding a Labour or Conservative partisan identification by a factor of 1, 2 or 3 according to whether it is 'not very', 'fairly', or 'very' strongly held. This is then divided by 3 so that we are effectively left with a sort of weighted average Labour and Conservative partisanship for each group. The weighted Conservative partisanship score is then subtracted from the weighted Labour partisanship score so that a net partisanship evaluation may be arrived at. This final quotient has a range running from -100 (that is, all respondents within a certain group are very strongly Conservative) to +100 (all respondents are very strongly Labour). Table 5.7 presents these weighted partisanship scores for trade unionists and non-unionists, broken down by occupational group, in 1964 and 1987.

The interesting feature of this table is that trade unionism now makes more difference to the partisanship of non-manuals than it does to that of manuals - quite the reverse of the pattern found in the 1960s. In fact, little seems to have happened to the overall pattern of non-manual partisanship; trade unionism still reduces the Conservative advantage considerably, indeed, to virtually the same extent (by 27.6 points in 1964, and by 27.4 points in 1987).

Table 5.7

Weighted partisanship by occupation and unionisation; Labour's lead over the Conservatives, 1964 and 1987

	1964		1987	
	Union	Non-union	Union	Non-union
Manual	37.4	4.5	21.3	8.8
Non-manual	-8.6	-36.2	-0.1	-27.5

For manual workers, however, the difference made by union membership is much slighter now (20.4 points slighter, to be precise). In this way we see very clearly, then, the weakening overall impact of union membership upon the partisan identification of manuals between 1964 and 1987.

So the partisan loyalties of trade union members have dwindled. Before leaving the subject of union members and partisan identification, however, it is worthwhile posing one further question: To what extent have the various parties been able to mobilise their nominal level of potential support amongst union members? That is, what proportion of partisan trade unionists vote for 'their' party? An answer to this question might even offer a preliminary insight into the potential impact of unions upon the issue assessments that voters make. To recall, most theories suggest in some way or another that voting behaviour comprises the dual elements of long standing predisposition and the assessment of significant short term political factors. Partisan identification is, of course, one of the main indicators of predisposition. By comparing vote and basic partisanship, therefore, we can obtain an idea of how far short-term influences might be intervening between the two. If there is relatively little difference between partisanship and vote, then it may simply be that it is enough for trade union membership to inspire general partisan identity from which voting alignment follows. If, on the other hand, there is a considerable discrepancy between the two, we would have some indication that other factors - very possibly short term factors - are influencing unionists to reject their basic loyalties at election time.

Such differences as there are between voting and partisanship are clearly demonstrated in Table 5.8, which shows the percentage of partisans that each of the main parties was able to rely upon for support at the elections of 1964 and 1987, by union and occupational status. It is obvious that, at least for

Labour and the Conservatives, nearly all partisans voted for 'their' party in 1964. It is equally clear that such was no longer the case in 1987; Labour was definitely 'under-performing' in relation to the number of partisans that it

Table 5.8
Vote as a percentage of partisanship, by occupational status and unionisation, 1964 and 1987

	1964			
	Non-manual		Manual	
	Union	Non-union	Union	Non-union
Conservative	101.8	101.6	103.7	106.8
Labour	96.6	105.3	104.5	94.0
Other	101.7	87.6	55.8	101.3

	1987			
	Non-manual		Manual	
	Union	Non-union	Union	Non-union
Conservative	103.7	99.0	99.0	104.8
Labour	89.4	87.6	91.2	88.3
Other	108.4	112.1	127.9	122.0

Note: These figures are obtained by comparing the percentage of the electorate that the parties won at a general election with the percentage of declared partisans that they had within the electorate.

had, losing out, it would seem, to both the Liberal-SDP Alliance, who formed a major part of the 'Other' category, and the Conservatives. Hence, we have a clear suggestion that by 1987 short term political factors were indeed intervening to influence people to vote for a party other than that to which they normally felt allegiance. The balance of short term factors having most probably run against Labour at the 1987 election - notwithstanding widespread admiration of its campaigning revival after 1983 - the party obviously suffered. By 1987, union membership seemed to make little or no difference to the mobilisation rate of Labour's partisans. Union members were not noticeably more likely to vote for the party they professed to identify with than non-members. The most notable aspect of this change concerns Labour and the manual working class, once again; in 1964, the difference between the Labour Party mobilisation rates of unionised and non-unionised manuals was fully 10.5 percentage points, whereas it was just 2.9 points by 1987.

We might conclude that short term factors are generally becoming more important to Labour partisans given that mobilisation rates are straying further away from 100%. And perhaps most importantly, table 5.8 gives us an early indication of the fact that any electoral decline that the Labour Party may have suffered cannot be attributable solely to declining partisanship. That is, if voters have turned away from Labour it is not only due to the fact that, as a group, less of them feel any general sense of long term attachment to the party; this may well have happened, but the point is that the party is additionally less able to count on the vote of those who *do* retain such an attachment.

Perhaps, it would be wise to issue a brief caveat at this point. It is now clear that union membership is less able to reinforce long term loyalties, especially those of manual workers. However, this does not necessarily mean that union membership is destined to lose all impact on voting behaviour in Britain. For instance, the potential for union impact on the short term factors affecting voting decisions may be unimpaired. This depends on the question of electoral salience, which was referred to earlier (see page 132). Trade unions were electorally salient issues at the elections of 1974, and again in 1979, although tensions between different types of unions - blue and white collar, public and private sector - may well have undermined the cohesive impact of trade unionism on voting behaviour. 1974 clearly represented a high point for union salience in recent British political history,[10] but it is possible that unions may again be salient in future elections.

To summarise what we have discovered so far then, it would seem that Labour has been decreasingly able to mobilise the support of its declared partisans at election time; this is especially true of manual workers, where union membership no longer helps much. This may well reflect the weakening of partisanship; vague affinity is relatively easily overcome at election time if the balance of short run factors runs negatively for a party. However, although it is clear that the effect of union membership upon vote and partisanship has declined since 1964, this decline has not by any means been monotonic; in particular, unionisation was important in 1974, but was not so decisive in determining voting choice in 1987. The pattern of electoral change throughout the period tends to suggest that short term considerations about the state of political relations between the Labour Party and the trade unions may have affected the voting decisions of union members. In chapter 6, we shall be examining the relationship between union membership and short term issue assessments in more detail, but before that we need to concentrate further on the interplay between social and political factors; the unions, of course, have played an historically vital role in the political mobilisation of the British working class, and this leads us to pose the question of whether they are still important to the phenomenon of class voting.

Unions and class voting

> One of the hallmarks of class-inclusive explanations has been the assimilation of virtually all social influences from production or workplace contexts directly into the occupational class cleavage (Dunleavy & Husbands 1984: 9).

The orthodox position of partisan identification writers on the role of trade unions in British electoral mobilisation is that they have reinforced class identification and solidarity via a process of socialisation (see, for instance, Franklin 1985: 112-113). The most basic reason for questioning the relevance of union membership for class voting, however, is simply that it is probably no longer accurate to think of unions as 'class typical' institutions. Patrick Dunleavy has demonstrated that with a control for the influence of production sector there is little overall association between class and unionisation (Dunleavy 1980). Table 5.9 sets out very simply the manual/non-manual breakdown of the unionised and non-unionised groups in our data. It is not only clear that the proportion of non-manuals has generally grown since 1964, but that it has advanced particularly within the group of unionised respondents. In fact, the proportion of non-manuals among trade unionists has more than doubled to exceed two-fifths, compared with the more modest advance among non-unionists, where they account for slightly more than half the total.[11]

Table 5.9
Occupational status by unionisation, 1964 and 1987

	1964		1987	
	Union	Non-union	Union	Non-union
Non-manual	17.6	44.0	43.6	55.3
Manual	82.4	56.0	56.4	44.7
	100.0	100.0	100.0	100.0

So by 1987, the composition of our unionised sample was not heavily biased towards the working class. This is important in relation to the orthodox view that unionisation affects voting behaviour by socialising members into a sense of class identity and loyalty. Clearly, this hardly seems plausible any longer.

This in itself is interesting since it provokes the obvious question of whether this changing occupational profile alone can go far towards explaining Labour's losses among union members. Is it the case that electoral change has followed, not from class dealignment as such, but rather from the simple fact that there are less and less manual workers to be found within the union-based electorate? To some extent we have already had an indication that this is unlikely to be a wholly convincing argument given the heavy rate of desertion among manual unionists. However, we can test this proposition more precisely. To do so, it is necessary to make a projection of the share of the electorate that the various parties would have obtained among union members at the 1987 election had the *only* source of electoral change since 1964 been the changing relative sizes of occupational groups. Thus, we assume that, in 1987, the same relationship held between occupation and vote amongst union members as in 1964, and that the only source of electoral change is the differing relative sizes of manual and non-manual groups. This can be done in a straightforward manner by weighting the conditional probabilities of voting a certain way in 1964 by the 1987 occupational group frequencies.[12]

Table 5.10 compares this simulated vote with the actual vote in the 1987 union sample; the fairly considerable difference between the two indicates that the changing rate of non-manual employment amongst the unionised can only offer a very limited explanation of the group's change in voting behaviour between 1964 and 1987. Had this factor been the only source of electoral change, the Conservatives would have received the support of 1.7% more of the unionised electorate in 1987 than they actually did, and Labour of fully

Table 5.10

Union members' vote in 1987, projected from 1964 solely on the basis of changing rates of occupational status

	Projected vote	Actual vote
Conservative	29.2	27.5
Labour	48.7	37.9
Other	11.5	24.3
Abstained	10.6	11.2
	100.0	100.1

10.8% more; by contrast, the minor parties in our data would have received 12.8% less support than they did, and the rate of abstention would have been 0.6% lower. We therefore have to look either to other potential demographic sources of change as yet unconsidered, but which might be connected with class (for instance, the growing rate of home ownership[13]), or to political sources of change.

So, as suspected, the increasingly white collar nature of trade union membership is not on its own an adequate explanation of Labour's losses. At this point it is important to turn our attention to the following questions, therefore: firstly, has class dealignment occurred among trade union members? (Indeed, are unions of any remaining importance for class mobilisation?) And secondly, if class dealignment has taken place among trade union members, then why? In assessing the first question, we may analyse the data in terms of three basic but useful measures of 'class voting'; firstly, it can be seen that the proportion of respondents voting according to their occupational class generally declined between 1964 and 1987, but this is especially true of union members. Across this period, the percentage of trade unionists voting according to their occupational class fell from 60.1% to 39.1%, whereas the corresponding decline among non-unionists was far less dramatic - from 48.6% to 43.0%.

The second, and perhaps most widely employed measure found in the literature on electoral behaviour has been the *Alford Index* (Alford 1963). This is calculated by subtracting the percentage of the middle class - or strictly speaking, the non-manual group in our case - that supports Labour from the percentage of the working class (the manual group) supporting the party. Whereas there was virtually no change in the Alford Index for non-unionists between 1964 and 1987 (it moving from 19.1 to 20.4), there was a very distinct fall in the index for the unionised group of respondents (it falling from 38.2 to 14.7). Thus, the Alford Index indicates that, if anything, it is now the non-unionists who are more inclined to vote in a class typical way.

However, the Alford Index has been criticised on various grounds, and particularly in the sense that it 'confuses relative with overall support' (Heath et al 1985: 41); that is, a decline in overall support for Labour within all classes may produce a drop in the Alford Index even when the relative pattern support it receives from the two classes is unchanged.[14] Consequently, a more appropriate measure of 'relative class voting' may well be the odds ratio, which we have already met. In the context of class voting, we may calculate the two-party ratios by taking the odds on a manual worker voting Labour rather than Conservative and comparing them to the odds on a non-manual worker doing so; as before, we 'compare' these odds in the form of the ratio of one set of odds to the other. In this case, an odds ratio of 1:1 would indicate that there was no class voting, the relative strengths of the two parties being identical among manuals and non-manuals. We can once again calculate third-party and anti-Conservative odds ratios, of course, but there is one further type of ratio of interest now. As we saw in the last chapter, Elinor Scarbrough has argued that a more appropriate way of calculating an odds ratio on class voting is to divide the odds on a manual worker voting Labour rather than anything else by the odds on a non-manual employee voting Conservative rather than anything else (see footnote 4.8). In this way, we are constructing a ratio of the level of ideal-typical working class behaviour to the level of ideal-typical middle class behaviour.

Examining the odds ratios on class voting for unionists and non-unionists we do indeed find a picture of considerable change between 1964 and 1987. On the basis of these ratios we would infer that class voting was higher among union members than among non-members in 1964, but that by 1987 the reverse was true, given a considerable fall in class voting among members and a moderate increase among non-members. Indeed, we cannot really say that unionism remained of any importance to class voting in 1987, given these results. This is so, irrespective of how we actually operationalise the measure of class voting, and it should be noted that the odds ratios all confirm the initial impression emerging from the Alford Indices. These ratios, along with the Alford Indices are presented in Table 5.11.

Table 5.11

Measures of class voting: Alford indices and odds ratios for unionists and non-unionists, 1964 and 1987 [15]

	1964		1987	
	Union	Non-union	Union	Non-union
Alford Index	38.2	19.1	14.7	20.4
Odds Ratio				
Two-party	4.7	3.5	2.2	4.0
Third-party	5.0	2.6	1.8	3.3
Anti-Conservative	2.6	2.8	1.7	2.2
Scarbrough ratio	2.8	0.4	1.5	0.5

Nevertheless, we should take care not to exaggerate; it remains apparent that trade union membership still seems to help Labour in some ways. In particular, Labour maintains a lead over the Conservatives among manual workers only when they are unionised; however, such advantage as they do have within this group has been significantly curtailed since 1964, declining from 45 percentage points down to just 20.8. By comparison, it has remained practically constant among non-unionists, changing from 2 to 3.5 (see table 5.12).

Table 5.12
Labour's lead over the Conservatives, by unionisation and class, 1964 and 1987

	1964		1987	
	Union	Non-union	Union	Non-union
Manuals	40.0	2.0	20.8	3.5
Non-manuals	-13.0	-42.4	-4.3	-35.7

This is the point at which the matter of alternative models of socio-economic class becomes most pertinent. We have made a case about the decline of class voting among trade union members which is based on the assumption that the simple manual/non-manual distinction is an adequate definition of 'class'. This, as has already been acknowledged, is a questionable assumption, although it is true that no model of socio-economic class is entirely beyond criticism, on either conceptual or operational grounds (see footnote 5.3). Nevertheless, at the very least, it would surely be prudent to check whether our major findings with respect to class voting still hold when an alternative to the manual/non-manual scheme is employed. A variation of the Goldthorpe-Heath model of socio-economic class is suitable for this purpose.

This is a Weberian model which conceives of class in terms of socio-economic interests. Manual labourers have comparatively poor security of employment, limited access to fringe benefits and little authority in the workplace. Collective action is typically their only source of economic power. The salaried manager or bureaucrat represents an obvious contrast, since security, authority and promotional prospects are all likely to be greater for him or her. Professionals occupy a similar economic location in many respects and can therefore be considered as part of the same social stratum. Then there are various other economic groups, which for the sake of simplicity, yet without doing violence to the data or the theory, can be combined together to form an intermediate class that falls between the working class and the salariat. This intermediate class includes routine non-manual employees with limited autonomy and prospects at work, small independent entrepreneurs and the self-employed, and manual foremen and technicians who have a certain authority over the bulk of the manual workforce (Heath et al 1985: 14-16).

Tables 5.13 and 5.14 present the story of unions and class voting in terms of this three-fold alternative model of class. There is little need for lengthy discussion of these tables, since they confirm in almost every detail the message emerging from the previous class voting measures. The indices and odds ratios are consistently slightly higher when the Goldthorpe-Heath variable is used, indicating that it probably captures the nature of socio-economic class more successfully in modern Britain, but the pattern of change is virtually identical.

Table 5.13

Voting by union membership for the Goldthorpe-Heath classes, 1964 and 1987

1964

	Salariat		Intermediate		Working Class	
	Union	Non-union	Union	Non-union	Union	Non-union
Conservative	41.6	62.4	28.3	52.4	19.4	28.5
Labour	24.9	15.4	42.7	23.6	67.8	47.6
Other	28.4	16.1	13.0	15.4	4.4	9.4
Abstained	5.1	6.2	16.0	8.3	8.4	14.6
	100.0	100.1	100.0	100.0	100.0	100.1

1987

	Salariat		Intermediate		Working Class	
	Union	Non-union	Union	Non-union	Union	Non-union
Conservative	32.0	52.4	31.3	47.6	22.9	26.9
Labour	25.8	10.4	36.1	18.2	44.0	37.9
Other	32.0	25.8	23.1	20.3	20.6	17.5
Abstained	10.2	11.4	9.6	13.9	12.5	17.7
	100.0	100.0	100.1	100.0	100.0	100.0

It is clear, once again, that class voting among trade union members declined radically between 1964 and 1987. Again, this owes much to the dramatic loss of support Labour sustained among working class trade unionists; of all the cells in table 5.13, this is the one manifesting the biggest decline over the period. And once more, we find that the incidence of class voting has probably not declined among non-members. If anything, rather the opposite if one concentrates upon two-party and third-party voting effects.

Table 5.14

Alford indices and odds ratios on class voting for Goldthorpe-Heath classes, 1964 and 1987

	1964		1987	
	Union	Non-union	Union	Non-union
Alford Index	42.9	32.2	18.2	27.5
Odds Ratios				
Two-party	5.8	6.7	2.4	7.1
Third-party	6.4	5.1	1.9	5.1
Anti-Conservative	3.0	4.2	1.6	3.0
Scarbrough ratio	3.0	0.6	1.4	0.6

Note: Alford indices are calculated by subtracting Labour's percentage of support within the salariat from its percentage of support within the working class. Similarly, the odds ratios are based on a comparison of working class and salariat only; the intermediate class is redundant in all these calculations.

It may of course be argued that the mere fact of manual workers voting for Labour - or not, as the case may be - cannot be taken to constitute 'class voting'; some evidence of genuine *class consciousness* may be required too. Whilst our data does not permit us to distinguish the voting behaviour of 'class devotees who actually live a class ideology' (Sartori 1968: 12), we might at least focus upon the relationship between voting and *subjective class*. Does the self-perception of working class status increase the probability of voting Labour, and if so, is trade union membership important to the development of working class identity?

David Robertson has said that, electorally speaking, 'Labour requires class consciousness...the Conservatives do not' (Robertson 1983: 86), and it has to be said that even in 1987, four-fifths of all Labour supporters regarded themselves as working class.[16] Even so, there was a decline in the proportion of working class identifiers opting for Labour between 1964 and 1987, indicating that subjective class is less sufficient a reason for voting Labour

Table 5.15
Vote by subjective class for union members and non-members, 1964 and 1987

1964

	Union				Non-union			
	Middle Class		Working Class		Middle Class		Working Class	
	A.	U.	A.	U.	A.	U.	A.	U.
Cons.	42.5	57.8	17.5	19.4	64.8	63.7	30.0	43.5
Lab.	19.9	21.8	69.8	68.0	8.5	22.4	43.8	36.6
Other	27.6	13.6	5.9	4.3	18.1	9.5	12.5	8.9
Abst.	9.9	6.8	6.8	8.3	8.5	4.5	13.7	11.0
	99.9	100.0	100.0	100.0	99.9	100.1	100.0	100.0

1987

	Union				Non-union			
	Middle Class		Working Class		Middle Class		Working Class	
	A.	U.	A.	U.	A.	U.	A.	U.
Cons.	38.6	38.5	18.0	28.6	56.9	56.6	24.3	41.0
Lab.	25.4	26.5	50.8	32.2	13.7	8.7	40.3	22.5
Other	24.6	26.5	21.0	27.2	20.4	20.9	19.9	20.3
Abst.	11.4	8.5	10.2	12.0	9.0	13.8	15.6	16.2
	100.0	100.0	100.0	100.0	100.0	100.0	100.1	100.0

Note: 'A.' indicates 'Aware' respondents, and 'U.' 'unaware' respondents. The former are those who offer a specific class identity without being prompted. 'Unaware' respondents are those who initially reply that they 'do not know' to which class they feel they belong, but choose between middle and working class when prompted.

than it was hitherto. This holds more or less regardless of union membership or degree of class awareness, although once again we find that the heaviest loss of support is clearly found amongst the unionised. Labour support fell by 19 percentage points among members readily aware of their working class identity, and by fully 35.8 points among those less aware. The corresponding losses for non-members with working class identities were 3.5 points and 14.1 points. Looking at table 5.15, it can be seen that these changes not surprisingly affect the lead that Labour is able to maintain over the Conservatives. Within the 'aware' section of the unionised working class, Labour's lead has dropped by 19.5 percentage points since 1964, and by 35.8 points within the 'unaware' group. Again, changes are not so dramatic within the ranks of the non-unionised; indeed, Labour's lead actually increased slightly (by 2.2 points) amongst the non-unionised aware working class.

A more sophisticated check can be performed by calculating levels of 'subjective class voting' in terms of Alford Indices and odds ratios again. These are presented in table 5.16. Not surprisingly perhaps, 'class voting' appears to be a stronger phenomenon when we define it in terms of subjective awareness rather than on the basis of simple occupational categorisation. Nonetheless, for trade union members, there has been a palpable decline in its strength across the years since 1964. Each of the various types of odds ratio confirms this, as does the Alford Index.[17] The most striking point about the vote-subjective class relationship which emerges from a consideration of the odds ratios, however, is probably the existence of an interaction with unionisation *across time* for those not so immediately aware of their class identity. Quite simply, in 1964 trade union membership seemed to be important in enhancing the level of class voting *amongst those who were less aware of subjective class*; by 1987 this was no longer the case. Overall, we can say that trade union membership appeared to make no difference to the level of what may be called subjective class voting amongst those most aware of class either at the beginning or at the end of our period; if a respondent is particularly aware of class and class identity anyway, there is probably no reason why the fact of being a union member should actually *increase* the probability of voting in line with this prior awareness. But those less immediately aware of their class identity were considerably more likely to vote according to that identity if they were also union members in 1964. The odds ratios suggest that this was no longer so by the late 1980s, however.

So trade union membership no longer increases the likelihood of subjective class voting, yet it should not be forgotten that subjective class still has an impact on voting behaviour. Table 5.15 demonstrated that Labour maintains a notable lead over the Conservatives within what I have called the aware working class. Although it may seem unlikely given the foregoing analysis, it still needs to be asked, therefore, if union membership can be significant in terms of influencing subjective class identity in the first place. This is tantamount to asking if unions can be important in generating (a degree of) class consciousness. 'Class consciousness', of course, means somewhat more than nominal class identity alone. At its most developed, perhaps, it implies Sartori's class ideologist who sustains a radical perspective over a series of related issues, incorporating perceptions of exploitation in modern industrial society and an alternative vision of the distribution of power and resources. It is perhaps hard to conceive of British unions as directly mobilising a radical class consciousness in these terms. However, this is not necessarily to say that

Table 5.16

Alford indices and odds ratios for 'subjective class voting' by unionisation, 1964 and 1987

	Union		Non-union	
	Aware	Unaware	Aware	Unaware
1964				
Alford Index	49.9	46.2	35.3	14.2
Odds Ratios				
Two-party	8.5	9.2	11.2	2.4
Third-party	9.2	7.6	8.7	2.0
Anti-Conservative	3.5	5.7	4.3	2.3
Scarbrough ratio	3.1	1.6	0.4	0.3
1987				
Alford Index	25.4	5.7	26.6	13.8
Odds Ratio				
Two-party	4.3	1.6	6.9	3.7
Third-party	3.0	1.3	4.3	2.9
Anti-Conservative	3.1	1.6	4.1	1.9
Scarbrough ratio	1.6	0.8	0.5	0.2

Note: Alford indices are calculated for differences between the rate of Labour support given by those perceiving themselves to be working class and those perceiving themselves to be middle class. Odds ratios use self perceived class similarly. For instance, the two-party ratio is calculated in terms of the odds on a subjectively working class individual voting Labour as opposed to Conservative, divided by the odds on a subjectively middle class individual doing so.

trade unions in Britain have been uninfluential in moulding the values typical of the labour movement and the working class. Whatever, we can at least try to resolve one basic question; can the membership of modern British trade unions be regarded as affecting a key component of class consciousness, that of subjective identity?

Previous research affords no clear expectations; Duncan Gallie has recorded that the fact of belonging to different types of unions (that is, general or craft unions) in Britain has no discernible effect on class-linked attitudes (Gallie 1983: 114). On the other hand, research conducted in the 1970s suggested that 'the data undeniably point towards union membership serving to assist in the development of a corporate class consciousness amongst British unionists' (Hill 1979: 282[18]). Table 5.17 suggests that, although unions might formerly have had an effect upon the subjective class identity of manual workers, this impact has certainly diminished.

Table 5.17
Subjective class by unionisation for manual workers, 1964 and 1987

	1964		1987	
	Union	Non-union	Union	Non-union
Middle class	11.8	22.6	16.7	21.9
Working class	88.2	77.4	83.3	78.1
	100.0	100.0	100.0	100.0

Amongst non-union manuals there has been little change in subjective class identity; among union members, there has been a decline in working class identification, however, with the result that there is hardly any union effect apparent at all now. In 1964 10.8% more trade unionists than non-unionists saw themselves as working class, whereas only 5.2% more did so in 1987. This impression of a slight relationship between union membership and subjective class awareness is confirmed by a multiple classification analysis, moreover. When subjective class identity is used as the dependent variable, unionisation appears to be the weakest of all social background influences; the beta coefficients for the relevant social background factors are as follows:

	Beta coefficient		Significance of effect	
	1964	1987	1964	1987
Occupation	0.20	0.13	0.00	0.00
Unionisation	0.05	0.06	0.00	0.00
Housing	0.08	0.12	0.00	0.00
Parental occupation	0.09	0.17	0.00	0.00
Education	0.26	0.20	0.00	0.00
Multiple R^2	0.21	0.20	0.00	0.00

Why has class dealignment occurred among union members?

We have discovered that genuine political and class dealignment has occurred among trade unionists since the 1960s, and the changing occupational profile of memberships alone does not account for this change. Why has this happened? Processess of social change such as class decomposition and mobility might be considered as potential explanations, but they generally turn out to be of limited help.

Class decomposition refers to the view that class communities are breaking up and class values and identities are eroded; consequently, class itself ceases to be such a powerful cue for social and political behaviour. However, recent commentators have tended to argue that claims of internal class decomposition have been exaggerated (Marshall et al, 1988). Most people in Britain remain aware of class and maintain some class identity. Moreover, if thoroughgoing decomposition were taking place, then we might expect to find evidence of an increase in the size of the non-manual Labour vote and of the manual Conservative vote ('cross-class voting'). In fact, there is little to suggest that this has really been the case; between 1964 and 1987 non-manual Labour support hardly changed - rising by 1.6 points among union members, and falling by 4.4 points among non-members - whilst Conservative manual support dropped by 4.6 points among non-unionists and remained virtually unchanged among unionists (up 2.3 points). Clearly, these shifts in support are nothing like sufficient to account for the changes in alignment that we have witnessed. Instead, the shift away from Labour among manual trade unionists is largely accounted for by changes towards the arguably class-neutral options of minor party support or abstention. In any case, those who actually retain a sense of working class identity - the least likely components of any process of class decomposition - are precisely the ones who manifest the highest rates of dealignment. Between 1964 and 1987, the proportion of the trade union electorate voting Labour declined by 19 points amongst the aware working class, but actually increased by 5.5 points amongst their middle class counterparts. The pattern is repeated among those less aware of class identities, with the working class offering 35.8 points less support to Labour in 1987, and the middle class offering 3.6 points more support (see table 5.15).

What about the impact of other forms of social change that may be potentially relevant? It has already been pointed out that *class mobility* in the limited sense of movement from manual to non-manual status is of no use in accounting for the heavy rate of Labour dealignment occurring among the core of 'stationary' manual trade unionists. (Second generation manual trade unionists, as a group, have reduced their support for Labour by 25.1 percentage points since 1964.) But what other social factors might throw light on the matter? In Chapter 3 we learnt that union memberships are, amongst other things, increasingly comprised of semi-skilled and unskilled workers, women and public sector employees (see page 81). Could any of these changes help explain manual dealignment? In principle, they could if it were the case that any of these groups proved less inclined to support Labour than other manual unionists. However, empirical evidence has tended to suggest the precise opposite. These categories of employee tend to be *more* inclined to vote for the Labour Party, if anything (Dunleavy and Husbands 1985: 132-133; Rose and McAllister 1986: 58). Our data confirms this.

Manual workers are considerably more heavily unionised in the public sector (nearly half of all respondents being members), and certainly more inclined to vote Labour; 55.9% of public sector manual unionists chose Labour in 1987, compared to 45.4% in the private sector. Neither does the skill level of manual trade union members offer any answers, there being practically no difference between the electoral alignment of skilled respondents on the one hand and semi-skilled or unskilled respondents on the other. 49.3% of the former and 50.9% of the latter opted for Labour in 1987. Finally, female manual unionists proved more likely to support the party, some 57.7% of them swinging Labour's way, compared to only 47.3% of their male counterparts. In summary then, social change, though hardly irrelevant, comes nowhere near providing a satisfactory explanation of electoral change amongst manual trade unionists.

Having already dismissed the explanatory power of purely organisational factors in chapter 2, we are left with political sources of change. Chief among the likely political factors emerging from our discussion so far would seem to be the effect of political relationships between the Labour Party and the trade unions. However, there is another factor which merits our attention first - the impact of housing policy in Britain since 1979. After their election in 1979,

Conservative governments sought to extend private home ownership through a policy of legalising and encouraging the sale of low-rent local authority accommodation to tenants. This has produced a situation in which many working class households have entered into home ownership for the first time, and - given the importance of housing as a determinant of voting behaviour - there is much speculation about the consequences of this for political alignment. Might the execution of this policy go some way towards explaining Labour's losses among manual trade unionists? Indeed, Esping-Andersen has demonstrated just how crucial a role state housing policy can play in affecting the electoral support of Social Democratic parties in Scandinavia. In effect, post-war housing policies in Sweden and Norway have been constructed so as to provide universalistic benefits for consumers, whereas the Danish strategy has been to provide selective benefits in the housing market. As a consequence, Esping-Andersen argues, housing status has become a line of social and political fragmentation in Denmark which has undermined the potential for social democratic electoral support. There is an obvious prima facie relevance for Britain (Esping-Andersen 1985: 265-270).

However, two points which detract from the argument emerge from a consideration of this question. Firstly, it should be borne in mind that there is really a dual aspect to the phenomenon we are investigating; one is the sheer decline of manual trade unionist support for Labour between 1964 and 1987, but the other is the variation in the pattern of this support at the general elections of 1970, 1974 and 1979. These are the elections at which the unions and industrial relations were most salient for voting decisions, and subsequent elections have in many ways simply been consolidations of the 1979 pattern of manual unionist alignment. In these terms, the housing policy of the Thatcher governments is an irrelevance, given that it cannot have had any electoral effect until the 1983 election at the earliest. But even if housing is unhelpful with regard to the electoral pattern of the 1970s, it may in principle still provide some insight into the overall losses the party has suffered since 1964, if it can be shown that manual union members proved more likely to purchase council homes than their non-union counterparts. This is the second point to concentrate upon with respect to the influence of housing policy. In fact, our data shows that members were no more likely to purchase than non-members; in 1987, just 1.6% of unionised manual respondents claimed to have bought homes from a local authority, compared to 2.4% of non-union manuals. These numbers are in any case far too small to offer much help in explaining the rate of electoral change we have observed. It must be concluded from this, therefore, that housing cannot help explain the particular shift away from Labour of the unionised working class.

This leaves us with the second possible political factor - the impact of party-union relations. Such an explanation is clearly suggested by the way that union members' patterns of electoral support seem to have reflected the political and industrial history of the period between 1966 and 1979. This impression is deepened when considered in the light of important sociological research. Of particular relevance is the classic work conducted by Goldthorpe and his colleagues on working class values in the 1960s, which suggested that 'affluent' workers - whom we may take to be increasingly typical of union memberships - bore a limited sense of communal loyalty or solidarity. Interestingly, whilst identifying themselves clearly as working class, most of these workers were discovered to have an 'individualist' or 'privatist' outlook. That is, where the 'traditional' working class unionist was embedded in a set of mutually reinforcing life situations which predisposed him towards Labour (that is, a socialisation process), a new 'affluent' unionist was more inclined to regard both the unions and the Labour Party in instrumental and calculative terms (Goldthorpe et al, 1969). This is not necessarily to say that class sensitivities and politics are disappearing within these sections of the working class (although we have seen that there was some decline in working class self identification amongst manual unionists after 1964), for awareness of relative inequality may well remain. However, commitment to the Labour movement seems to be relatively contingent.

Goldthorpe's work has not been entirely uncontroversial. It may be that the labourist British working class has always been instrumental; given that the Labour Party historically forewent a strategy of ideological encapsulation this would not be altogether surprising. From our point of view, however, it does not much matter precisely *when* the working class became identifiably instrumental, so long as it is clear that this is an appropriate attitudinal description by the time of the party-union conflicts of the 1960s and 1970s. If this is an accurate generalisation about modern British working class consciousness, then some light is shed upon the basis of our political explanation of electoral change; since affective loyalty cannot be counted upon among Labour's 'core' followers, it is vital that the party succeeds in providing the economic and industrial climate best suited to the realisation of their material aspirations. If it fails to 'deliver the goods' in these terms, then there is no obvious reason why these voters should continue to support Labour, given their instrumentalist outlook. Indeed, it is not hard to imagine how the bitter conflicts between the party and the unions during the 1960s and 1970s would have disillusioned Labour's core of manual trade unionists. The sense of betrayal felt by many with what they once regarded as 'their' party would only have served to diminish further Labour's fund of affective loyalty. The initial electoral retreat for these voters in 1970 was largely into abstention;

by 1979, many union members were moving towards a Conservative Party which was promising, amongst other things, an end to incomes policy (see table 5.1).

This perspective, in turn, raises further questions. Firstly, why precisely is it that so much of the British working class takes such an instrumentalist outlook? And secondly, how is it that the Labour Party has had so much difficulty in 'delivering the goods' in material terms when in office? Neither answer is free of complexity, nor of a certain amount of contentious speculation. Without going into these matters in depth, however, it is worth saying that the trade unions themselves may be relevant to the answers. For one thing, Marshall and his colleagues - amongst others - have gone to some length to argue that, historically, working class consciousness owes much to the unions in Britain. Specifically, they point to the lack of a definite class objective which has beset the British working class, and they ascribe this largely to the 'failure of class organisations to convert sectional and conventional struggles into solidaristic and legal ones. The decentralised structure of free collective bargaining militates against such a process' (Marshall et al 1988: 268). Furthermore, I have already argued that the failure of Labour's corporatist strategy in the 1960s and 1970s turns largely upon the decentralised character of the trade union movement. Under such circumstances national planning and incomes policies fall apart amidst a welter of sectional claims and internecine struggles over the suppression or maintenance of pay differentials. And as economic and industrial strategies begin to falter, it encourages further fragmentation of the labour movement. Indeed, failure of economic strategy can be of the utmost consequence for party-union relations, as Esping-Andersen has pointed out:

> Sustained full employment is the single most important means of preventing dualism and fundamental cleavages among wage earners; it is the ultimate precondition for trade union strength and labour movement unity (Esping-Andersen 1985: 317).

Before concluding this discussion of the causes of class dealignment among manual union members, one final point is worth adding. We have asserted that a combination of political and social factors helps explain the class dealignment of manual union members. Much more than this we cannot say. In particular, it is virtually impossible to be exact in demarcating the contributions of purely 'social' from purely 'political' factors. The two are inextricably interlinked in various ways. For instance, though happy to contend that the pattern of estrangement and reconciliation between the Labour

Party and the unions must to some extent lie behind the basic pattern of dealignment-realignment-dealignment displayed by union members as a group at the elections of 1970, 1974 and 1979, we might reflect that it is hard to know how purely 'political' a factor this phenomenon of estrangement really is. For one thing, it should not be forgotten that the initial cooling in relations followed, in some measure, from the strategic decision of the leadership in the early 1960s to shed its 'cloth cap' image and become a catch-all phenomenon, indeed, even a 'natural party of government'. And, of course, this 'declassiste' strategy was in turn largely a *response* to the fact of social change. After three successive election defeats there was a widespread - if not monolithic (nor necessarily correct) - perception that Labour was suffering the electoral consequences of not adapting to the circumstances of a newly mobile and affluent society. The general point is that Labour's 'political' problems with the unions may have partly resulted from social change and perceptions of social change.

Conclusion

To summarise the argument then, we might say that class voting has in general declined since 1964 - though by no means disappeared - and the importance of trade unions to class voting has weakened considerably. Moreover, whilst a majority of Labour voters continue to regard themselves as working class, the impact of unionism upon subjective class identity has declined to near insignificance, at least among manuals. In a sense, none of these changes may seem entirely surprising given that unions on the whole are no longer class-typical organisations. Yet social change alone does not seem to provide a satisfactory account of the decline of union influence on class voting. Indeed, the most interesting point about the shift away from Labour over the years is that it seems to have been most notable within those groups usually considered to lie at the 'core' of the party's traditional support - the stationary manual workers, union members and those with working class self-perceptions. The diminished affective loyalty of these groups allied to the political tensions often apparent between Labour and the unions best accounts for the electoral behaviour of trade unionists.

There remains to be considered in greater detail one aspect of social change which, it has been argued, may also dilute the strength of class voting, especially amongst trade unionists; this is the production sector effect. If the unions are no longer important in mobilising a class vote, could they then be important for the mobilisation of a new line of socio-political cleavage? And since we are moving on to the question of alternative electoral cues to class, it is also worthwhile considering the matter of unionists' attitudinal profiles. Do unions influence their members' synoptic values or issue assessments? It is to these matters that we now turn.

Notes

1. The data sets employed throughout are *Political Change in Britain, 1963-1970* (directed by David Butler and Donald Stokes), and the subsequent *British Election Studies* of 1974 and 1979 (directed by Ivor Crewe, James Alt, Bo Sarlvik and David Robertson) and of 1983 and 1987 (directed by a team led by Anthony Heath). I gratefully acknowledge the ESRC Data Archive based at the University of Essex for making these data sets available to me.

2. Table 5.1n gives the odds for unionists and non-unionists respectively, and the final ratio between the two sets of odds which indicates how distinct trade union voting is. (All odds and ratios have been rounded to 1 decimal place.)

Table 5.1n
Voting odds and odds ratios for unionists and non-unionists, 1964-1987

	A	B	C	A	B	C
		1964			*1966*	
Two-party	2.5	0.7	3.8	3.1	0.8	3.7
Third-party	1.4	0.4	3.2	1.5	0.5	2.7
Anti-Conservative	3.3	1.2	2.9	4.2	1.4	3.0
		1970			*1974 (February)*	
Two-party	2.2	0.6	3.5	2.4	0.6	4.1
Third-party	1.0	0.4	2.5	1.0	0.3	2.8
Anti-Conservative	3.3	1.2	2.8	3.9	1.3	3.0
		1974 (October)			*1979*	
Two-Party	3.1	0.7	4.6	1.6	0.6	2.6
Third-party	1.1	0.4	3.0	0.8	0.4	2.0
Anti-Conservative	4.9	1.5	3.2	2.7	1.2	2.3
		1983			*1987*	
Two-party	1.2	0.5	2.4	1.4	0.6	2.4
Third-party	0.5	0.3	1.9	0.6	0.3	2.0
Anti-Conservative	2.7	1.4	1.9	2.6	1.4	1.9

Note: A = Union members' odds, B = Non-members' odds, C = Odds ratio

3. Throughout, we shall be relying largely on the simple manual/non-manual dichotomy when speaking of 'class', although it is not intended as a surrogate for a fully theorised class scheme; in this sense it would have to be regarded as an inadequte account of contemporary class structure. For this reason, a more elaborated model of socio-economic class will be introduced at various key points in the analysis, and comparisons drawn.

In British voting studies various alternative class schemes have been employed such as the fundamentally Weberian ones favoured by Robertson (Robertson 1984) and Heath (Heath et al 1985), or in a more Marxisant vein, the model preferred by Patrick Dunleavy (Dunleavy and Husbands 1985). The sociological division between Marxist and Weberian class analysis has been critically reviewed by Marshall and his colleagues. They set themselves the specific task of comparing the relative merits of the class schemes proposed by John Goldthorpe (neo-Weberian) and Erik Wright (Neo-Marxist) (Goldthorpe 1980, Wright 1979, Wright 1985). Overall, they concluded that Goldthorpe's approach held considerably greater value. Wright's model was constructed on the assertion that class relations are revealed in matters of ownership of the means of production, on the one hand, and in relationships of domination (supervision and decision-making) at work, on the other. This was fundamentally criticised on two grounds; firstly, it was claimed that there were major problems in the way that class categories are actually constructed employing these criteria. Consequently, Marshall is apt to question just how many of Wright's 'proletarians' really are proletarians, and how many of his 'managers' are managers. In the second place, Marshall attacks the 'incoherence' of Wright's empirical findings. In particular, he is unconvinced of Wright's view that British society is genuinely 'polarised', with large sections of the intermediate social groupings being engulfed either by the proletariat or the bourgoisie. Goldthorpe more credibly emphasises the existence of the categories which lie both demographically and politically between the working and service classes (Marshall et al 1988: passim).

I have therefore chosen to incorporate Anthony Heath's tripartite variation of the Goldthorpe class scheme into my work (see page 122). However, there is no need to discard the simple manual/non-manual distinction entirely. In the first place, it remains basically informative and, notwithstanding the various embellishments found in sociological theory, it is a central feature of all of these class schemes. Moreover, Ivor Crewe has argued in favour of the manual/non-manual dichotomy on the grounds that Heath's scheme, though a welcome departure in theory, becomes too restrictive in practice (see pages 100-101, above). The manual/non-manual distinction is simple and easily comparable. It should not be without significance for devotees of any of the major schools (though, admittedly, it risks satisfying none of them). There is a further reason for incorporating the manual/non-manual scheme. We consciously attempt to emulate what is probably the most comprehensive model of class voting that has been specifically designed for the period that interests us (comprehensive, that is, in the sense that it does not rely solely upon the criterion of occupation) - that of Franklin (Franklin 1985). And Franklin employs the straightforward manual/non-manual distinction as an occupational variable. For these reasons I have decided to leave the simple manual/non-manual division at the centre of my approach, although room has been made for broad comparison with the Goldthorpe-Heath model wherever that seems appropriate. This is most relevant when we touch upon the question of trade unionists and class voting.

It should also be noted that it would be ideal if we could further control for Labour-affiliation when crosstabulating unionisation by vote. Unfortunately, it is not possible to distinguish between unions that are Labour-affiliated and others in all of the data sets employed. However, the manual/non-manual distinction does overlap with this to some extent.

4. The odds from which which the odds ratios reported in table 5.2 are derived are as follows:

	Manual		Non-manual	
	Union	Non-union	Union	Non-union
1964				
Two-party	3.2	1.1 (= 3.0)	0.7	0.3 (= 2.3)
Third-party	1.9	0.6 (= 3.2)	0.4	0.2 (= 1.7)
Anti-Conservative	3.9	1.8 (= 2.1)	1.5	0.6 (= 2.3)
1987				
Two-party	1.9	1.1 (= 1.7)	0.8	0.3 (= 3.1)
Third-party	0.8	0.5 (= 1.5)	0.4	0.2 (= 2.6)
Anti-Conservative	3.4	2.2 (= 1.5)	2.0	1.0 (= 2.0)

5. Of course, mobility in the narrow sense intended here is not the only sort of social change that could have affected manual workers; there are other ways in which social change might affect even those who are not mobile. For example, the embourgeoisement theory, which was for a while influential during the 1950s and early 1960s, was an attempt to account for the impact of social change on the static manual working class. Similarly, the seminal *Affluent Worker* study conducted by Goldthorpe and Lockwood (and which I believe to be relevant to the behaviour of trade unionists) describes changes in the lifestyles and values of manual workers.

6. Of course, it is not unusual for electoral researchers to employ *multiple regression* techniques. However, this does necessitate the arguably questionable manipulation of what is essentially *categorical level* data so that it may be entered into a regression equation as *interval level* data. It has been argued that the ordinary least squares multiple regression approach remains appropriate even with a categorical level dependent variable, so long as this variable's distribution is not heavily skewed (that is, so long as one of its categories contains at least 25% of the total distribution), and the sample is reasonably large (Gillespie 1977). However, I have been inclined to reject the regression technique here since most of the independent variables are also categorical. This is not really the sort of data that regression was designed to analyse. I have generally preferred the straightforward multiple classification analysis technique because it tells us what we want to know, and it is specifically designed to express a relationship between a set of nominal level independent variables and an interval level dependent variable. It therefore seems entirely adequate for our needs. (The dependent variable in this case is simply the proportionate Labour vote; thus, for an independent variable like trade union membership, we would obtain a reading for the variable's categories in terms of the proportion voting for Labour - for example, members = 0.37, non-members = 0.23. That is, 37% of trade unionists vote Labour compared to 23% of non-unionists.)

The beta coefficients quoted throughout this chapter are based on the eta statistic; this essentially expresses the explained variance in the dependent variable as a proportion of the total variance. More precisely, the explained variance is taken to be that part accounted for by the categories of the independent variables. We may illustrate this with an example in which we have as our dependent variable vote (with Labour vote coded as '1', and all other votes coded '0'), and one independent variable, union membership, with just two categories, member and non-member. If we had a situation in which all the members voted for Labour and all the non-members voted for other parties, we could say that the two categories of the unionisation variable explain all of the variance in voting behaviour. In other words, total variance could be accounted for entirely by 'between-group' variance. Were there also some fluctuation in the voting behaviour of individuals within the categories of union status, then we would have a further source of variation in the dependent variable; it could not be explained by variation between the categories alone.

Between-group variance itself is calculated in terms of the difference between the mean of each category and the grand mean for the entire sample, squared and multiplied by the number in each category; *within-group variance* is calculated in a similar fashion except that we are now considering the differences between the individual scores and the grand mean. The beta coefficients are standardised partial regression coefficients, and significance levels are quoted throughout. These significance levels are based upon the F-ratio statistic, and it will be noted that most of the main effects for the multiple classification models presented in the book are significant at the 1% level or better; the independent variable most likely to prove statistically insignificant in the voting models is that of education. The multiple R^2 for each overall model and the significance of each overall model is reported, although it should be borne in mind that the construction of models that explain the greatest possible variance in voting behaviour is not a primary concern in this work. Rather, the central focus of interest is the strength and significance of individual effects within each model - above all, that of unionisation, of course. It is the importance of this variable relative to others that lies at the heart of the matter, as far as this study is concerned. Throughout, interaction effects between independent variables are generally ignored in the multiple classification models since very few proved statistically significant. Indeed, it is important to the procedure that this should be so, since the beta coefficients assume additive, rather than interactive, effects. As a general point, if there are strong interaction effects in a model, the multiple classification scores become meaningless. This implies, of course, that we are dealing throughout with linear models based on additive, rather than multiplicative, effects (see Nie et al 1975: Chapter 22.) That we can trust the multiple classification results is confirmed by the pattern of some of our major findings; for example, the growing importance to vote of housing and the slight weakening of occupation, plus the significance of attitudinal variables in the 1980s are far from extraordinary findings. Other researchers using alternative statistical techniques (such as multiple regression or logit modelling) have made similar discoveries.

7. The social background variables employed in the model were coded as follows:

Occupation	-	manual=1, non-manual=0
Unionisation	-	member=1, non-member=0
Housing	-	council tenant=1, other=0
Education	-	minimum leaving age=1,other=0
Parental class	-	father manual=1, non-manual=0

As stated above, we follow Franklin in taking these variables to constitute the basis of a model of class voting in Britain since 1964 (though it is not possible to construct a full multi-stage causal model using the multiple classification technique). The logic behind the coding of the variables should be fairly clear; we have already discussed the case of occupation of course, which is one of the potentially problematic variables. The division between those who rent their accommodation from a municipal authority and other individuals makes sense on two counts. Firstly, it may work via the socialisation process. The provision of low-cost accommodation by local authorities has tended to reinforce patterns of class segregation and socialisation, especially in inner city areas (Franklin 1985: 18). The alternative explanation of the impact of housing location on vote is quite simply that it is a matter of collective interest to vote Labour if you live in accommodation rented from a local authority. This is the view ascribed to by consumption sector theorists (Saunders 1981). In so far as housing location is concerned, it is simply in one's interest to vote Labour if one is a council tenant because Labour is far more likely to support the provision of resources which can be used for the maintenance of council property and for the subsidising of council rents.

The basis for the division of the education variable is the minimum school-leaving age. In 1964 this was 15, but by 1987 it had been increased by one year. At one time it might have been possible to make an interesting distinction between the type of schools that individuals frequented - Grammar, Secondary Modern, Technical or Private. However, with the introduction of the Comprehensive system of education this was no longer a clear basis for the differentiation of socialisation patterns by the 1970s. For children who stay on beyond the minimum leaving age, it is likely that some sort of segregation will occur, in that they will continue to mix - at least within the school environment - only with other such children.

Since our purpose at this point is to assess the relative importance of unionisation compared to other elements of social location, partisan identification and parental partisan identification have been excluded from the model. These are really psychological factors which intervene between social location and vote. It is not necessary to test the Michigan model itself in order to obtain a picture of the relative importance of union membership compared to other social determinants of the vote. We therefore end up with a social background model of vote which might be diagrammatically portrayed in the following way:

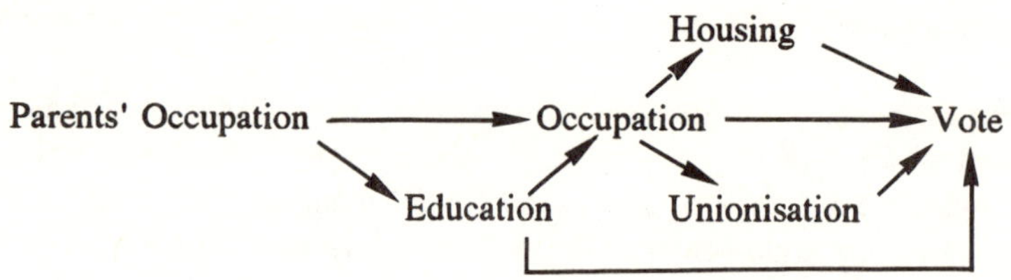

Finally, it is worth dealing with the question of how socio-economic class should be properly conceived, a point that we have already touched upon in note 5.3. For the sake of comparison, the social background model of vote can be re-executed substituting for the manual/non-manual distinction the more theoretically rounded definition of class suggested by Goldthorpe and Heath. This variable is coded: Salariat = 1, Intermediate = 2, Working class = 3.

This model produces the follwing results:

	Beta coefficient		Significance of effect	
	1964	1987	1964	1987
Economic class	0.21	0.17	0.00	0.00
Unionisation	0.15	0.12	0.00	0.00
Housing	0.11	0.21	0.00	0.00
Parental class	0.15	0.13	0.00	0.00
Education	0.05	0.03	0.00	0.15
Multiple R^2	0.19	0.15	0.00	0.00

It takes but brief comparison with the original social background model of vote to see that this alternative tells essentially the same story; true enough, the impact of class conceived in the Goldthorpe-Heath sense is slightly greater in both 1964 and 1987, but within the model the relationship of the various parameters to one another remains the same. That is, the impact of class, parental class, unionisation and education has declined to some extent or other since 1964, whilst that of housing has been enhanced. The actual sizes of these parameters are similar in both models, moreover.

8. It should be pointed out however, that when a term for the production sector variable is added to our social background model of vote in 1987, the strength of the beta coefficient for unionism does not change radically (falling from 0.11 to 0.08). For a similar model of the 1983 election, there is no change at all in the unionisation beta when a sectoral effect is added (it remaining at 0.09). This tends to indicate that the effect of sectoral location in cross-cutting the alignment of unionists may not be particularly important. That is, controlling for production sector did not appear to weaken the union-vote relationship at all in 1983, although there are signs that by 1987 it might have done so slightly.

9. Table 5.2n presents the partisanship odds for unionists and non-unionists respectively. One sees quite clearly that for each type of odds, the fluctuation

Table 5.2n
Partisanship odds and odds ratios for unionists and non-unionists, 1964-1987

	A	B	C	A	B	C
		1964			*1966*	
Two-party	2.6	0.7	3.6	3.1	0.7	4.1
Third-party	1.7	0.5	3.2	1.6	0.5	3.0
Anti-Conservative	3.1	1.0	3.0	4.0	1.1	3.6
		1970			*1974 (February)*	
Two-party	2.3	0.7	3.4	2.3	0.7	3.5
Third-party	1.5	0.5	3.0	1.2	0.5	2.5
Anti-Conservative	2.9	1.1	2.7	3.3	1.1	3.0
		1974 (October)			*1979*	
Two-party	2.3	0.7	3.3	2.0	0.7	2.8
Third-party	1.1	0.5	2.5	1.0	0.5	2.1
Anti-Conservative	3.4	1.5	2.3	3.0	1.2	2.5
		1983			*1987*	
Two-party	1.7	0.7	2.5	1.5	0.7	2.3
Third-party	0.9	0.5	2.0	0.9	0.5	1.9
Anti-Conservative	2.5	1.2	2.1	2.3	1.1	2.1

Note: A = Union members' odds, B = Non-members' odds, C = Odds ratio

is much greater for union members than for non-members. Thus, whilst the two-party odds do not fluctuate from a stable baseline of 0.7 for non-members, they drop from a high point of 3.1 down to a 1987 low of 1.5 for trade unionists; for third-party partisanship, the non-members' ratio remains constant at 0.5 but the members' ratio varies between 1.6 and 0.9, whilst for anti-Conservative partisanship the respective variations are between 1.5 and 1.0, compared to 4.0 and 2.3.

10. The electoral salience of questions central to the party-union relationship is illustrated by table 5.3n. Labour relations appeared among the three issues most frequently nominated as important by voters during the election campaigns of the 1970s, but never since.

Table 5.3n

Leading issues nominated as most important facing the country at general elections, 1964-1987

1964	1. The economy (15%) 2. Housing (14%) 3. Pensions(11%)
1966	1. The economy (48%) 2. Housing (16%) 3. Commonwealth (14%)
1970	1. Prices (35%) 2. *Labour relations* (13%) 3. Other economic problems (11%)
Feb.74	1. Prices (55%) 2. *Labour relations* (18%) 3. Other economic problems (6%)
Oct.74	1. Prices (72%) 2. Other economic problems (6%) 3. *Labour relations* (5%)
1979	1. Prices (29%) 2. Unemployment (22%) 3. *Labour relations* (14%)
1983	1. Unemployment (80%) 2. Prices (4%) 3. Defence (4%)
1987	1. Unemployment (66%) 2. Health (8%) 3. Defence (6%)

Note: Figures in brackets are percentages of respondents nominating an issue as the most important currently facing the country.

Source: Gallup Political Index

11. The question of the changing occupational profile of union membership was dealt with to some extent in chapter 3 of course. It is interesting to compare our data with the most recently available information on the manual/non-manual breakdown of trade unions (refer to table 3.4).

12. The calculations for this simulation of the 1987 vote, which assumes a constant class-vote relationship but changing manual/non-manual proportions amongst union members, are as follows:

First, we weight the total frequencies of the manual and non-manual categories in the union sector for 1987 by the proportion of each of these groups voting for the various parties in 1964:

	Manual	Non-manual
Conservative	.205 x 470 = 96.4	.403 x 370 = 149.1
Labour	.655 x 470 = 307.9	.273 x 370 = 101.0
Other	.044 x 470 = 20.7	.206 x 370 = 76.2
Abstained	.097 x 470 = 45.6	.117 x 370 = 43.3
	470.6	369.6

Next, one simply adds the sums in the rows to get the new overall simulated frequencies found in each of the voting categories. These are:

Conservative	96.4 + 149.1	= 245.5
Labour	307.9 + 101.0	= 408.9
Other	20.7 + 76.2	= 96.9
Abstained	45.6 + 43.3	= 88.9
	470.6 + 369.6	= 839.8

From here, it is simply a question of calculating the percentages of the entire union sample (=839.8) that these frequencies correspond to.

13. In fact, it has been pointed out by Heath et al that housing, whilst important as a predictor of voting behaviour at any given *point in time*, is not very useful as an explanation of electoral *change*. This is for two reasons; firstly, the major change in housing status over the period that interests us has been the decline of the private rental sector as the proportion of private owners has grown. Those in the private rental sector have always been inclined to fall between owner-occupiers and local authority tenants in terms of their voting preferences, and therefore the extent of the change in voting behaviour following this has been 'muted'. Secondly, whilst the absolute sizes of housing groups and social classes have been changing, they have not altered much relative to each other. Broadly the same proportion of the working class lives in council-rented accommodation as did at the beginning of the period; and the same can be said of the proportion of the middle class that are home-owners. (The relative size of these classes has changed, of course.) Thus, housing is unable to offer any additional explanation of electoral change (or more specificically, of class dealignment) to that already offered by class (Heath, Jowell and Curtice 1985: 51). We shall be returning to an essentially similar point when considering the possible impact of Conservative housing policy upon working class trade unionists in the 1980s.

14. Heath quotes an example of the effect of this, by starting out with the information that in 1945 62% of manuals voted Labour compared with 28% of non-manuals, giving an Alford Index of 34. If Labour's support fell to 33% among manuals and to zero among non-manuals, this would result in an Alford Index of 33 points, less than in 1945. 'But surely we would want to say that such a situation where Labour drew all its votes from the working class represented a much higher degree of class alignment than in 1945' (Heath et al 1985: 41).

15. The formulas for the different odds ratios quoted in table 5.11 are:

Two-party -

(Labour vote/Conservative vote) among manuals
(Labour vote/Conservative vote) among non-manuals

Third-party -

(Labour vote/Non-Labour vote) among manuals
(Labour vote/Non-Labour vote) among non-manuals

Anti-Conservative -

(Non-Conservative vote/Conservative vote) among manuals
(Non-Conservative vote/Conservative vote) among non-manuals

Scarbrough method -

(Labour vote/Non-Labour vote) among manuals
(Conservative vote/Non-Conservative vote) among non-manuals

The actual odds for 1964 and 1987 break down in the following way:

	Union		Non-union	
	Manual	Non-manual	Manual	Non-manual
1964				
Two-party	3.2	0.7 (=4.7)	1.1	0.3 (=3.5)
Third-party	1.9	0.4 (=5.0)	0.6	0.2 (=2.6)
Anti-Conservative	3.9	1.5 (=2.6)	1.8	0.6 (=2.8)
Scarbrough	1.9	0.7 (=2.8)	0.6	1.6 (=0.4)

	Union		Non-union	
	Manual	Non-manual	Manual	Non-manual
1987				
Two-party	1.9	0.9 (=2.2)	1.1	0.3 (=4.0)
Third-party	0.8	0.4 (=1.9)	0.5	0.2 (=3.3)
Anti-Conservative	3.4	2.0 (=1.7)	2.2	1.0 (=2.2)
Scarbrough	0.8	0.5 (=1.5)	0.5	1.0 (=0.5)

16. The exact breakdown of party support by subjective class is provided in table 5.4n:

Table 5.4n
Subjective class by vote, 1987

	Working class		Middle class		
	Aware	Unaware	Aware	Unaware	
Conservative	18.9	32.5	23.3	25.3	= 100.0
Labour	50.8	30.8	10.2	8.1	= 99.9
Other	30.3	33.4	17.0	19.3	= 100.0
Abstained	33.6	37.3	11.9	17.2	= 100.0

17. The odds ratios and Alford indices tend to suggest that subjective class voting has declined generally, but especially among unionists. The only group that has not changed its behaviour much in this regard is the non-unionised unaware one (that is, the one amongst which subjective class voting is probably lowest anyway); the two-party and third-party odds ratios for this group have not weakened since 1964, whilst they have for the unionised group. The full sets of odds, along with resulting odds ratios are reported in table 5.5n.

18. R.H. Hill suggested that trade unions are likely, in principle, to have some impact upon class identity and consciousness given that 'the emphasis upon collective solidarity and the orientation towards the collective resolution of common grievances stress normative ideals quite contrary to the individualistic ethic of the dominant ideology' (Hill 1979: 270). In examining the data he tested for the confounding effects of sex, occupation and workplace, but discovered that union membership had a distinct effect on radical class-linked attitudes regardless of these factors. Moreover, he also accepted the possibility that the relationship might not necessarily indicate anything about the positive influence of unions, since it could be explained simply by the particular propensity of those with a radical outlook to join a union. He controlled for this by examining separately the attitudes of those who were compulsory union members (through closed-shop arrangements) and those who were genuinely voluntary members. He discovered that both compulsory and voluntary members shared similarly high levels of class consciousness (ibid: 274-280). Clearly, Hill's work (conducted on data gathered in the early 1970s) supported the orthodox view that unions influenced people's political dispositions through the medium of class. He summarised his view by concluding that 'on the whole then, the data reviewed here suggest that union membership and participation is linked to a higher level of class consciousness amongst British workers, although this

consciousness remains within the bounds set by the less than revolutionary role played by the unions themselves' (ibid: 282). It seems possible that even this relationship may have become attenuated by the 1980s.

Table 5.5n
Odds on subjective class voting, 1964 and 1987

		Union		Non-union	
1964					
Two-party	a.	4.0	0.5 (= 8.5)	1.5	0.1 (= 1.2)
	b.	3.5	0.4 (= 9.2)	0.8	0.4 (= 2.4)
Third-party	a.	2.3	0.4 (= 9.2)	0.8	0.1 (= 8.7)
	b.	2.1	0.3 (= 7.6)	0.6	0.3 (= 2.0)
Anti-Cons.	a.	4.7	1.4 (= 3.5)	2.3	0.5 (= 4.3)
	b.	4.2	0.7 (= 5.7)	1.3	0.6 (= 2.3)
Scarbrough	a.	2.3	0.7 (= 3.1)	0.8	1.8 (= 0.4)
	b.	2.1	1.4 (= 1.6)	0.6	1.8 (= 0.3)
1987					
Two-party	a.	2.8	0.7 (= 4.3)	1.7	0.2 (= 6.9)
	b.	1.1	0.7 (= 1.6)	0.6	0.2 (= 3.7)
Third-party	a.	1.0	0.3 (= 3.0)	0.7	0.2 (= 4.3)
	b.	0.5	0.4 (= 1.3)	0.3	0.1 (= 2.9)
Anti-Cons.	a.	4.9	1.6 (= 3.1)	3.1	0.8 (= 4.1)
	b.	2.5	1.6 (= 1.6)	1.4	0.8 (= 1.9)
Scarbrough	a.	1.0	0.6 (= 1.6)	0.7	1.3 (= 0.5)
	b.	0.5	0.6 (= 0.8)	0.3	1.3 (= 0.2)

Note: a - 'Aware', b - 'Unaware'

6 Trade Unionist Voting Behaviour Since 1964: Sectoral Effects and Political Attitudes

The idea that production sectors operate in an electoral context has been developed chiefly by Patrick Dunleavy (Dunleavy 1980). His notion is that a potential new socio-political cleavage exists between those located in the public and private sectors of employment. A further subdivision exists within the private sector between large scale *(corporate sector)* and small scale *(market sector)* firms. Sectoral groups may be drawn into political conflict as a result of the emergence of a fiscal crisis of the state which forces an increasing burden of taxation on to the private sector. The market sector is particularly susceptible to the effects of this burden given that it is unable to pass on its extra costs to the consumer in the same way as corporate sector firms which wield a significant degree of monopoly power.

Sectoral cleavages cross-cut class cleavages and affect unionisation rates considerably; according to Dunleavy and Husbands, in fact, by the mid-1970s, any apparent relationship between class and unionisation was simply 'a classic case of spurious correlation' (Dunleavy and Husbands 1985: 130). Instead, unionisation varied according to sector, being high in the public and corporate sectors, and low in the market sector. This is interesting since it provokes the thought that the political role of the trade unions may come to lie increasingly in the mobilisation of sectoral conflicts rather than class-based ones. If the majority of union members are in the public sector, then the unions may become increasingly involved in issues which primarily have a public-versus-private aspect, rather than a working class-versus middle class one. In cutting across class loyalties, sectoral effects may also account for class dealignment. When Dunleavy first mooted the possibility of a sectoral effect in British politics, in the wake of the 1979 general election, it must have seemed plausible. Following the breakdown of the Labour government's bitterly contested public sector pay policy, it seemed possible that the party suffered the defections of erstwhile supporters amongst private sector unionists, who were angered that their public sector counterparts seemed to be able to get away with what they themselves could not - that is, militant industrial action without risking their jobs. So much for the speculation; what is the evidence for the existence of such a cleavage?

In fact, in so far as the 1979 election is concerned, Dunleavy was unable to demonstrate that there was any,

> ..additional direct effect from sectors to voting, over and above the indirect effect operating through trade union membership (Dunleavy and Husbands, 1985: 133).

In other words, sectors were only important in that they provided the context for differentiated levels of unionisation - and it was unionisation itself that had the direct impact on vote. By 1983, however, it is claimed that a genuine sectoral effect did occur, expressing itself chiefly in the way that non-manuals in the public sector were considerably more likely to vote Labour than their private sector counterparts. Table 6.1 reveals, however, that by 1987 this effect had virtually disappeared as private sector non-manuals swung to Labour while (the non-unionised) public sector swung away from Labour. Such changes hardly conform to the expected pattern of a sectoral effect, though perhaps there is some union-sector interaction implied in the maintenance of Labour support by unionised public sector non-manuals. With regard to manual workers we are again left wondering if it is a question of a union-sector interaction rather than an unmediated sectoral effect; among the non-unionised, both sectors manifest swings to Labour, though among the unionised, only the public sector produces such a swing. This notwithstanding, it is hard to avoid the overall impression that sectoral differences have diminished; the average sectoral difference in table 6.1 is 8.75 percentage points in 1983, but just 3.42 points in 1987.

However, effects of the type we are contemplating are complex and not easily absorbed through studying a cross-tabulation. An appropriate way of confirming the overall importance of sectoral effects for voting behaviour is once again the multiple classification analysis. Thus, when a term for sectoral effect is added to our basic social background model of the vote, the indications are that its impact is almost negligible in 1983[1]. The modest

Table 6.1
Vote by sector, class and unionisation, 1983 and 1987

Occup'n	Sector	Unionisation	Labour		Cons'ive		Other		Labour-Cons.	
			83	87	83	87	83	87	83	87
Manual	Public	Union	45	57	20	25	35	22	25	22
		Non-union	35	46	35	32	29	19	0	14
	Private	Union	47	46	29	27	24	27	18	19
		Non-union	37	45	33	35	30	20	4	10
Non-Manual	Public	Union	32	33	30	39	38	28	2	-6
		Non-union	26	18	53	52	21	30	-27	-34
	Private	Union	12	30	52	41	36	29	-40	-11
		Non-union	10	17	62	58	28	25	-52	-41

Source for 1983 figures: Dunleavy and Husbands, 1985: 133.

increase in the overall net impact of sector on vote in 1987 can hardly be regarded as significant, though it does perhaps serve to emphasise the variable's potential influence. The beta coefficients produced for such a model are:

	Beta coefficient		*Significance of effect*	
	1983	1987	1983	1987
Occupation	0.14	0.17	0.00	0.00
Unionisation	0.10	0.08	0.00	0.00
Housing	0.23	0.21	0.00	0.00
Education	0.01	0.01	0.45	0.53
Parental occupation	0.08	0.14	0.00	0.00
Production sector	0.03	0.05	0.07	0.00
Multiple R^2	0.13	0.15	0.00	0.00

Viewed one way, this actually confirms something which Dunleavy and Husbands themselves demonstrate. They produce evidence which seems to show, as much as anything, the relative weakness of the sectoral effect on voting. In a logit model of voting in 1983, they insist, for theoretical reasons, on entering first a term for the sector-vote relationship. Rather as with multiple regression analysis, the order in which independent variables are entered into models of this type will affect the amount of variance which they are able to explain. The earlier they are introduced, the stronger the effects are likely to be. Despite this, the sector-vote relationship explains less than any other term in the model.[2]

Furthermore, it must be emphasised that nothing about table 6.1 suggests the development of the production sectoral cleavage might explain the growing class dealignment of manual workers. In 1983 there was virtually no difference between private and public sector manual employees in terms of the level of support that they offered the Labour Party; and this held equally for both union members and non-members. Neither was there any shift from Labour in 1987 by private sector manual union members (which the theory of sectoral effects would lead one to expect), although it is true that they did not actually swing towards the Party in the way that their public sector counterparts did.

Nonetheless, the production sector argument is an interesting one with potential bearing on the future political role of the unions. It would not be wise to dismiss its importance entirely, therefore. Even if there is hardly an abundance of convincing evidence confirming the direct impact of sector upon vote as yet, it is conceivable that sectoral factors might be starting, in some tangible way, to impinge upon the political consciousness of voters in Britain. For instance, sectoral interests might well affect the way in which people make certain issue assessments, even if they are rarely a direct determinant of the voting choice itself. The unions could be instrumental in this. For example, the unions are in a uniquely influential position to run campaigns aimed at drawing the electorate's attention to the nature of the effects of privatisation and public spending cuts on the level and quality of public services in health, education and welfare (see Taylor 1987b). This implies that, with help from the unions, Labour could win votes by exploiting and promoting certain sectorally relevant issues. Although Dunleavy himself is unwilling to countenance the general usefulness of issue-based explanations of voting behaviour, it is interesting to consider the question of whether sectoral location appears to be in any way related to voters' political attitudes.

This is best achieved with attitudinal scales. For instance, an impression of the relative impact of sector on attitudes can be gained by creating a scale from responses to questions about issues which could plausibly be considered relevant to either class or sectoral interests. Using the 1987 data set, such a scale has been constructed from questions about the trade off between local authority services and taxes, about political and financial support for public or private educational and health services, and about the desirability of privatisation and public spending cuts.[3] In twentieth century Britain, all of these questions have been debated largely in terms of class ideology. Such questions have been central to the classic two-party, two-class model of political conflict. For the working class, the state has been crucial in meeting the requirements of its collective interest. However, it might be argued that these are questions which are now more relevant to matters of sectoral interest. Issues of public spending cuts, of the encouragement of private education and health services, and of privatisation are all of paramount concern to those employed in the public sector. These are the citizens who may stand to lose their jobs, or at least find themselves working under new constraints and pressures, as a result of the implementation of such policies. Consequently, a prima facie case may be made suggesting that attitudes concerning these questions could be influenced by either class or sectoral interest.

Having constructed an attitudinal scale from people's responses to the relevant questions, a multiple classification analysis may be performed with position on this attitudinal scale as the dependent variable, and with occupational class and sector as the independent variables. This gives us some notion of the relative importance of sectoral location. The betas produced were 0.13 for class and 0.07 for production sector; what this means in terms of location on the attitudinal scale is easily demonstrated (bearing in mind that -1.00 represents the far right of the scale and 1.00 represents the far left):

Attitudinal location of occupational and sectoral groups

Non-manual	0.35
Manual	0.45
Private sector employees	0.38
Public sector employees	0.43

	Beta coefficient	*Significance of effect*
Occupation	0.13	0.00
Production sector	0.07	0.00
Multiple R^2	0.02	0.00

It is clear from this analysis, that sectoral differences are only half as great as class differences. This result can be supplemented by a similar analysis of the importance of occupational sector for voters' more general ideological values. These underlying, or 'synoptic' values, as they have been called - and of which more below - can be similarly constructed into an attitudinal scale with precisely the same properties. On such a scale there is virtually no difference between private and public sector workers, as confirmed by the beta coefficient of just 0.01 for sectoral location (at a significance level of only 0.724) when a multiple classification analysis is performed. Thus, whilst sectoral interest has virtually no apparent influence upon voters' broad ideological stances, it may have some, albeit rather slight, significance for certain types of directly relevant political question. Whilst not blinding ourselves to its potential significance for trade unionists' political consciousnesses, therefore, it must be concluded that sectoral location is hardly of profound importance as yet, and certainly does not provide as clear a basis for attitudinal or electoral variation as occupational class.

Trade unions and issue assessments

We have seen that unions can no longer be regarded as important instruments of class socialisation; apparently, their influence on electoral behaviour does not yet work through the sectoral cleavage either. However, there remains the possibility that unions maintain some capacity for influencing voters' attitudes. In chapter 4 we saw that there is a distinction between the broad underlying values which voters hold in the long term and the evaluations they make of certain issues that may be salient in a particular short term context. Both are political attitudes, and it is their connection with unionisation which we will be examining in the rest of this chapter. We will start with short term issue assessments. Can trade unions influence the short term assessments made by their members at election time?

The first way in which we can approach this question is to add a term representing respondent's issue assessments to our basic social background model of vote. We can then see how much impact trade unionism continues to have independently of issue assessments. This approach allows us to focus on whether unions affect voting only via their prior impact on issue assessments. In the course of chapter 4, various issue models were reviewed and it was concluded that one of the most realistic and empirically useful was the retrospective performance model pioneered by Fiorina. It is interesting to adopt such an approach in looking at the behaviour of union members. Specifically, a variable has been constructed which is designed to tap evaluations of past performance by the incumbent government over a range of salient public issues. These assessments have been weighted according to the importance that each respondent ascribed to the issue's impact on the voting decision, and according to the respondent's perception of the capacity of *any* government to take effective action on an issue.[4] (An interesting account of the significance of retrospective issue assessments for voting choice in Britain can be found in Whiteley, 1983.)

Unfortunately, the sort of data that would permit one to construct this type of issue variable only exists in our 1987 data set. However, it is probably not essential that we consider issue effects for 1964 given that it is well established that such effects were generally less prevalent at that time. Moreover, we know that union membership was more closely associated with class and partisan identity then. The beta coefficients for all the social background variables in our model of vote are reported in Table 6.2.

Table 6.2
The impact of issue assessments and social background on vote, 1987

	Beta coefficient		*Significance level*
Occupational class	0.15	(0.17)	0.00
Unionisation	0.06	(0.08)	0.00
Housing	0.19	(0.21)	0.00
Education	0.00	(0.01)	0.89
Production sector	0.03	(0.05)	0.08
Parental occupational class	0.10	(0.14)	0.00
Multiple R^2	0.26	(0.15)	0.00

Note: Figures in parenthesis show beta coefficients prior to the addition to the model of a term for retrospective assessment.

The overall model explains 26% of the variance in voting, compared with 15% when the retrospective issue assessment variable is omitted. Interval scales such as the retrospective assessment one do not produce beta coefficients under the multiple classification procedure, but it is certain enough that it is an important variable in the model. Indeed, analysis of sums of squares reveals that over half of all the explained variance in the model is attributable to the impact of retrospective assessment (55% to be precise, at a significance level of 0.00). Clearly, retrospective evaluation of governmental performance on issues is the single variable most strongly related to voting choice; in addition, three of the social background variables remain of some importance (occupational class, housing and parental occupation). In common with most of the other variables in the model, the unionisation parameter is weakened slightly when retrospective assessments are added. To recall, unionisation produced a beta coefficient of 0.08 in the social background model of vote, and this is reduced to 0.06 when the effect of retrospective judgements is added. Therefore, it would seem that unionisation retains some direct impact on vote which is independent of issue evaluations, though it is not particularly strong.

However, this only serves as preliminary evidence regarding the way in which trade unions now influence voting decisions. We still need to seek out direct evidence of unionisation's influence on the way in which people think about political issues. The first way in which we can do this is by simply checking if trade union membership affects the retrospective assessment variable itself. This can be done by running a multiple classification analysis with retrospective assessment as the dependent variable. As in the case of sectoral attitudes, the retrospective assessment variable is a scale running from -1 (indicating 100% pro-Conservative assessments, *and* that all relevant issues are considered very important to vote, *and* that governments are generally considered to be capable of taking effective action on these issues) to +1 (indicating an extreme anti-Conservative evaluation). Given this, we may examine the differences between the average positions on the scale of various social groups, including trade unionists and non-unionists.

Table 6.3

Average positions of social group members on retrospective performance scale, 1987

Union	0.09	Non-union	0.04
Manual	0.07	Non-manual	0.04
Council tenant	0.09	Non-council tenant	0.04
Minimum schooling	0.06	Further schooling	0.04
Manual father	0.07	Father non-manual	0.02
Public sector	0.08	Private sector	0.04

Whilst non-union members are apparently more likely than members to regard the 1983-87 Conservative government's record favourably, the difference does not appear great at first glance. On the other hand, it is important to regard the impact of union membership in the context of other social background factors which might influence attitudes and judgements. Compared to these other factors, unionisation is not such an insignificant influence. It distinguishes voters in terms of the retrospective assessments they make as strongly as any other social variable, in fact. The difference of five scale points between unionists and non-unionists is equalled only by differences on the housing and parental occupation variables. Five points may not sound a large difference, but this should probably be understood largely as an artefact of the way the scale is constructed. Beyond this, one should acknowledge that social location may not generally influence retrospective evaluations strongly. Nevertheless, trade unionists prove to be more anti-Conservative/pro-Labour than any other social group except council tenants in the retrospective evaluations they make. This impression of relative importance is confirmed by the beta coefficients for all social background factors which are reported in table 6.4. Only parental occupation produces a stronger effect.

Table 6.4
The impact of social background on retrospective issue assessments of voters, 1987

	Beta coefficients	*Significance of effect*
Occupational class	0.04	0.05
Unionisation	0.06	0.00
Housing	0.06	0.00
Education	0.03	0.14
Production sector	0.06	0.00
Parental class	0.10	0.00
Multiple R^2	0.03	0.00

Trade unions and underlying political values

So far, we have concentrated on analysing the importance of union membership in influencing the short-term assessments people make of governmental performance. However, it may also be important to understand something of trade union impact on people's underlying values. This obliges us to move back into the domain of long term predispositions, even though we continue to focus upon attitudinal effects. One of the most insightful but straightforward accounts of the role of underlying values has been given by the *How Britain Votes* team, who assert that:

> ..voting choices are not made on the basis of a conscious weighing in the balance of alternative policies..electoral choice is based on a much broader, more synoptic evaluation of parties than the consumer theory allows for...Factors such as policies, record in office, putative ability to implement a programme, leadership, unity of purpose may all come into it, but none is paramount..It is the fit between the general character of the party and the voter's own general ideology which, we believe, best accounts for electoral choice (Heath et al 1985: 99).

Is it at all likely that trade unions might have some influence over the development of these synoptic values in their members? Heath and his colleagues echoed David Robertson and others in arguing that general ideological predispositions are best regarded as dividing along two distinct attitudinal dimensions in the case of the British electorate. One of these dimensions reflects class linked attitudes, whilst the other reflects the continuum between social liberalism and authoritarianism. This is a useful notion upon which to base an examination of the ideological profile of trade unionists.

Heath argues that certain issues are particularly sensitive to underlying ideology, and therefore serve as good indicators of synoptic values. In particular, questions about nationalisation or privatisation, and about income redistribution are acute indicators of traditional class values in modern Britain. On the other hand, attitudes towards health and social services, the death penalty or nuclear disarmament are effective indicators of degree of social liberalism (ibid: 117-118). Where have trade unionists stood on such issues since the 1960s? Table 6.5 indicates the extent to which they have opted for left wing and liberal responses to all these questions.

We can obtain a rough idea of the connection between unionisation and synoptic values by simply subtracting the non-union percentages from the union percentages in table 6.5. This gives a sort of index of union distinctiveness on such values, and it is interesting to note two things about this (see table 6.6). Firstly, on two of the four attitudes which can be measured both in 1964 and 1987 (nationalisation and health and social services) it is obvious that the index has dropped considerably. On one other attitude (the death penalty) there has been little overall change in the gap between union members and non-members, although there is one difference in 1987; by this election it was the non-members who were slightly more in favour of capital punishment. On the final attitude (nuclear disarmament) the gap between

Table 6.5
The synoptic attitudes of trade unionists, 1964 and 1987

	Union		Non-union	
	1964	1987	1964	1987
Class Values				
Income redistribution	N.A	52.2	N.A	40.8
Nationalisation	42.0	21.1	21.1	15.8
Liberal Values				
Health & social services	87.4	95.3	74.2	90.2
Death penalty	18.7	19.5	21.5	16.3
Nuclear disarmament	9.4	26.6	8.3	19.2

Note: Figures are percentages opting for left wing responses to questions tapping class values and for liberal responses to questions tapping degree of social liberalism.

members and non-members has grown a little. However, the proportions of both groups in favour of disarmament grew considerably between 1964 and 1987, and the actual gap in the latter year was hardly a great one. The second notable point is that by 1987 trade unionists were more likely to hold left wing and liberal attitudes than non-unionists for all of the indicators we have checked. However, in no case is the union/non-union gap especially considerable, with the possible exception of the question of the redistribution of income.

Table 6.6
Index of union distinctiveness

	1964	1987
Nationalisation	20.9	5.3
Income redistribution	N.A	11.4
Health & social services	13.4	4.2
Death penalty	-2.8	3.2
Nuclear disarmament	1.1	7.4

The picture of how distinct union members' values are, can be further elaborated in a spatial sense. That is, the distribution of attitudinal preferences along the two underlying ideological dimensions can be visually represented on a map of electors' values. This is achieved by a straightforward process of combining crosstabulations. Similar questions about nationalisation (a class values indicator), the death penalty and nuclear disarmament (liberal values indicators) were asked in both 1964 and 1987, and the responses can be coded similarly for all these questions for both years. This means that we can make very direct comparisons of these attitudes across time. On the two dimensional maps which can be created from these attitudes, in the manner of Heath and his colleagues, left wing responses fall to the west of one dimension and liberal responses to the north of the other; consequently, Labour's 'heartland' theoretically lies to the north west, the Conservatives' to the south east and, the Liberal Democrats' forerunners to the north east. Table 6.7 shows the distribution of trade unionists and non-unionists on these ideological maps.

Table 6.7
An ideological map of union members and non-members, 1964 and 1987: Nationalisation by capital punishment

		More Nationalisation		No Change		More Privatisation	
		1964	1987	1964	1987	1964	1987
Anti-death penalty	union	10.2	5.4	6.9	9.9	2.1	4.5
	non-union	6.3	3.7	12.6	8.7	3.4	4.0
Not sure	union	1.0	1.0	2.2	3.1	0.4	1.2
	non-union	1.8	0.9	4.8	3.9	1.2	1.6
Pro-death penalty	union	31.0	14.4	32.9	38.6	13.4	21.8
	non-union	13.0	11.0	40.2	37.3	16.6	29.1

As an ideological map, table 6.7 is in one respect, perhaps, not entirely what one would expect, since there is a strong tendency for both unionists and non-unionists to favour the death penalty in both years. Nevertheless, it can be observed that members are more likely than non-members to be found in the most north westerly cell, especially in 1964; conversely, non-members are more likely than members to be found in the most south easterly cell, especially in 1987. Differences are not great in the most north easterly segment of the map for either year. Overall, this suggests that members and non-members do differ somewhat, though not greatly, in their basic political values. An especially notable feature of the table is the rightward shift of trade unionists on the question of nationalisation, and this may have served to draw members closer to non-members in an ideological sense.[5]

To what degree precisely do the underlying values of union members differ from those of non-members? The simplest way of answering this question is to repeat the process of subtracting the non-union percentages from union percentages in each of the cells in table 6.7. This produces the index of union distinctiveness reported in table 6.8, which reveals that the differences between members and non-members were greater in 1964 than in 1987. Indeed, the union/non-union gap was greater in 1964 in 8 out of the 9 cells on our ideological map; the average cell difference between members and non-members in 1964 was 4.8 percentage points, compared to just 1.9 for 1987. Clearly, the basic ideological values of trade unionists are no longer so very different from those of non-unionists.

Table 6.8
Index of union members' ideological distinctiveness, 1964 and 1987

	More Nationalisation		No Change		More Privatisation	
	1964	1987	1964	1987	1964	1987
Anti-death penalty	3.9	1.7	-5.7	1.2	-1.3	0.5
Not sure	-0.8	0.1	-2.6	-0.8	-0.8	-0.4
Pro-death penalty	18.0	3.4	-7.3	1.3	-3.2	-7.3

Note: Figures are differences between unionists and non-unionists (produced by subtracting non-union percentages from union percentages in each of the cells in table 6.7). Average cell difference 1964 = 4.8, average cell difference 1987 = 1.9.

The impression of a diminishing ideological gap between trade unionists and non-unionists can be confirmed by recourse, once more, to the technique of multiple classification analysis. The general synoptic values we have been examining individually or in two-dimensional space, can be combined into an overall ideological scale which is constructed in a similar fashion to the retrospective performance scale. Thus, an additive attitudinal scale can be created from electors' responses to the questions about nationalisation, income redistribution, health and social services, the death penalty and nuclear disarmament. Unfortunately, the 1964 survey included no question on income redistribution, which means that this scale is not strictly comparable to the 1987 ideological scale; nonetheless, the scales must be similar enough to be strongly indicative. The scale runs, as before from -1 to +1, with -1 representing the point at which a respondent opts only for right wing alternatives on the various issues comprising the scale, and +1 that at which he or she opts solely for left wing alternatives. Table 6.9 shows how the various social categories, including unionists and non-unionists, differ on this scale. Given the aforementioned proviso about the lack of strict comparability in the two scales, one has to be careful about accepting at face value the apparent leftward shift of all groups over the period between the two surveys. (If this actually is an accurate reflection of reality, then it probably owes

Table 6.9

The average position of various social groups on synoptic values scales, 1964 and 1987[6]

	1964		
Union	-0.07	Non-union	-0.15
Manual	-0.12	Non-manual	-0.12
Council tenant	-0.09	Non-council tenant	-0.13
Father manual	-0.12	Father non-manual	-0.12
Minimum schooling	-0.12	Further schooling	-0.11
	1987		
Union	0.08	Non-union	0.08
Manual	0.10	Non-manual	0.07
Council tenant	0.12	Non-council tenant	0.07
Father manual	0.08	Father non-manual	0.09
Minimum schooling	0.09	Further schooling	0.06
Public sector	0.08	Private sector	0.09

much to the considerable movement of mass opinion on the disarmament issue. It is quite clear that the 1987 sample is far more in favour of nuclear disarmament than the 1964 sample.) One also has to be careful about inferring change directly from cross-sectional rather than panel data. Nevertheless, the evidence is very suggestive. We appear to have confirmation of the finding that ideological differences between trade unionists and non-unionists have diminished - indeed, utterly disappeared, according to this analysis of variance. This is best illustrated by an examination of the betas for trade unionism and the other social background variables when the attitudinal scale is treated as dependent upon them. The betas suggest that unionisation is actually the most important social determinant of ideological position in 1964, whereas it is the least important (and statistically least significant) by 1987.

Table 6.10

The impact of social background on the general ideological values of voters, 1964 and 1987

	Beta coefficient		*Significance of effect*	
	<u>1983</u>	<u>1987</u>	<u>1983</u>	<u>1987</u>
Occupational class	0.04	0.05	0.00	0.02
Unionisation	0.12	0.00	0.00	0.95
Housing	0.05	0.04	0.00	0.03
Education	0.02	0.04	0.07	0.08
Parental class	0.03	0.04	0.01	0.06
Production sector	-	0.01	-	0.72
Multiple R^2	0.02	0.01	0.00	0.00

Note: Production sector is excluded from the 1964 analysis since it does not exist as a variable in the 1964 data set.[7]

Overall, it would seem that in so far as trade union membership continues to affect voting behaviour it does so only partly through its capacity to influence people's attitudes; it appears to have some influence upon short-term issue assessments, but little continuing impact on underlying ideological values. Combined with the knowledge that unions have lost their capacity to affect partisan commitment, this latter finding implies the general inability of unions to inspire any of the long term influences that affect voting behaviour. Rather, unionisation is limited to influencing the short term assessments that go some of the way to making up voting choice - possibly through interacting with emerging sectoral interests. If any social background factors influence underlying ideology at all, they would seem to be limited to those that remain connected in some way with class in Britain - occupation, parental occupation, housing and education. These are the only social factors which have statistically significant (though not necessarily strong) effects on ideology, according to the analysis conducted here. These factors may well affect voting decisions through one of three paths - the direct one, through influencing long term ideology or through influencing short term performance assessments. Unionisation and sector have little ideological connection, and their influence upon voting behaviour is probably only either direct or via short term assessments. Thus, we end up with a potential model of the effect that union membership has on vote which looks rather like that portrayed in figure 6.1.

Figure 6.1

A model of voting choice, incorporating ideology, issue assessments and social background

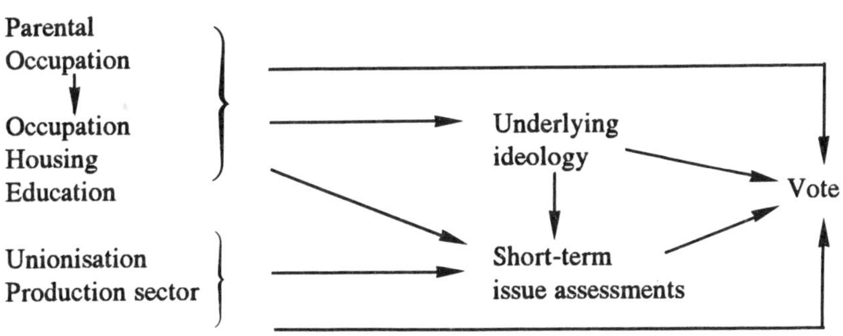

This model can be tested using the multiple classification procedure by adding the retrospective assessment and general ideological scales to the basic social background variables, and entering them subsequently to the latter. This model explains 28% of the vote, with housing and occupation emerging as the most important explanatory social background variables, as table 6.11 indicates. All told, the social background factors account for slightly over half of all explained variance in the model (52%), whilst the combined effect of the attitudinal variables (ideology and restrospective assessment) accounts for the remainder. It is likely that one or the other of the attitudinal variables has greater impact than any single social background variable, though we cannot directly confirm this through multiple classification analysis.

Table 6.11
Beta coefficients of social background influences on vote, after controlling for ideology and retrospective performance evaluations, 1987

	Beta coefficients	*Significance of effect*
Occupation	0.14	0.00
Unionisation	0.06	0.00
Housing	0.18	0.00
Parental occupation	0.10	0.00
Education	0.00	0.53
Sector	0.03	0.00
General ideology	-	0.00
Retrospective assessments	-	0.00
Multiple R^2	0.28	0.00

In summary, trade unions have little continuing influence over long term predispositions. We have already seen that their effect on partisan and class identity is diminished; now it seems that they exert little or no influence over synoptic values. Unions seem to have little capacity to socialise people in terms of underlying values, social identities or political loyalties. In short, Butler and Stokes' view of the influence of unions on the political behaviour of the British electorate has become obsolete. Unions may, nevertheless, retain a residual capacity to influence the short term assessments that their members make at election time, especially if those members are concerned about crisis in the public sector.

Notes

1. Note that production sector was coded '1' if the respondent was employed in the public sector, and '0' if in the private sector. Of course, Dunleavy would not welcome the idea of including in the model variables such as parental class and education, which reflect socialisation effects, along with the other terms which, for him, reflect the direct impact of group interests. But it should be noted that the *eta* coefficient for production sector - that is, the uncontrolled coefficient for vote and sector - is no higher than 0.03 in 1983 and 0.04 in 1987. Thus, the simple bivariate relationship between vote and sector, without taking into account the impact of any other variable, is still low.

2. The key results that Dunleavy and Husbands obtain from their preferred logit model of the influence of production sector upon vote in 1983 are recorded in table 6.1n. The G^2 statistics reported indicate the degree of independent variance within a table that is accounted for by any given relationship. One sees clearly that, despite being the first term introduced into the model, the sector/vote relationship only contributes an independent conditional G^2 of 8.38%; even the term for the association between union membership and vote explains more of the variance than this, despite being the final effect introduced into the model, sequentially speaking. Equally obviously, the most important single effect in the entire model appears to be that for the relationship between class and vote.

Table 6.1n
The relative importance of the relationship between sector and vote

Relationship	Conditional G^2
Sector-vote	8.38%
Gender-class-vote	14.76%
Class-vote	92.83%
Unionisation-vote	9.03%

The G^2 statistic is the counterpart of the familiar R^2 in regression - it indicates the proportion of variance explained.

Source: Dunleavy and Husbands 1985: 136

3. The questions from which this particular attitudinal scale was constructed were the following:

- i. Are you in favour of more nationalisation/privatisation of companies by government?
- ii. Should the government reduce public spending generally?
- iii. Should local authorities generally choose to increase services and rates or reduce spending?
- iv. Should the government encourage private medicine?
- v. Should the government get rid of private education?
- vi. Should the government put more money into the NHS?
- vii. Should the government spend more on education?

When the sense of the reply was such that it represented a left wing response it was given a value of +1; right wing replies were coded -1, and 'Don't Knows' 0. The values of these coded responses were simply added together, and then divided by the number of valid responses so that the range of the scale ran from -1 (only right wing attitudes preferred) through to +1 (only left wing attitudes). A reliability test was performed on this scale which produced a Cronbach Alpha coefficient of 0.50.

4. The retrospective assessment scale is constructed in a similar fashion to the scale described in the preceding note. Respondents were asked how well they thought the Conservative government had handled a number of issues over the previous four years (unemployment, prices, taxes, health and social services, crime, education and defence). Responses were coded from +1 (unfavourable to the Conservatives) to -1 (favourable to the Conservatives). These initial 'scores' were then weighted by two if the respondent perceived that governments in general had the potential to 'do a lot' about the issue, but only by half if governments were not regarded as especially competent to deal with the problem. In addition, a score was weighted by two if the issue was seen as having been 'quite important' to the respondent's vote, and by three if it was regarded as having been 'very important'. Again scores were divided by the number of valid responses in order to give a scale running from -1 to +1. A Cronbach Alpha reliability coefficient of 0.74 was recorded for this retrospective evaluation scale. When a term for this scale was added to the basic social background model of vote the following picture of the distribution of variance emerged, in terms of the sum of squares:

Variance	*Sum of squares*
Explained by retrospective assessment	79.70
Explained by social background	53.53
Explained by interactions of independent variables	12.92
Total explained variation	146.15
Residual	372.23
Total Variation	518.39

5. It should be noted that the essential picture emerging from table 6.7 was confirmed in an alternative version of the ideological map constructed from voters' positions on the issues of nationalisation and nuclear disarmament.

6. Again, the method of synoptic value scale construction was such that it ran from -1 (completely right wing preferences) to +1 (completely left wing preferences). The questions from which the scales were constructed were the following:

1964:

i. There's a lot of talk about nationalising industry. Which of these statements comes closest to what you yourself feel should be done?

a. A lot more industries should be nationalised.
b. Only a few more industries should be nationalised.
c. No more industries should be nationalised, but the industries that are nationalised now should stay nationalised.
d. Some of the industries that are now nationalised should be denationalised.
e. No opinion/Don't know.

ii. Do you feel that the government should spend more on pensions and social services, or do you feel that the spending for social services should stay about as it is now?

iii. Would you like to see the death penalty kept or abolished?

iv. Which of these three statements comes closest to what you yourself feel should be done?
a. Britain should keep her own nuclear weapons independent of other countries.
b. Britain should have nuclear weapons only as part of a western defence system.
c. Britain should have nothing to do with nuclear weapons under any circumstances.

1987:

Essentially the same questions were included with regard to nationalisation, the death penalty and nuclear disarmament, whilst the following questions were added:

i. Should income be redistributed towards ordinary working people or not?

ii. Should the government put more money into the NHS?

Cronbach Alphas of 0.26 for 1964 and 0.55 for 1987 were recorded.

7. It must be acknowledged that the general ideological scale employed here risks giving a misleading impression in one sense, since it attempts to collapse two distinct value dimensions into one. As an alternative, therefore, two separate synoptic values scales tapping liberal and class attitudes respectively, were also created. This yielded some interesting results. It seemed reasonable to suppose that combining both sets of values into a one-dimensional scale might weaken its reliability. However, when separate scales were constructed solely from the liberal attitude indicators on the one hand, and only from the class attitude indicators on the other, it was discovered that reliability was not in fact enhanced. Thus, the Alpha coefficients for the liberal values scales were 0.16 for 1964 and 0.34 for 1987. An additive class scale could not be constructed for 1964 since there was only one indicator (attitude on

nationalisation), but for 1987 it was 0.53. Thus, in all cases, reliability tests indicated that there was little advantage in disaggregating general ideological scales in this way.

Nonetheless, multiple classification analyses of the alternative ideological scales revealed patterns which the overall one-dimensional scale might have obscured. The details of the attitudinal models are reported in table 6.2n. On the one-dimensional scale for 1987, no social variable appeared to have much of an effect on underlying values; the alternatives suggest that housing, occupation, parental class, and to a lesser extent, unionisation and sector all

Table 6.2n
Social background and disaggregated synoptic values scales, 1964 & 1987

	Beta coefficients		*Significance of effects*	
	Liberal values	Class values	Liberal values	Class values
1964				
Occupation	0.04	-	0.00	-
Unionisation	0.06	-	0.00	-
Housing	0.05	-	0.00	-
Parental class	0.04	-	0.80	-
Education	0.02	-	0.10	-
Sector	-	-	-	-
Multiple R^2	0.01	-	0.00	-
1987				
Occupation	0.03	0.13	0.10	0.00
Unionisation	0.03	0.07	0.09	0.00
Housing	0.04	0.15	0.07	0.00
Parental class	0.03	0.11	0.11	0.00
Education	0.12	0.01	0.00	0.80
Sector	0.05	0.07	0.02	0.00
Multiple R^2	0.02	0.09	0.00	0.00

have some influence on class values, however. Liberal values seem to be notably affected by educational experience, on the other hand. Nothing appears to have influenced liberal values greatly in 1964, but we may assume that the above-mentioned class linked factors all had at least as much impact in 1964 as in 1987.

Given the discovery in chapter 5 that class voting and identity have weakened among union members, it is a little surprising to find that they do retain some distinctly class-related attitudes after all. Though interesting, three observations need to be made about these findings, however. Firstly, it should be borne in mind that these alternative scales may not be such reliable indicators, especially in the case of the liberal values variable. Secondly, they do not necessarily alter greatly the central argument about the position of unions. Relative to other social background factors, union membership still has little association with fundamental values in 1987. It is the equal weakest influence on liberal values, and only education has less impact on class values. Thirdly, even if we do tentatively accept that class-related values are to some extent connected with unionisation, we can infer nothing about causality within the relationship. It is not possible to state categorically that trade unions influence class attitudes; it is just as likely that class-conscious individuals are especially inclined to join unions on ideological grounds. Given the growth of white collar unionism and the geographic dispersion of union membership, there are strong grounds for doubting that trade unions continue to influence the ideological predispositions of their members.

Note also that, for the sake of completeness, a version of the 'final' model of vote for 1987 (see table 6.11) was run with disaggregated ideological variables. The overall explanatory value of this model did increase notably (from 28% to 37%); the details of this model are as follows:

	Beta coefficients	*Significance of effect*
Occupation	0.11	0.00
Unionisation	0.03	0.00
Housing	0.14	0.00
Parental occupation	0.07	0.00
Education	0.02	0.59
Sector	0.01	0.00
Retrospective assessments	-	0.00
Liberal values	-	0.00
Class values	-	0.00
Multiple R^2	0.37	0.00

61.2% of the explained variance within this model is accounted for by the attitudinal variables, and the remainder by the social background factors. It is interesting also to observe that union membership now has very little remaining independent impact upon vote; class and housing are the only social background factors that really maintain any influence.

7 Trade Unions and the Future of the Labour Party

Since the early 1960s the electoral behaviour of British trade union members has given the lie to the notion that they can generally be assumed to sustain a political commitment to the Labour Party. Although the pattern of their support has fluctuated somewhat, an underlying trend is apparent, and it is not a trend that Labour can draw comfort from. Considerably fewer unionists have voted for the party in the general elections since October 1974, and fewer have been inclined to express a strong partisan identification with it. In the opening chapter it was noted that previous analysis of this phenomenon was either too brief or too vague to be really enlightening. Hopefully, our understanding of what has happened over the past quarter of a century is a little better now.

It was suggested initially that there could be, broadly speaking, three possible types of explanation of the changing voting behaviour manifested by union members - social, political and organisational. To start with the latter first, we confronted the possibility that the reduced organisational input of the unions into the Labour Party might have somehow resulted in a weaker political mobilisation of their own memberships. A review of the organisational links between the party and the affiliated unions quickly dispelled this notion. It is quite clear that this organisational relationship cannot be considered to have weakened significantly since the early 1960s; affiliated membership is a greater proportion of total party membership than ever and, consequently, so is the financial dependence of the national party organisation upon the unions. (There is no way of knowing precisely how the financial link between the party and the unions has altered at the local level, although it is clear that it is, and probably always has been, weaker than at national level.) The role that the unions played in the Labour Party's policy making activity in 1987 remained as significant as it did at the beginning of the period, though we are now confronted with the possibility of reform of the block vote. The number of unions which remain wedded to the idea of sponsoring members of parliament has not declined since 1964, and the development of bodies like TULV, the TUCC and TUFL demonstrates that the unions are prepared to seek new ways of making their organisational relationship with the party more effective (as, indeed, does the growing commitment to political education). The success of the campaigns over the retention of political funds in 1985-86 summed up the value the unions continue to place on the link with the party - whilst rendering its electoral decline among their members more of a paradox, perhaps. Whatever, the organisational factor cannot convincingly be paraded as the key reason underlying this decline - though it may well remain important for the future performance of the Labour Party at the polls. We must perforce turn to social and political factors for an understanding of the electoral changes that have occurred.

The weakened association between union membership and class behaviour in the electoral context is more likely to be explained by the continuing erosion of the distinctive class character of unions than by their increasing relevance for the mobilisation of the production sector cleavage. As yet there is little or no hard evidence to persuade one of the importance of this line of socio-political conflict for voting behaviour in Britain, although its potential cannot be ignored. An interaction between social and political factors seems to be the most plausible way of explaining the particularly notable dealignment of a part of Labour's core constituency - manual trade unionists who identify with the working class. In the first place, pioneering sociological work in the 1960s demonstrated that certain sections of the working class were clearly instrumental in outlook; in the second place, political relationships between the party and the unions have passed through several phases of tension, periods which coincide closely with shifts in manual unionists' electoral alignment. It seems logical to contend that the disillusion arising from these periods of tension is likely to have affected the voting behaviour of manual trade unionists, given their instrumentality. One might also speculate as to whether Labour would have been so electorally vulnerable to the impact of this party-union conflict if it had historically attempted the ideological encapsulation of the British working class. There is evidence to suggest that ideological mobilisation serves as a form of partisan reinforcement that can withstand specific disappointments with aspects of party performance

(Whiteley 1983). It should be added that the likelihood of satisfying the instrumental aspirations of all trade unionists has probably diminished with the growing diversity of union interests. Furthermore, we have noted that the weakening control some union leaderships have been able to exert over their memberships has exacerbated party-union tensions at certain times, notably in the late 1960s and 1970s.

This may go a long way towards providing a satisfactory explanation of the declining association between unionisation and voting behaviour, and the change in members' electoral alignment. But what explains the remaining electoral influence that unions have? In view of our finding that the connection between unionisation and the long term factors underlying voting choice has weakened, it would seem that such importance as unionisation does retain flows largely via short term factors like issue and performance assessments. That unions should now influence vote in this way is hardly surprising given the weakening class and partisan loyalties of their memberships. Individuals without strong identities and loyalties are forced to reassess their position at each electoral consultation. It is interesting and important to note that this means we cannot simply say that trade unions are less important for electoral behaviour in Britain than they formerly were. Though the multiple classification analyses examined in chapters 5 and 6 clearly indicate the declining influence of unionisation between 1964 and 1987, it is not certain that things will remain this way. If unionisation now works largely through its influence on short term assessments, then its overall influence will surely fluctuate according to its connection with salient election campaign issues. For example, should industrial relations once more become a salient issue in the context of an election campaign, it is quite possible that trade union membership will again become a prominent correlate of voting behaviour.

Perhaps we can be more precise about how unions might affect the short term evaluations that people make. For a start, there is one immediately obvious sense in which unions can affect issue assessments - namely, in so far as they are 'an issue' themselves. This is why the salience of industrial relations is important for the unions. Despite the problematic relations of the last twenty five years, Labour is still undoubtedly perceived as being connected with the unions, as somehow being a spokesman for the special interest of the unions. It is therefore inevitable that the Party's popularity suffers in times of newsworthy and (invariably unpopular) industrial unrest. In this sense, the unions were critically important influences on the outcomes of the elections of 1974 and 1979, and they were of some significance in 1970.

But it is, of course, also possible that the unions will be increasingly significant in affecting the issue perceptions of voters through their organisation of publicity campaigns which are not directly a question of industrial relations. In this respect, we have already mentioned the potential that the unions have over issues relating to the provision of public services. Moreover, in the mid-1980s the unions argued forcibly that the significance of the political fund ballots lay precisely in the need to protect the right to run campaigns of this sort. Indeed, in an article co-authored by Labour's first national Trade Union Liaison Officer, it was pointed out that non-partisan political activity by unions has been increasing.

> The return to free collective bargaining after 1980 was an earthquake in the bargaining system. Far from involving less political activity, the demise of incomes policy and the Conservative government's attack on unions and the public sector have stimulated a surge in political campaigning. Battles over anti-union legislation, privatisation, local authority and NHS cuts, compulsory tendering, cuts in nationalised industries' spending and a host of other issues have all demanded ever-growing political resources (Upham and Wilson 1989: 8).

These authors continue to note that such political activities are not necessarily limited to issues which directly affect the interests of members; it is apparent that union affiliations and contributions to bodies like the CND, Amnesty International, the NCCL, War On Want and Anti-Apartheid groups have also burgeoned. This tends to dovetail with the impression that unions can influence the evaluations voters make of short-term policy issues such as past governmental performance. To reiterate then, it is not inconceivable that unions may be highly influential again for the outcome of an election, but only when they have a direct bearing on salient campaign issues. Without this, the residual impact of unionisation is likely to be distinctly limited, as in 1983 and 1987.[1] This weakened residual effect is a consequence of the lost social and ideological distinctiveness of trade unions.

However, to play any sort of effective role in helping the Labour Party electorally, it may be important for the unions to maintain a reasonably positive general public image; their 'word' will otherwise lack credibility. It is clear that, since the 1960s in particular, they have often been unpopular with the British public, especially during periods of industrial unrest (see table 7.1). Still, while this is widely recognised, it may be easy to exaggerate. Table 7.1 suggests that, even during the dark days of the 'winter of discontent', a majority of people continued to regard unions positively. By the late 1980s union poularity may even have achieved an all-time high in Britain. Perhaps this largely reflects the fact that they appear to have been tamed after a decade

Table 7.1
General popularity of trade unions in Britain, 1964-1987

	Good Thing	Bad Thing	Don't Know
1964	70	12	18
1965	57	25	18
1966	63	20	17
1967	60	23	17
1968	66	18	16
1969	57	26	17
1970	60	24	17
1971	62	21	17
1972	55	30	16
1973	61	25	14
1974	54	27	19
1975	51	34	16
1976	60	25	14
1977	53	33	14
1978	57	31	12
1979	51	36	13
1980	60	29	11
1981	56	28	16
1982	59	30	11
1983	63	25	12
1984	61	30	10
1985	65	24	10
1986	67	22	12
1987	71	17	12

Note: These responses were made to the question 'generally speaking, and thinking of Britain as a whole, do you think that trade unions are a good thing or a bad thing?'

Source: Gallup Political Index

of costly disputes, high unemployment and tough legal regulation. Yet Labour and the unions will understand the importance of sustaining union image. It may well be significant in this respect that certain aspects of the Conservative governments' legislation concerning the unions appear to have caught the public imagination, especially those relating to the internal democracy of union procedures. Not surprisingly, perhaps, the present Labour leadership clearly recognises this; certainly, a future Labour government would be unwilling to remove all of the provisions of the Conservative legislation, as we saw in chapter 3. Indeed, for Labour the credibility and general standing of the unions may be vital; the ability of the Party to construct an effective working relationship with the unions when in power will surely be crucial to its chances of enacting a successful economic policy. If Labour still wishes to assert that 'unions have a central role to play in a successful economy' (Labour Party 1989: 21), then it will have to convince voters about the democratic and responsible nature of union leaderships, and about the economic consequences of union actions. In this light, Labour and the predominant forces within the TUC at the beginning of the 1990s must be seen to be making positive moves; for instance, the 1990 TUC endorsed Labour's proposed package of positive rights for employees, which promises to maintain strike ballots, the election of union officials and restrictions on secondary action (Harper 1990).

In addition to any issue influences that unions might have, their organisational significance should not be overlooked. Given the erosion of strong partisan loyalties, more votes than ever may be 'up for grabs' at forthcoming elections and this means that the role of organisational input and campaigning at election time becomes more important than ever. Skilfully managed campaigns which concentrate on shifting issue agendas onto advantageous ground have a great potential for swaying votes. It is estimated that one-fifth of the electorate changed their minds about who to vote for during the 1987 election campaign (Miller et al 1989: 111). Again, Labour seems ready to recognise this now (see Webb 1991). If so, then the significance of the unions for Labour's future electoral performance may become increasingly acute, for as we have seen, it is not really too great an exaggeration to say that Labour's organisation is provided by the unions. Since the crushing defeat of 1983 the unions have shown signs of their willingness to help in, indeed, even press for, a complete renewal of the party's overstretched organisational resources (particularly via TUFL). It is not easy to test directly for the electoral impact of union-supplied organisational resources, but it is no less significant a factor for that.

Nevertheless, some caveats should be stated regarding the unions' organisational input. Two things in particular should be borne in mind. In the first place, the drive for party membership among trade unionists may prove a somewhat fanciful notion. The party's aim is to supplement its affiliated membership with a million individual members; many of these, it is hoped, will be current levy-paying union members who will instead pay a comparatively modest individual membership fee in the future. If achieved this would represent the mobilisation of a substantial new block of committed support. However, the Labour Party and the trade unions should be wary of setting themselves unattainable targets. The present individual membership figure lies at around 200,000 which makes the stated goal of one million members extremely ambitious. The mass membership social democratic party in European politics is by now something of an anachronism; Kirchheimer pointed this out clearly enough over twenty years ago. Although Labour is obviously looking forward in many ways, the expectation of suddenly transforming itself into that which it has never really been seems optimistic, to say the least.

The second caveat regarding the future of the unions' organisational role within the party concerns the example provided by the campaigns over political funds. On the face of it, of course, this must be a source of inspiration for all those concerned to transform the unions into genuine agents of mass political mobilisation. Against all the odds, apparently, the unions rekindled their glimmering mobilisational potential and successfully awoke the political consciousness of their members. This achievement should not be underestimated, yet neither should one leap to over-simplistic conclusions. The very specific nature of the political funds question itself needs to be recognised. As we have seen, the best evidence available to the party and the unions prior to the ballots hardly indicated an impressive groundswell of support for the link between the two. What did stir ordinary members was the apparent attempt by the government to deny the unions any sort of a voice in the political arena. This, it seems, affronted their basic sense of political fairness. In many ways, it could be regarded as a matter of fundamental democratic rights, and it was up to the rank and file to preserve the right of unions to express themselves in the political arena on matters of direct concern to them. Even those refusing to pay the political levy, or those in unions not affiliated to the Labour Party, could be prevailed upon to protect this right. It does not necessarily follow that the majority of union members are closet Labour activists just waiting to be energised. According to Fatchett, it should not even be taken for granted that future political fund ballots (assuming that the present legislation remains in place) will inevitably be won. Should they next take place in the context of an unpopular Labour government, for example, the results could be very different (Fatchett 1987: 105). The effectiveness of the unions in stimulating political interest and commitment among their members is likely to be simply a matter of the particular issue and political circumstances under which campaigning is conducted. Members' reactions will thus be quite unpredictable and varied.

So trade unions chiefly maintain a capacity for influencing voting behaviour through the mobilisation of the organisational resources at their disposal on behalf of the Labour Party, and through their impact on short term campaign-specific factors. What they can no longer be expected to do is play a role as an agent of class mobilisation. As a whole, the profile of the union movement is not greatly distinguishable from that of the wider public. It follows from this that there is little likelihood of, or point in, the unions attempting to re-generate support on the basis of appeals to class interests and identities, of course. The days of this are over for the union movement. Consequently, the appeals that the Labour Party must make to trade unionists are usually going to be those that they make to the wider electorate. There may be certain appeals to particular sections of the union membership, of course - especially the public sector, perhaps. However, there is little scope for constructing appeals that will effectively unify the entire union movement as such; class-specific appeals to unionists are even less likely. The unions are too heterogeneous, and they are not working class enough. The vast majority of union members are no longer loyal working class Labour partisans, so it is incumbent upon the party to get its general issue appeal, credibility and image right. This is as important in attracting the support of members as it is in attracting that of non-members.

Nothing said in this book precludes the possibility of a revival of Labour's fortunes within the ranks of trade unionists, of course. Indeed, one opinion poll taken in the summer of 1990 suggested a dramatic Labour resurgence among union members, as Conservative and minor party support collapsed (see table 7.2). However, this is almost certainly a result of the balance of short term effects, which were running strongly against the Conservatives, and somewhat against the Liberal Democrats, at the time. The key point to note is that Labour's apparent revival affected non-unionists as well, and the difference between members and non-members is therefore very similar to that reported in 1983 and 1987 (see table 5.1). Union *distinctiveness* has not increased.

Table 7.2
Political preference by unionisation, 1990

	Union members	Non-members	Union-Non/union
Conservative	25	36	-11
Labour	61	48	13
Other	10	12	-2
None	4	4	0
	100	100	

Source: British Political Opinion (MORI), August 1990.

Finally, something of an old chestnut. What are the implications of our analysis for the question of the separation of the party from the unions? There are those who would prefer to see political parties funded largely by the state, so that they may be comparatively independent of the influence of major vested interests. Leaving aside the normative justifications of such an argument, what of the likely electoral benefit to the Labour Party? One should be careful of alluring, but deceptive vistas. Whilst it is true that the party might enjoy a new freedom in constructing policy and arguing through its values, and would no longer be associated with the perennially unpopular unions, the long term consequences are far from predictable. For one thing, it should be borne in mind that the unions have, historically speaking, mostly played a stabilising role within the party. For long periods the major unions have deployed their considerable power within the party's councils to shore up the position of the usually moderate leadership. Were this to be foregone, it is not inconceivable that constituency activists would become the dominant force within the party. Since they have traditionally been radical, it follows that such a party might soon develop a militant socialist profile. It would be naïve to suggest that this is likely to enhance the Labour Party's attractiveness for most of the British electorate. To remain in the mainstream of party political competition in Britain, Labour probably has to maintain a status on the centre left. There is much in the history of the past decade to confirm such a view.

Whatever, this hypothetical point is for all practical current purposes superfluous, for an imminent split is inconceivable in the wake of the political fund ballots. The unions and the party fought hard to maintain - amongst other things - their financial link. Whilst a concern for this might not have been uppermost in the minds of all who voted for retention of the funds, few members would surely have been so unaware as to overlook the implications that their decision would have for the Labour Party. Yet equally few were worried enough about the party-union connection to vote against political funds. Thus, the link has received some sort of a popular sanction, and unless there is a radical shift towards state funding of political parties, it will remain as the basis upon which Labour will hope to progress for the foreseeable future. The task for Labour is how to build a sustainable relationship with the unions which will not repel large sections of the electorate, including union members themselves. This almost certainly requires avoiding a return to anything that smacks of the 'tired' old corporatism of the 1970s (Taylor R, 1987: 432), and it most definitely involves the development of an approach to incomes which will not alienate public sector trade unionists. Without actually seeming to draw the unions too closely into the process of developing industrial and social policy, the party must be able to count upon them as reliable supporters of its economic and industrial strategies. Internally, the party is attempting both its own organisational and political renewal; externally, it is attempting the popularisation of the link with the unions, by seeking to give the impression that unions will no longer be in a position to dominate the relationship. The extent to which it achieves electoral success in the 1990s will depend in no small measure upon the effectiveness of these initiatives and the impact of what has been a singularly trying decade upon the attitudes of union leaders and activists.

Notes

1. It might be added that recent indications do not suggest that labour affairs and industrial relations are set for an imminent return to the heart of the political agenda. For instance, a poll of electors conducted by MORI in the summer of 1990 did not record a single respondent who regarded unions and strikes as the most important issue facing the country.

Table 7.1n
Electors' views of the most important issues facing the country, 1990

	Most important issue	One of the two most important issues
Prices	13%	32%
Defence	21%	31%
NHS	5%	28%
Unemployment	8%	26%
Economy	12%	25%
Poll Tax	8%	24%
Unions/Strikes	0%	1%

Source: British Political Opinion (MORI), September 1990.

References

Apart from the following, I have drawn upon various unpublished sources of information provided by the Labour Party - mainly TULV, TUFL and TUCC documents. I am particularly indebted to staff at the TUC, TGWU and the Labour Party library at Walworth Road for the provision of these.

Alford, RR (1963) *Party and Society: Anglo-American Democracies* (Chicago: Rand McNally).

Alt, JE (1979) *The Politics Of Economic Decline* (Cambridge: CUP)

Alt, JE and Chrystal,K. (1983) *Political Economics* (Brighton: Harvester).

Alt, JE, Sarlvik, B and Crewe, I (1976) 'Partisanship and Policy Choice: Issue Preferences in the British Electorate', *British Journal of Political Science*, 6.

Anderson, P (1965) 'Problems of Socialist Strategy' in Anderson,P and Blackburn,R (eds) *Towards Socialism* (London: Collins).

Bain, GS (1983) 'Union Growth: Dimensions, Determinants and Destinies' in Bain, GS, (ed) *Industrial Relations in Britain* (Oxford: Basil Blackwell).

Barnes, SH (1966) 'Ideology and the Organisation of Conflict', *Journal of Politics*, Vol. 28.

Barnes, SH (1974) 'Italy: Religion and Class in Electoral Behaviour' in Rose,R (ed) *Electoral Behaviour: A Comparative Handbook* (London: Collier-Macmillan).

Barnes, SH and Kaase, M (1979) *Political Action: Mass Participation In Five Western Democracies* (Beverly Hills: Sage).

Barnes, D and Reid, E (1980) *Government and the Trade Unions: The British Experience, 1974-1979* (London: Heinemann).

Barton, T (1986) 'British Class Politics: Reports of its Death Have Been Greatly Exaggerated', Paper presented to the *Trends In Voting Behaviour* workshop of the ECPR, (Gothenburg).

Bell, D (1960) *The End Of Ideology* (NYC: Collier).

Blackaby, FT (1979) *British Economic Policy 1960-1974* (Cambridge: CUP).

Blackburn, R *Union Character and Social Class: A Study of White Collar Unionism* (London: Batsford).

Bochel, J and Denver, D (1971) 'Canvassing, turnout and party support: An experiment', *British Journal of Political Science*, 1.

Budge, I and Farlie, D (1983) *Explaining And Predicting Elections: Issue Effects And Party Strategies In 23 Democracies* (London: George Allen & Unwin).

Butler, D and Kavanagh, D *The British General Election of February 1974* (London: Macmillan).

Butler, D and Pinto-Duschinsky, M (1971) *The British General Election of 1970* (London: MacMillan).

Butler, D and Stokes, D (1969) *Political Change in Britain* (Harmondsworth: Penguin); Second edition 1974.

Campbell, A, Converse, P, Miller, WE and Stokes, D (1960) *The American Voter* (NYC: John Wiley).

Cmnd. 2577 (1965) *Machinery of Prices and Incomes Policy* (London: HMSO).

Cmnd. 2808 (1965) *Prices and Incomes Policy: An Early Warning System* (London: HMSO).

Cmnd. 3073 (1966) *Prices and Incomes Standstill* (London: HMSO).

Cmnd. 3235 (1967) *Prices and Incomes Policy After June 30th 1967* (London: HMSO).

Cmnd. 6507 (1976) *The Attack on Inflation: The Second Year* (London: HMSO).

Cmnd. 7293 (1978) *Winning The Battle Against Inflation* (London: HMSO).

Cmnd. 8778 (1983) *Democracy In Trade Unions* (London: HMSO).

Coates, K and Topham, T (1986) *Trade Unions and Politics* (Oxford: Basil Blackwell).

Converse, PE (1964) 'The Nature of Belief Systems in Mass Publics', in Apter, D *Ideology And Discontent* (NYC: Free Press).

Crewe, I (1984) 'The Electorate: Partisan Dealignment Ten Years On', *West European Politics*, 6.

Crewe, I (1985) 'Great Britain' in Crewe, I and Denver, D (1985)

Crewe, I (1986) 'On the Death and Resurrection of Class Voting: Some Comments on How Britain Votes', *Political Studies*, 34 (4), 620-638.

Crewe, I, Sarlvik, B and Alt, (1977) 'Partisan Dealignment In Britain 1964 - 1974', *British Journal Of Political Science*, 7.

Crewe, I and Denver, D (1985) *Electoral Change In Western Democracies: Patterns And Sources Of Electoral Volatility* (Beckenham: Croom Helm)

Crossman, RHS (1979) *Diaries Of A Cabinet Minister: The Condensed Version* (London: Methuen).

Crouch, C (1979) *The Politics of Industrial Relations* (London: Fontana).

Crouch, C (1982) 'The peculiar relationship: The party and the unions' in Kavanagh, D (ed), *The Politics Of The Labour Party* (London: G. Allen and Unwin).

Crouch (1990) 'The United Kingdom: The rejection of compromise' in Baglioni, G and Crouch, C *European Industrial Relations* (Los Angeles: Sage).

Dalton, RJ and Flanagan, S (1984) 'Parties Under Stress', *West European Politics*, 6.

Dorfman, GA (1979) *Government Versus the Trade Unions in Britain Since 1968* (London: Macmillan).

Downs, A (1957) *An Economic Theory Of Democracy* (NYC: Harper & Row).

Drucker, H (1979) *Doctrine and Ethos in the Labour Party* (London: George Allen and Unwin).

Drucker, H (1982) 'The Influence of the Trade Unions on the Ethos of the Labour Party' in Pimlott, B and Cook, C (eds) *Trade Unions in British Politics*, (London: Longman).

Dunleavy, P (1980) 'The Political Implications of Sectoral Cleavages and the Growth of State Employment', *Political Studies*, Vol. 28, 364-383, 527-549.

Dunleavy, P and Husbands, CT (1985) *British Democracy at the Crossroads: Voting and Party Competition in the 1980s* (London: George Allen and Unwin).

Epstein, L (1967) *Political Parties In Western Democracies* (NYC: Praeger).

Esping-Andersen, G (1985) *Politics Against Markets: The Social Democratic Path To Power* (Princeton).

Fatchett, D (1987) *Trade Unions and Politics in the 1980s* (NYC: Croom Helm).

Fenley, I (1980) 'Labour and the trade unions' in Cook, C and Taylor, I *The Labour Party: An Introduction To Its Structure, History and Policies* (London: Longman).

Fiorina, MP (1977) 'An Outline of a Model of Party Choice', *American Journal of Political Science*, 21.

Fisher, JT (1988) *Part III of the Trade Union Act 1984: A Failed Attempt To Break The Consensus Of British Political Finance?*, Unpublished dissertation, City of London Polytechnic.

Fisher, JT (1991) 'Trade Union Political Funds and the Labour Party', Paper to conference on*Elections, Parties & Public Opinion in Britain* (Oxford).

Forester, T (1976) *The Labour Party And The Working Class* (NYC: Holmes & Meier).

Franklin, MN (1985) *The Decline of Class Voting in Britain: Changes in the Basis of Electoral Choice, 1964-83* (Oxford: Clarendon Press).

Freyman, J (1980) *When Labour Votes: The Partisan Alignment of British Trade Unionists, 1964-1974* (Ann Arbor: UMI).

Gillespie, MW (1977) 'Log-linear techniques and the regression analysis of dummy dependent variables', *Sociological Methods And Research*, 6.

Goldthorpe, JH Lockwood, D Bechofer, F and Platt, J (1969) *The Affluent Worker in the Class Structure* (Cambridge: CUP).

Goldthorpe, JH (1980) *Social Mobility And Class Structure In Modern Britain* (Oxford: Clarendon Press).

Goodman, G (1988) 'Labour and the unions: No time for a divorce', *New Socialist*, October/November.

Grant, D (1987) 'Mrs. Thatcher's Own Goal: Unions and the Political Fund Ballots', *Parliamentary Affairs*, 40/1.

Hackett, G (1985) 'Electricians Volunteer for the Crossfire', *New Statesman*, 30 April.

Hague, R (1983) 'Confrontation, incorpororation and exclusion: British trade unions in collectivist and post-collectivist politics', *West European Politics*, 6/4.

Hammond, E (1988) 'Crossed wires?', *New Socialist*, October/November.

Harrison, M (1960) *The Trade unions and the Labour Party Since 1945* (London: Allen and Unwin).

Harper, K (1990) 'TUC backs Labour union law package', *The Guardian*, 4 September.

Harrop, M (1986) 'Voting and the Electorate', in Drucker, H, Dunleavy, P, Gamble, A and Peele, G *Developments In British Politics* (London: Macmillan).

Harrop, M and Miller, WL (1987) *Elections And Voters: A Comparative Introduction* (London: Macmillan).

Hatfield, M (1978) *The House The Left Built: Inside Labour Policy Making, 1970-1975* (London: Victor Gollancz).

Healey, D (1989) *The Time Of My Life* (London: Michael Joseph).

Heath, A, Jowell, R and Curtice, J (1985) *How Britain Votes* (Oxford: Pergamon).

Hill, RH, (1979) *Sources Of Variation In The Class Consciousness Of The British Working Class* (Ann Arbor: UMI).

Himmelweit, HT, Humphreys P and Jaeger, M (1981) *How Voters Decide* (Milton Keynes: Open University Press): Second edition 1985.

Hobsbawm, E (1981) 'The Forward March of Labour Halted?' in Jacques, M and Mulhearn, F *The Forward March Of Labour Halted?* (London: New Left Books).

Hodgson, G (1981) *Labour at the Crossroads: The Political and Economic Challenge to the Labour Party in the 1980s* (Oxford: Martin Robertson).

Hughes, C and Wintour, P (1990) *Labour Rebuilt: The New Model Party* (London: Fourth Estate).

Hughes, J (1968) 'Democracy and Planning: Britain 1968' in Coates, K *Can The Workers Run Industry?* (London: Sphere).

Inglehart, R (1971) 'The Silent Revolution in Europe: Political Change in Post-industrial Societies' *American Political Science Review*, 66.

Inglehart, R (1977) *The Silent Revolution: Changing Values And Political Styles Among Western Publics* (Princeton: University Press).

Inglehart, R and Rabier, JR (1986) 'Political Realignment in Advanced Industrial Democracies' *Government And Opposition*, 21.

Jackson, MP (1982) *Trade Unions* (London: Longman).

Johnson, RW and Ellis, J (1974) 'Members From the Unions', *Fabian Research Series 316.* (London: Fabian Society).

Key, VO (1955) 'A Theory of Critical Elections', *Journal Of Politics*, 17.

Kirchheimer, O (1966) 'The Transformation of Western European Party Systems' in LaPalombara, J and Weiner, M (1966) *Political Parties and Political Development* (Princeton: PUP).

Klingemann, HD (1979) 'Measuring Ideological Conceptualizations' in Barnes, SH and Kaase, M.

Kogan, M and Kogan, D (1982) *The Battle For The Labour Party* (London: Fontana).

Korpi, W (1981) 'Social Policy and Distributional Conflict in the Capitalist Democracies: A Preliminary Comparative Framework' *West European Politics*, Vol. 4.

Kuchler, M (1984) *Maximising Utility At The Polls? A Replication Of Himmelweit's 'Consumer Model Voting' With German Election Data of 1983* Unpublished paper presented at the European University Institute, Florence, Italy.

Labour Party: Annual Reports of the National Conference and of the NEC 1964, 1965, 1966, 1967, 1970, 1971, 1974, 1975, 1978, 1979, 1980, 1983, 1984, 1987, 1988 (London: Labour Party).

Labour Party (1987) *Britain Will Win: Labour Manifesto* (London: Labour Party).

Labour Party (1988) *Promoting Our Values: Special Report On Building Finance And Membership* (London: Labour Party).

Labour Party (1989) *Meet The Challenge, Make The Change: Final Report Of Labour's Policy Review For The 1990s* (London: Labour Party).

Labour Research (1987) 'Unions face fall-out from industrial decline' *Labour Research*, September.

Lane, JE and Ersson, S (1987) *Politics And Society In Western Europe* (London: Sage).

Lane, JE and Ersson, S (1989) *Politics And Society In Western Europe* (second edition) (London: Sage).

Leopold, JW (1986) 'Say yes to a voice: An analysis of the campaign for the retention of trade union political funds, 1984-86', *Industrial Relations Journal*, 17/4.

Lievesley, D and Waterton D (1985) 'Measuring Individual Attitude Change' in Jowell, R and Witherspoon, S. *British Social Attitudes: The 1985 Report* (Aldershot: Gower).

Lipset, SM (1964) 'The Changing Class Structure in Contemporary European Politics', *Daedalus*.

Lipset, SM and Rokkan, S (1967) *Party Systems And Voter Alignments* (NYC: Free Press).

Lloyd, J (1988) 'Parting of the Ways', *Marxism Today*, March.

Lockwood, D (1966) 'Sources of Variation in Working Class Images of Society', *Sociological Review*, (14) 249-267.

MacInnes, J (1987) *Thatcherism At Work* (Milton Keynes: Open University Press).

MacIntyre, D (1985) 'Left and Right Join Forces To Fight Legislation', *The Times*, 29 August.

Maguire, K (1991) 'Hardliners' call to scrap Tory union law fails', *The Daily Telegraph*, 4 September.

Maguire, M (1983) 'Is There Still Persistence? Electoral Change In Western Europe, 1948-1979' in Daalder, H and Mair, P.

Mair, P (1983) 'Adaptation and Control: Towards an Understanding of Party and Party System Change' in Daalder, H and Mair, P (eds) *Western European Party Systems: Continuity and Change* (Beverly Hills and London: Sage).

Mair, P (1984) 'Party Politics in Contemporary Europe: A Challenge To Party?', *West European Politics*, 6.

MARPLAN (1984) *Poll Amongst Trade Unionists* (London: MARPLAN), January.

Marsh, A (1988) *The Trade Union Handbook* (London: 3rd Edition).

Marshall, G, Newby, H, Rose, D and Vogler, C (1988) *Social Class In Modern Britain* (London: Hutchinson).

Massey, D and Miles, N (1984) 'Mapping Out the Unions', *Marxism Today*, (May).

May, TC (1978) *Trade Unions And Pressure Group Politics* (Farnborough: Saxon House).

McIlroy, J (1985) 'All change at Blackpool', *New Statesman*, 30 August.

McLean, I (1982) *Dealing In Votes* (Oxford: Martin Robertson).

Middlemas, K (1979) *Politics In Industrial Society: The Experience Of The British System Since 1911* (London: Andre Deutsch).
Miller, WL (1978) 'Social Class and Party Choice in England', *British Journal of Political Science*, 8.
Miller, WL (1980) 'What was the Profit in Following the Crowd? The Effectiveness of Party Strategies on Immigration and Devolution', *British Journal of Political Science*, 10.
Miller WL, Broughton D, Sonntag N, & McLean D (1989) 'Political change in Britain during the 1987 campaign' in Crewe I and Harrop M *Political Communications: The General Election Campaign Of 1987* (Cambridge: CUP).
Miller WL, Clarke HD, Harrop M, Leduc L, and Whiteley P (1990) *How Voters Change: The 1987 British Election Campaign In Perspective* (Oxford: Clarendon).
Miller, WL (1984) 'There Was No Alternative: The British General Election of 1983', *Parliamentary Affairs*, 37.
Miliband, R (1972) *Parliamentary Socialism: A Study in the Politics of Labour* (London: Merlin).
Minkin, L (1980) *The Labour Party Conference* (Manchester: MUP).
Minkin, L (1986) 'Against the tide: Trade unions, political communication and the 1983 general election' in Crewe, I and Harrop, M *Political Communication: The General Election Campaign Of 1983* (Cambridge: CUP).
Moore, RS (1975) 'Religion as a source of variation in working class images of society', in Bulmer, M *Working Class Images Of Society* (London: Routledge, Kegan Paul).
MORI (1982) *Political Opinion in Great Britain*, August.
MORI (1985) *Union World 1,000* (London: MORI), February.
Mosley, P (1984) '"Popularity Functions" and the Role of the Media: A Pilot Study of the Popular Press', *British Journal of Political Science*, 14.
Nairn, T (1965) 'The nature of the Labour Party' in Anderson, P and Blackburn, R *Towards Socialism* (London: Collins).
Nie, NH, Hadlai Hull, C, Jenkins, JG, Steinbrenner, K and Bent, DH (1975) *SPSS: Statistical Package for the Social Sciences* (New York: McGraw-Hill).
Nie, N, Verba, S and Petrocik, J (1976) *The Changing American Voter* (Cambridge, Mass: Harvard University Press).
Nielsen, HJ (1985) *British Attitudes Towards Trade Unions*, (Copenhagen: Institute of Political Science Working Paper).
Norris, P (1990) *British By-Elections: The Volatile Electorate* (Oxford: Clarendon).

Page, BI and Brody, RA (1972) 'Policy Voting and the Electoral Process: The Vietnam War Issue', *American Political Science Review*, 66.

Paldam, M (1981) 'A Preliminary Survey of the Theories and Findings on Vote and Popularity Functions', *European Journal of Political Research*, 9.

Panitch, L (1976) *Social Democracy And Industrial Militancy* (Cambridge: CUP).

Park, T, Lewis, M and Lewis P (1986) 'Trade unions and the Labour Party: Changes in the group of trade union sponsored MPs', *Political Studies*, xxxiv.

Parkin, F (1971) *Class Inequality and Political Order: Social Stratification in Capitalist and Communist Societies* (London: MacGibbon and Kee).

Pedersen, M (1979) 'The Dynamics of European Party Systems: Changing Patterns of Electoral Volatility', *European Journal of Political Research*, 7.

Pedersen, M (1983) 'Changing Patterns of Electoral Volatility in European Party Systems, 1948-1979: Explorations in Explanation', in Daalder and Mair.

Pelling, H (1971) *A History Of British Trade Unionism*, 2nd Edition (Harmondsworth: Penguin).

Pinto-Duschinsky, M (1980) *British Political Finance, 1830-1980* (Washington DC, American Enterprise Institute).

Pinto-Duschinsky, M (1989) 'Financing the British general election of 1987' in Crewe, I and Harrop, M *Political Communications: The General Election Campaign Of 1987* (Cambridge: CUP).

Poguntke, T (1987) 'New Politics and Party Systems: The Emergence of a New Type of Party?' *West European Politics*, 10.

Price, R and Bain, GS (1976) 'Union growth revisited: 1948-74 in perspective' *British Journal of Industrial Relations*, XIV/3.

Pulzer, P (1967) *Political Representation and Elections in Britain* (London: Allen & Unwin).

Richter, I (1973) *Political Purpose In Trade Unions* (London: Allen and Unwin).

Robertson, D (1984) *Class and the British Electorate* (Oxford: Basil Blackwell).

Rose, R (1974) *Electoral Behaviour: A Comparative Handbook* (London: Collier-Macmillan).

Rose, R (1980) *Class Does Not Equal Party: The Decline Of A Model Of British Voting* (Strathclyde: CSPP).

Rose, R and McAllister, I (1986) *Voters Begin to Choose: From Closed-Class to Open Elections in Britain* (London: Sage).

Rose, R and Urwin, D (1970) 'Persistence and Change in Western Party Systems Since 1945', *Political Studies*, 18.

Sartori, G (1968) 'The Sociology of Parties: A Critical Review' in Stammer, O (ed) *Party Systems, Party Organisations and the Politics of the New Masses* (Berlin: IPW).

Saunders, P (1981) *Social Theory And The Urban Question* (London: Hutchinson).

Scarbrough, E (1984) *Political Ideology And Voting* (Oxford: Clarendon Press).

Scarbrough, E (1986) *The British Electorate Twenty Years On: Reviewing Electoral Change And Election Surveys* (Colchester: Essex Papers in Politics and Government).

Schumpeter, JA (1952) *Capitalism, Socialism And Democracy* (London: G. Allen & Unwin); Fifth edition.

Simpson, B (1973) *The Trade unions And The Labour Party* (London: Allen and Unwin).

Sonquist, JA and Morgan, JN *The Detection of Interaction Effects* (Ann Arbor: Monograph 35, Michigan University).

Stallard, W (1987) 'Policy making in the Labour Party: The Liaison Committee in opposition and in government, 1970-1979', *Teaching Politics*, 16/1, January.

Stewart, M (1977) *The Jekyll and Hyde Years: Politics And Economics Since 1964* (London: Dent).

Taylor, AJ (1987a) *The Trade Unions And The Labour Party* (London: Croom Helm).

Taylor, AJ (1987b) 'The Politics of Non-Partisan Trade Unions: The British Case', *Politics*, (7), pp8-13.

Taylor, R (1978) *The Fifth Estate: Britain's Unions In The 1970s* (London: Routledge, Kegan, Paul).

Taylor, R (1987) 'The Trade Unions and the Labour Party: Time for an Open Marriage', *Political Quarterly*, 58.

Torode, J (1984) 'The Mood of the Politically Motivated', *The Guardian*, (August 2nd).

TUC (1974) *Report Of The General Council* (London: TUC).

TUC-PLP Liaison Committee (1983) *Partners In Rebuilding Britain* (London).

Undy, R Ellis, V McCarthy, WEJ and Halmos, AM (1981) *Change In The Trade Unions: The Development Of The United Kingdom's Unions Since 1960* (London: Hutchinson).

Upham, M and Wilson, T (1989) 'Natural allies: Labour and the unions', *Fabian Tract 534* (London: Fabian Society).

Webb, PD (1986) 'British Democracy at the Crossroads' (Review), *Political Quarterly*, 57.

Webb, PD (1987) 'Union, Party and Class in Britain: The Changing Electoral Relationship, 1964-1983', *Politics*, 7.

Webb, PD (1991) 'Election campaigning, organisational transformation and the professionalisation of the British Labour party' *European Journal Of Political Research*.

Weir, B (1985) 'The American Tradition of the Experimental Treatment of Elections: A Review Essay', *Electoral Studies*, 4.

Wellhofer, ES (1979) 'Strategies for Party Organisation and Voter Mobilisation: Britain, Norway and Argentina' *Comparative Political Studies*, Vol. 12/2.

Wertheimer, E (1929) *A Portrait Of The Labour Party* (London: Putnam).

Westergard, J (1965) 'The Withering Away of Class: A Contemporary Myth' in Anderson, P and Blackburn, R *Towards Socialism* (London: Collins).

Whiteley, P (1983) *The Labour Party in Crisis* (London: Methuen).

Whyte, JH (1974) 'Ireland: Politics Without Social Bases', in Rose,R (ed) *Electoral Behaviour: A Comparative Handbook* (London: Collier-Macmillan).

Williams, F (1950) *Fifty Years March: The Uses Of Labour* (London: Odhams)

Wright, EO (1979) 'The Class Structure Of Advanced Capitalist Societies' in Wright, EO, *Class, Crisis And The State* (London: Verso).

Wright, EO (1985) *Classes* (London: Verso).

Wrigley, C (1982) 'Trade unions and politics in the First World War' in Pimlott, B and Cook, C *Trade Unions In British Politics* (London: Longman).

Index